D1100316

How the Internet Undermines Democracy
Donald Gutstein

Published in 1999 by Stoddart Publishing Co. Limited
34 Lesmill Road, Toronto, Canada M3B 2T6

Distributed in Canada by General Distribution Services Limited
325 Humber College Blvd., Toronto, Canada M9W 7C3
Tel. (416) 213-1919   Fax (416) 213-1917
Email Customer.Service@ccmailgw.genpub.com

Distributed in the U.S. by General Distribution Services Inc.
85 River Rock Drive, Suite 202, Buffalo, New York 14207
Toll-free tel. 1-800-805-1083 Toll-free fax 1-800-481-6207
Email gdsinc@genpub.com

03 02 01 00 99 1 2 3 4 5

Cataloguing in Publication Data

Gutstein, Donald, 1938–   .
E.con: how the Internet undermines democracy

Includes bibliographical references and index.
ISBN 0-7737-6056-3

1. Internet (Computer network) – Social aspects – Canada.
2. Internet (Computer network) – Government policy – Canada.
3. Internet (Computer network) – Economic aspects – Canada.   I. Title.

HM221.G867   1999   303.48'33   C99-931462-9

Cover design: Bill Douglas @ The Bang
Design and typesetting: Kinetics Design & Illustration

Printed and bound in Canada

Canada

THE CANADA COUNCIL | LE CONSEIL DES ARTS
FOR THE ARTS | DU CANADA
SINCE 1957 | DEPUIS 1957

*We acknowledge for their financial support of our publishing program the
Canada Council, the Ontario Arts Council, and the Government of Canada
through the Book Publishing Industry Development Program (BPIDP).*

contents

Acknowledgements

Many individuals contributed to the writing of this book. Eddie Kim, Cheryl Linstead, Katherine Manson, and Jackie Mosdell assisted with the research. Students in my information rights course in the School of Communications, Simon Fraser University, helped in the development of my ideas by constantly challenging my arguments. Bob Anderson, Robert Babe, Ellen Balka, Brian Lewis, Stuart Rush, and David Smith read early chapters of the manuscript. Of course, any errors are mine alone. At Stoddart, managing editor Don Bastian has been a pleasure to work with. His professionalism and calmness at the eleventh hour have been very much appreciated. Freelance copy editor Janice Weaver made the manuscript much more readable. Finally, the book would not have happened without the love, sacrifice, and encouragement of my partner, Mae Burrows, and our son, Josh Gutstein. Josh is learning that in his family, people's right to information is a strongly held value.

introduction

When the Internet came along, I was excited. Like many others, I believed that the increased access to information and communication provided by this publicly funded medium would lead to enhanced participation in democracy. From my position in the communication school at Simon Fraser University, I had taxpayer-supported access to the Internet and its seemingly limitless resources, which I could use in my teaching and research. I eagerly signed up for a variety of mailing lists and revelled in the plethora of information that was delivered to my e-mail address every day. As more citizens gained access to this vast information-generating engine, it seemed like a new era was dawning. Expanded and reinvigorated democracy could not be far behind.

In the early 1990s, CA*net, the Internet in Canada, was funded by taxpayers through university computing departments and the National Research Council. Users would dial up a university or other access point. From there, they would be connected to a regional network such as BCnet or Onet, which linked them to CA*net, the national backbone, which then passed them on to another regional network or to the U.S. and the global Internet. Soon, commercial service providers were beginning to appear on the scene, providing competition for

CA*net. But that wasn't necessarily a problem; CA*net could have been moulded into the Internet equivalent of the CBC in broadcasting. In 1928 the Aird Commission consulted extensively with Canadians before recommending the establishment of a public broadcasting service. The same process should have occurred for the Internet, so Canadians wouldn't be buried under an avalanche of commercial American content. A public information network, modelled along the lines of public broadcasting or public transit, would have provided informational benefits to all Canadians.

That didn't happen. A decision had been made, quietly, without public consultation, in contrast to the Aird Commission, that once private-sector services were established, there would be no role for CA*net, or for any kind of public information network. I discovered this fact when I stumbled across the Canadian Network for the Advancement of Research, Industry and Education (CANARIE), an industry-dominated organization supported and financed by the Mulroney and Chrétien governments. Its task was to upgrade CA*net and turn it over to the private sector – Bell Canada, as it turned out. CANARIE was in a conflict of interest from the beginning, since among its members were companies (including Bell) that were entering or planning to enter the business of providing Internet access and services. They would directly benefit from CA*net's demise. CANARIE also set out to build a faster computer network that would be available only to university and government researchers, but that also had to have commercial payoffs. A third task was to fund promising applications such as telelearning, telehealth, and electronic commerce, which could make profitable use of the network CANARIE was creating. This approach – privatizing a perfectly functional non-profit network and ensuring that all future developments were under the private sector's thumb – was wrong-headed, in my view. CANARIE made no provision in its programs for public information access. Non-profit and community projects were specifically excluded from support unless they had private-sector partners.

CANARIE was a creation of Industry Canada, the federal agency responsible for industrial development. During Kim Campbell's brief stint as prime minister, Industry Canada was bulked up to become the

super-ministry for the information highway, and was given responsibility for telecommunications, science and technology, patents and
trademarks, and corporate affairs. Through John Manley, Industry
Canada has become industry's advocate in the Chrétien Cabinet.
Its tentacles reach everywhere, into education through its SchoolNet
program, into libraries through LibraryNet, into scientific research
through its responsibility for federal granting councils and its control
over federal research labs, into international trade through its responsibility for patents and trademarks and the all-important area of
intellectual-property rights, and into health care through its health-
network initiatives. Industry Canada's goal, I concluded, was not to
increase access to information but just the opposite: to boost Canadian
economic growth by exploiting the country's public information
resources. I believe that Industry Canada and CANARIE are part of a
grand government-business strategy that could have dire consequences for the health of Canadian democracy.

The strategy unfolded something like this. Institutions providing
information services – schools, health-care organizations, libraries,
science research labs, the CBC – took a big hit during the great
budget-slashing assaults of the Chrétien government. Next, computer
networks designed to connect every library, school, and hospital in
Canada to the Internet were offered up, and gratefully accepted, as a
means to offset funding shortfalls. But along with these computer networks came the private sector, and that meant these institutions were
subjected to pressures to commercialize their resources. "Partnerships"
became the buzzword for federal and most provincial governments,
and these partnerships brought a vastly expanded system of copyright and intellectual-property rights. Copyright – the right of a
creator to impose a monopoly on the distribution of his or her work –
was originally conceived as a privilege bestowed by Parliament on
authors to encourage the creation of new ideas, which society needed
to continue its development. Today that privilege has been distorted
beyond all recognition by global information and media corporations,
which make billions of dollars from their control of intellectual property. In the past few years, they've been able to extend the term of
copyright protection beyond all reasonable duration, and to apply

copyright to the Internet, further enriching themselves. They're even trying to impose – so far unsuccessfully – protection on compilations of information, which would give them ownership of the facts in their databases. Canada's Ken Thomson owns tens of thousands of databases, and will be the world's greatest beneficiary if this perverse law is ever implemented.

With the networks under commercial control, an ironclad system of protection being lowered over the information commons like a shroud over the land, and frenzied efforts to put in place pay-per-view or pay-per-use schemes, Industry Canada and the Chrétien government unveiled their Connecting Canadians strategy. The goal of Connecting Canadians, according to a promotional package, "is to help Canadians become the most connected people on earth, ready to take advantage of the opportunities of today's new knowledge-based economy." From the perspective of democratic values, Connecting Canadians is really Conning Canadians, an attempt to turn public information resources that we all need into items of electronic commerce that many cannot afford.

And all this is to ignore Canada's long history of public entrepreneurship, which started a hundred years ago with Ontario Hydro, the Prairie telephone companies, and the railways and continued into the second part of this century with public broadcasting, Second World War Crown corporations, Atomic Energy of Canada Ltd., PetroCanada, and dozens more. Even the Internet, in Canada as well as the U.S., was developed through public entrepreneurship long before any corporations were interested. Most public organizations, including CA*net, are gone not because they failed or performed poorly, but because of a twenty-year propaganda campaign waged by corporate interests to discredit the public sector and persuade Canadians that the private sector could do a better job. Canadian history demonstrates that it's a myth that only the private sector can generate economic growth; this myth, however, has become the prevailing orthodoxy of our time.[1]

The opening chapter of this book addresses the impacts of Connecting Canadians on Canada's public information resources. It dissects the six priorities of the program, and shows how they depend on building high-speed computer networks and commercializing public information resources that have been created by government agencies like Statistics Canada and taxpayer-supported academic research. The chapter argues that Canadians have agreed to finance public information activities because they provide knowledge vital for our democratic way of life. With their commercialization, a foundation of democracy is being removed. The Internet promised to be the most democratic and liberating of new media, but commercial pressures and government policies have forestalled that type of development. An alternative form of development is proposed − a public information network that follows the model of public transit and benefits all of society, rather than the information highway model, which benefits those already well-off.

In the next chapter, I turn my attention to the disturbing situation facing our most treasured public information institution, the free library, which is supported by municipal taxation so all residents can have access to information on all subjects and on all sides of issues. The budget cuts implemented by recent federal and provincial governments have thrown into question the library's ability to provide its traditional services. At the same time, the information industry has seized the opportunity to make inroads into library activities. The ultimate challenge may be the corporate-controlled digital library, where fees are charged for high-quality information delivered over the Internet, and the only information available for free is of low quality; this will divide citizens into two classes − information rich and information poor.

In Chapter 3, I describe the coalescing of the telecommunications, broadcasting, and information-technology industries into an industry-government partnership that is determining the shape and direction of Canadian Internet developments. Key players are Industry Canada (the federal department responsible for connectedness) and CANARIE. This chapter investigates that organization, and examines its strategy for building a high-speed, high-bandwidth network and financing the development of telelearning, telehealth, and e-commerce applications that can make most profitable use of the network.

In the 1980s, telephone companies, which are a major force in CANARIE, realized that in the future profits would come from content and not carriage – from originating, storing, and manipulating messages, not just carrying them as the telcos had done for a century. Chapter 4 describes the telcos' successful move to full-blown information-industry players. They are now firmly entrenched in the content business.

Chapter 5 explains the rush to gain control over content, and in particular the largely successful efforts by the U.S. government and multinational information corporations to enclose the information commons by imposing a regime of strong intellectual-property protection. Each success in expanding protection – declaring software programs to be subject to copyright, tying intellectual property to trade (through NAFTA and GATT), imposing copyright restrictions on the Internet, extending the duration of copyright and patent protection – has enriched global corporate behemoths like Disney, Microsoft, News Corp., and Canada's Thomson Corp. Corporate interests are even trying to impose intellectual-property protection, so far unsuccessfully, on the facts contained in databases. Copyright was supposed to balance creators' rights against the right of society to benefit from new works. Today, society's interest has been virtually eliminated, and a regime has been put in place to ensure privatization and the commercial exploitation of public information resources.

Next I discuss the trend in university research to produce intellectual property of increasing value to researchers, university administrations, and the information industry. In the past, the results of academic research were published in journals and presented at conferences, and from there they would pass into the public domain. Now university research is being commercialized – CANARIE's networks and another government program called Networks of Centres of Excellence (NCE) have been set up to accomplish this goal – and researchers are expected to sign non-disclosure agreements with corporate backers. As a result, university research agendas are distorted and public-interest research loses out. This chapter describes the close collaboration between researchers and corporate interests at Canadian universities. It focuses on one NCE in particular, TeleLearning, which is controversial because some academics suspect that its intention is to replace teachers and classrooms with patented software and computer networks operated by university-corporate partnerships.

The goal of TeleLearning is to digitize and commercialize education curriculum so it can be bought and sold on the Internet. Canadian taxpayers spend $55 billion a year on education, which would be a huge market for the information industry – if it can turn education into a market. Chapter 7 describes efforts to "colonize" education, transforming it from a public-based, teacher-delivered resource into a private-sector, Internet-delivered commodity. Industry Canada's SchoolNet program and the Ontario and New Brunswick governments have gone furthest along this route, but hundreds of companies are planning to cash in on the education market. This chapter describes the machinations of two, IBM and Microsoft.

How is industry able to accomplish its takeover of public information? Aren't Canadians concerned about the whittling away of public information and the threats to democracy? Chapter 8 argues that corporate propaganda has successfully blurred national interests with business interests. A small sector of society has convinced Canadians that the public interest is the same as private interests: what's good for the information industry is good for Canada. This chapter critiques three myths that underlie the successes of the information industry and underpin the Connecting Canadians strategy: 1) deficits were caused by out-of-control spending on social programs (and information institutions), which had to be cut; 2) information technology (IT) benefits everyone, therefore we need IT in libraries and schools; and 3) only the private sector is capable of building the information networks we need. Once we see that these three propositions are myths, new kinds of networks serving the public interest become possible.

Despite corporate propaganda, Canadians have done much to develop information networks that meet community, rather than corporate, needs. The final chapter of this book describes activities whose common theme is an attempt to reclaim public information or to create a place for local and community information on the network. It describes the largely unsuccessful attempts by the freenet, or community network, movement to create locally based, non-commercial networks, and suggests that their lack of success was a result of their reliance on assistance from Industry Canada and the corporate sector, which both had an interest in ensuring that community networks would not succeed. More promising are networking initiatives by already well-organized sectors of society: trade unions, women's organizations, social-justice movements, and environmental groups, which use computer networks, such as the Association for Progressive Communications, to help achieve their objectives. The chapter suggests they must make democratic communication an additional goal. They must also forge alliances with librarians, community networkers, teachers, and others dedicated to public access.

What is also needed is a set of information rights for citizens in the twenty-first century, which would extend civil rights of the eighteenth century, political rights of the nineteenth century, and economic rights of the twentieth century. Until citizens are guaranteed such rights – privacy, access to information and to information services, literacy, the right to benefit from discoveries and inventions, the right of groups and nations to communicate their views and values – Connecting Canadians will remain captive to the information industry, and citizens will not enjoy the benefits of democratic networks.

connecting canadians . . . to what?

We will make the information and knowledge infrastructure accessible to all Canadians by the year 2000, thereby making Canada the most connected nation in the world.
— Speech from the Throne, September 23, 1997

Connecting Canadians is the Chrétien government's program for the age of the Internet. Part PR spin, part real development, it's a clutch of strategies whose goal, according to a government promotional package, is "to help Canadians become the most connected people on earth, ready to take advantage of the opportunities of today's new knowledge-based economy." Connecting Canadians is a relatively new concept in Canadian government thinking, first enunciated in the Speech from the Throne in September 1997, after the Liberals were re-elected. No question it's part hype. In fact, Canada ranks tenth in the world in terms of connectedness (as measured by PC ownership, Internet use, cost of a local telephone call, newspaper readership, and nineteen other variables), according to the 1999 Information Society Index study by World Times and International Data Corp. Canada was actually down two places from its 1998 ranking, and falls behind the U.S., Sweden, Finland, Singapore,

Norway, Denmark, the Netherlands, Australia, and Japan.[1] And even if the government is successful in connecting Canadians to the Internet, the main beneficiaries are likely to be large U.S. Internet companies like America Online and Amazon.com, which has become the third-largest book retailer in just over a year. Hooking up more Canadians, argues the Canadian Imperial Bank of Commerce's chief information officer, "will simply enable more Canadians to purchase online goods and services from established U.S. providers."[2]

But Connecting Canadians builds on developments that have been occurring in the U.S. and Canada since the 1960s, when computers and satellites came into general use and an information industry rose to prominence by using these technologies to turn information into a commodity that could be bought and sold across national borders. My concern is that Connecting Canadians is a misguided attempt to create a place for Canada in the global Internet economy by handing over − selling out, some might say − the nation's public information resources, resources assembled by the government and non-profit sectors over one hundred years of struggle and hard work, to the information industry.

The government says Connecting Canadians will help us take advantage of today's opportunities by focusing on six priorities. The first is to get Canadians on-line. By 2000, the government will have connected all 16,500 public schools and 3,400 libraries to the Internet; provided public Internet-access sites in 5,000 rural and 5,000 urban locations; and through the Canadian Network for the Advancement of Research, Industry and Education (CANARIE), an organization we will meet many times in this book, built the fastest computer network in the world. The second priority is to promote electronic commerce − doing business over the Internet − to make Canada a location of choice for developing e-commerce products and services, and to capitalize on the growth of on-line business. Third is to increase the availability of Canadian-produced content on-line by offering post-secondary courses, major cultural collections, and health information over the Internet, and by developing a home-grown multimedia industry that can capture some of the dramatic growth predicted for this sector. The fourth priority is to put government information and services on the Internet, providing seven-day, twenty-four-hour service to Canadians and leading the way for Canadian businesses and consumers to follow. Fifth is to connect municipal governments to local residents and businesses in an initiative the government calls Smart Communities (as if communities before were stupid). Sixth is to connect Canada to the rest of the world, or at least the rest of the developed world, with a view to attracting investment to Canada's industries.

Industry Minister John Manley, the federal Cabinet minister most responsible for Connecting Canadians, laid out these priorities at a Vancouver Board of Trade lunch I attended in December 1998. They went over well in that largely business audience. Being connected sounds good. Who would want to be unconnected, especially if it means missing out on the economic opportunities of the future?

Canada is well on its way to this brave new world of connectedness, Manley assured us, emphasizing only a few of the variables used in the Information Society Index. Among G-8 nations, we have the highest level of post-secondary school enrolment, the lowest annual residential telephone and Internet charges, and we rank second in Internet users. But we mustn't rest on our laurels, he warned. All other G-8 countries are doing this too. We are "in a global race where speed wins, and the countries that lead will dominate the knowledge-based economy." It will take "partnerships, a national vision, and the capacity to do it quickly" to succeed, he said. There is so much to do and so little time to do it.[3]

But this program isn't just about the economy, the minister continued. "Connecting Canadians will . . . build a stronger democracy through direct citizenship participation," Manley informed us, or at least his flashy PowerPoint presentation did. Yet he glossed over this point, perhaps because it reveals a fundamental contradiction in the entire connectedness enterprise. Connecting Canadians involves a Faustian bargain — to succeed in the knowledge economy, we may have to give up our democratic rights — and this is something Manley is wise not to dwell on. We will benefit from the Internet economy by forcing public libraries and archives to become content providers for the information industry, by commercializing the public-education curriculum and government-financed science research, and by privatizing health information. Connectedness depends on digitizing and privatizing public information resources so they can form the basis of commercial transactions on the Internet. These activities do not build a stronger democracy; they undermine democracy, a system that depends on the effective functioning of these institutions.

In my view, Manley has little interest in promoting citizen democracy. That's not his role in government. As minister of industry, he is supposed to promote the interests of business, which may often conflict with citizen interests and rights. In his Board of Trade presentation, Manley evidently could not bring himself to say the words that flashed on the screen at one point: "Connecting Canadians will . . . build a stronger democracy through direct citizenship participation." Instead, he said, "build new linkages between citizens and government," something quite different. These could be linkages to manipulate citizens, not empower them. Stronger democracy comes from stronger linkages *among* citizens and *to* the information services they require to make informed decisions. Many Canadians tried to create such linkages in the early 1990s by developing non-commercial computer-communications networks, or freenets, in cities and towns across Canada. Manley's support for these initiatives was lukewarm at best. He provided some funding to get them up and running, but expected them to wither away and die when commercial service providers appeared on the scene (a development he encouraged). In the Connecting Canadians world, Canadians will interact with government as individual consumers, not as citizens or members of communities.

Only one Connecting Canadians priority expressly mentions electronic commerce; but in fact, all six are attempts to impose electronic commerce on Canadians by convincing them it is the only alternative in the knowledge-based economy and then ensuring that it is. Bill C-54, the Protection of Personal Information and the Electronic Authentication Act, which Manley introduced in the House of Commons in October 1998, is an attempt to structure individual rights to suit the needs of the information industry (to minimize "the cost of privacy violation to potential economic growth," as *Business Week* describes similar American concerns). The act extends protections of personal information contained in the federal Privacy Act to federally regulated industries such as telecommunications, broadcasting, banking, and inter-provincial transportation. Three years after it is passed, the act will be further extended to the entire private sector. To this point, privacy laws in Canada (except for Quebec) have applied only to the public sector, and for years Canadians have been clamouring for basic protections in the private sector. The act is long overdue, but it would never have been entertained had it not been for most people's reluctance to shop on-line because of their concerns about the security of personal and financial information transmitted over the Internet. Big information interests, like IBM, Bell Canada, and Microsoft, want electronic commerce to proceed quickly. This legislation is designed to provide a level of comfort for individuals so they will use the Internet for shopping, not because a right to privacy is a basic entitlement of Canadians. As Manley said when he introduced the bill, "For electronic commerce to flourish, we need confidence in how our personal information is gathered, stored, and used, and clear rules for industry."[4]

There are important provisions in the legislation – it does, for instance, mandate the protection of personal information kept by private-sector organizations – but it is designed to suit the needs of industry, not the rights of citizens. The act will be administered by Industry Canada, not the Treasury Board (which is responsible for the government's information holdings and administers the Privacy and Access to Information acts), and Industry Canada's mandate is to serve and promote industry, not protect the rights of citizens. As its discussion paper says, the "legislation strikes a balance between industry's interest in compiling and using personal information and the *consumer's* right to have personal information adequately protected"[5] (emphasis added). Where is the citizen's right? Disaffected consumers can appeal to the federal privacy commissioner, but he can make recommendations only, not binding orders. This means that if a company chooses to ignore the commissioner's recommendation, an individual would have to take the lengthy, and possibly costly, step of appealing a company's information practices to the federal court.

The government defines electronic commerce broadly – it includes all transactions using electronic means – but leaves the key notion of transactions vague. Do transactions have to be market-oriented, involving buying and selling? No, "transactions are not limited to purchases of goods and services." Why then do you call it commerce? Because they "move along a spectrum beginning with information gathering and exchange, progressing to negotiation and decision to purchase, finally to completion of transaction and after sales support." So transactions are not limited to purchases, but they must lead in that direction. "As electronic commerce grows, the importance of sales transacted on-line is expected to increase."[6]

That's why Connecting Canadians is so worrisome. In fact, most priorities in the strategy are, like the privacy legislation, designed to boost electronic commerce. As an Industry Canada official admitted to her audience during a consultation regarding Bill C-54 in February 1998, "Let's face it, the information highway is e-commerce." Get all Canadians on-line so they can form a mass market for Internet advertisers and businesses. Connect schools so they can become purchasers of electronic educational services. Connect municipalities to create a market for municipal government and other local agency information. Connect libraries so their resources can be exploited electronically by business and the information industry. Develop tele-education and telehealth markets in the public sector, move them to the private sector, and then to the global market. Currently, people need to "go" to school, to move physically to the site of education, be it a public school, a college, or a university. But once education is electronified, education services can be consumed anywhere in the world, and there will be less need for schools and teachers and even for a public presence in establishing curriculum – the private sector will do it. Put government services on-line to provide opportunities for information vendors and information-technology companies to expand their businesses. "[E]lectronic commerce will become the preferred means to conduct [the Government of Canada's] business."[7] Most public-sector information resources are still free, but this will change once the following conditions are met: technologies are perfected for secure electronic transmission of personal and financial information, and for the use of micropayment systems that allow charges of a few cents a display screen to be levied efficiently; and copyright and patent laws are changed to protect ownership of information on the Internet.

Obviously, there's more to electronic commerce than selling information products provided by schools, libraries, universities, and government labs and agencies. Manley was the host for the Organization for Economic Co-operation and Development (OECD) Ministerial Conference on Electronic Commerce in Ottawa in October 1998, just days after he introduced Bill C-54. (In fact, it seems he introduced the legislation to impress the ministers.) The OECD is based in Paris, France, and represents the most-developed nations in the world, plus a sprinkling of less-developed countries like Mexico and South Korea. Former Liberal Party of Canada president Donald Johnston is the American-backed secretary-general of the OECD. With ministers from most OECD countries and high-level representatives from other international organizations (such as the World Trade Organization and the United Nations) present, it's clear that a global approach to electronic commerce was being effected – the conference was titled "A Borderless World." Like so much public policy today, e-commerce is also a public-private partnership. The official U.S. delegation, for instance, included representatives from Microsoft, Disney, AT&T, and MCI/WorldCom, and U.S.-sponsored representatives from Thomson Corp.'s West Publishing (Canadian) and Reed Elsevier's Lexis-Nexis (British-Dutch), two of the largest electronic-database publishers in the world.[8]

IBM president Lou Gerstner told the crowd of 800 invited guests and delegates that "the real revolution isn't about the end-user experience, and it's not even about the technology. [It's] about banks, universities, government agencies and commercial enterprises making fundamental changes in the way they currently do things."[9] Consumer purchases of books and music on the Internet garner newspaper headlines, but business-to-business trade will account for the greatest share of on-line commerce: airlines order parts electronically, increased sales by a computer manufacturer triggers an order for cardboard boxes and other supplies, a firm auctions used cars to dealers around the country, customers pay bills on-line, and so on.

Traditional intermediary workers, such as travel agents, retail sales staff, and call-centre operators, will be wiped out and an increased share of revenues will accrue to companies and their shareholders. Business likes this scenario so much that electronic commerce will skyrocket in usage, according to predictions. The World Trade Organization estimates that electronic business transactions will grow from $26 billion (U.S.) in 1998 to $300 billion in just two years. Canada's share, if it does nothing, will be about $13 billion in 2002. But by implementing the Connecting Canadians strategy and commercializing public information, the country can boost its share by another $20 billion.

Connecting Canadians, in other words, may be electronic theft. Much of the additional revenues will derive from private-sector sales of public information resources. Taxpayers, through their governments, provide money to develop computer networks and put government databases and library resources on the Net, but the Net is privately owned and operated and the private sector will reap the lion's share of revenues from e-trade.

The Internet in Canada started out as a network of universities and research labs in the 1980s, and coalesced into CA*net, which was a joint venture between universities and the federal National Research Council. By 1997, CA*net was no more, having been taken over by the Internet service unit of Bell Canada. Other telecommunications carriers and Internet-access providers also moved into the field. There is still much non-commercial material available on the Net: government Web sites provide access to thousands of documents; community, non-profit, and special-interest groups operate their own sites, with volumes of relevant, critical, and useful information; and universities maintain a major presence. But at the millennium, the Internet is predominantly a private-sector medium. Even the highly praised SchoolNet program (one of Manley's six priorities), which connects schools and libraries to the Internet, is a partnership of public-sector organizations (Industry Canada, provincial ministries of education, universities, and colleges) and private-sector companies (telephone and cable companies that want to provide connectivity and other services to schools; computer companies like Apple, IBM, and Sun

Microsystems, with their obvious interest; and information companies like the Globe and Mail, Southam, and Scholastic Canada, which
want to sell schools their information and education products). And
soon, SchoolNet-inspired initiatives will begin to earn e-commerce
revenues for public- and private-sector partners.

the fourth priority

The government's intentions in Connecting Canadians can be dis-
cerned most clearly in its fourth priority, putting government
information and services on the Internet. Most Canadians are unaware
of the vast information resources held by their federal, provincial, and
municipal governments. As taxpayers, they have paid billions of dollars over the years for every scrap of information in government files.
They have paid to fund research, collect statistics, publish health- and
consumer-education pamphlets, maintain archival records, undertake
a census every five years, publish financial accounts, ensure the dissemination of knowledge to the public through patent and copyright
statutes, administer freedom-of-information laws, provide weather
and climatic information, and much more. A system has been built up
since Confederation to distribute this information, and this system
consists of the communication and program arms of government
departments, the distribution and sales network of Supply and
Services Canada, the National Library of Canada's cataloguing and
dissemination functions, and the Depository Library Program, which
distributes government publications to libraries across the country.
Information has either been provided free, as part of the government's
duty to inform the public, or been offered for sale, sometimes in partnership with private-sector publishers, and this latter information
could be read in libraries.

If information has commercial value, then these government databases are the crown jewels. It's not surprising that the industry-
dominated Information Highway Advisory Council (IHAC), which
Manley set up in 1994 to advise him on information highway (later
Internet) policies, wanted to get its hands on the vast databases under
government control. It recommended in its final report: "The private

sector should be offered the opportunity to digitize, add value, and market government-owned materials, documents, etc., for which there is a perceived profit."[10] But if public or popular information is to survive, the government has a more important role to play than to act as a source of cheap content for information products, as James Madison foresaw in his oft-quoted observation to W.T. Barry:

> A popular Government, without popular information or the means of acquiring it, is but a Prologue to a Farce or a Tragedy: or perhaps both. Knowledge will ever govern ignorance; And people who mean to be their own Governors must arm themselves with the power which knowledge gives.

In response to IHAC's self-serving recommendations (self-serving because companies and industries represented by IHAC members were among those who would benefit from commercializing government information), the Chrétien government set up a task force on digitization, with high-level representation from twenty-one government ministries, agencies, and Crown corporations. The task force's report wasn't made public for more than a year after its completion, raising questions about how committed to public access the government really was.[11] The report did recognize, though, that government has a duty to continue to provide tax-supported access to essential information in support of the public good, as well as to expand commercial cost-recovery to the government's digital content. Beyond these words, though, there was little in the recommendations to ensure that government agencies would continue to provide free access to information, or that any fees that were charged were fair and reasonable, however those are defined. Today, nearly all information placed in government files is in digital format, but most information gathered over the past 150 years is not. The task force recognized that much essential information for the public good is contained in these files, and recommended that the government establish a central fund for digitizing so-called legacy collections (information gathered before computers were in general use). However, what is worrisome about the task force's view of government information is that it cites Industry Canada initiatives such as the Strategis Web site and

SchoolNet as examples of public-good activities, leading one to speculate about the wisdom of putting Industry Canada in charge of the public good. The question is still open: Will popular information remain free or will citizens be shut out by fees?

During the Internet's first few years, governments excelled at providing easy access to their departments and agencies, and to documents, studies, and reports. Industry Canada's Strategis site is the largest business information Web site in Canada, with more than 3 million documents on-line. Until 1999, these documents and Industry Canada services were freely available, having already been paid for by taxpayers. But at the end of 1998, Mpact Immedia Corp., a subsidiary of Bell Canada, the largest telephone company in Canada (and a member of Manley's IHAC), won a hotly contested contract to turn Strategis into "an area where business information and services could be purchased over the Internet."[12] People will be able to use the site to register for bankruptcy (a cheery thought); file for patents, trademarks, copyrights, and federal incorporation; purchase various licences; and do database searches – paying fees for each service. Mpact will be paid to install an e-commerce infrastructure for the Strategis site, will charge licensing fees for software, and will also earn a transaction fee for each purchase. Strategis, the company noted, was an important contract because many other government departments will be rolling out electronic-commerce projects in the near future. The government will be connecting Canadians and charging them for the privilege. This shouldn't be surprising, given the record of both the Mulroney and the Chrétien governments in managing their information resources.

The impact of the government's information policies can be seen first and clearest at Statistics Canada because of its high-profile position as the most important disseminator of government information; it is the agency where the struggle between the public's right to information and the information industry's right to profit from public information come into sharpest relief. The agency has a clear mandate under the Statistics Act to collect, analyze, and publish statistical information that describes "the economic, social and general conditions of the country and its citizens." Canadian taxpayers contribute more than $250 million a year to StatsCan — more in census years — to collect information on virtually every aspect of Canadian life. StatsCan tabulates details on the lives of Canadians from womb to grave, tracking births, deaths, health, finances, lifestyles, jobs, and education. The agency charts the economy, records changes in the prices of goods and services, measures what Canadians buy from and sell to foreigners, tracks how much money is in the economy, and much, much more. Every year the agency conducts hundreds of surveys and studies, and turns raw data into useful information products. Every five years it spends hundreds of millions of dollars to conduct a national census. Dissemination is a big part of its mandate. StatsCan not only sells millions of publications each year, but also has long-standing policies that govern providing public access free of charge to general statistical data; providing copies of publications free to several hundred Canadian depository libraries and to provincial statistical agencies; distributing the Statistics Canada Daily to the public through the news media; providing information in aggregate form about recent publications to ensure general news coverage; responding to half a million requests for general information each year, primarily by telephone; and staffing advisory offices across the country to provide a largely free information service to citizens.

Like other government agencies, StatsCan was required to make substantial cuts in its budget — a combined decrease of 22 percent between the late 1970s and the early 1990s — leading it to cut staff by 30 percent over that period. In the mid-1980s, the Mulroney government imposed a cost-recovery policy on some government agencies and then granted StatsCan special status to be able to retain revenues generated from publishing and information activities. Over the next decade, the stodgy number-crunching agency turned itself into a marketing-driven, private-sector-oriented "enterprise" that eliminated publications, raised prices, and moved decisively into electronic publishing, leaving many of its traditional users frustrated and bitter. It even opened an office in Calgary, where almost all of its business is selling customized data research to companies and individuals, and its staff of five — all of whom were private-sector recruits — spend their time out of the office building client relationships.

And while it courted the private sector, the agency eliminated some of its important traditional publications, like the *Canada Health Survey*, the only vehicle to systematically monitor the health status of Canadians. (This publication was later reinstated.) The agency also stopped collecting information on patients in psychiatric institutions, on primary medical care, on hospital costs and use, on the incidence and prevalence of diseases and disabilities, and on alcohol and drug use. There were serious gaps in information on poverty, economic productivity, Canada's international competitiveness, and the state of the environment, as well as a loss of information on such controversial issues as the extent of foreign control of the economy and a reduction in the quality of information on unemployment, small businesses, manufacturing, and corporate profits.[13]

Along with the cuts came steep rises in prices for some remaining publications. Ronald McMahon, Saskatchewan's chief statistician, provided some interesting examples of increased prices, using figures provided by the agency. A CD-ROM containing 450 megabytes of geographical information could be purchased from the U.S. Census Bureau for $7,500. StatsCan would charge $127,000 for the same amount of Canadian data, he reported.[14]

According to Denis DesJardins of StatsCan, "On average, the price of our publications . . . increased by a factor of less than four between 1985 and 1989." This was a new way of saying prices were jacked up, on average, nearly 400 percent.[15]

Cuts in published titles, along with the soaring cost of remaining publications, are consequences of the agency's decision to move into electronic publishing. In organizing its program of activities for the 1986 census, StatsCan, perhaps unwittingly, set in motion forces that led to today's problems. The agency recast itself as a retailer of printed publications for individual and business users, and as a wholesaler of electronic data to the information industry, which would repackage and redistribute the material; in return, StatsCan would receive royalties and licensing fees. However, as hard-copy products are replaced with electronic products, and as the private sector plays a larger role in the distribution of such products, traditional end users have been frozen out. Soon, StatsCan may reduce print publishing to a bare minimum, an obvious response to the Connecting Canadians strategy, and only those with technological skills and the money to pay will have access to StatsCan information. The result may be two classes of people: the information rich and the information poor. Ironically, Connecting Canadians will result in less access for many Canadians, an outcome that John Manley and the federal government must be aware of. There's another concern, too. The insertion of a third party – the private sector – between StatsCan and the citizens it is mandated to serve might drive the agency to produce only the data that private-sector distributors want (i.e., what business users who can afford to pay want). We will lose information and knowledge of vital interest to many Canadians who cannot pay for electronic access.

public information and democracy

Human societies have always been knowledge-based. For centuries, information was a community resource, and information exchange took place on a local and voluntary basis between individuals and communities. Local knowledge remains the foundation of many contemporary societies. What is unique about the so-called knowledge-based economy is that knowledge (and the information that underlies it) has been turned into a commodity, an item of commerce. This trend began in the 1960s, when computers and satellites first allowed electronic measuring of data flows and monitoring of transactions. These were confined largely to government agencies, research labs, and large firms, which had sophisticated data-processing capabilities. But the Internet makes possible the buying and selling of information and knowledge on a far broader scale; such transactions are available to anyone with a PC and an Internet connection, and who can afford to pay. That changes everything. So while the explosive growth in the use of the Internet seems to indicate greatly expanded access to Statistics Canada and other information in libraries, government offices, health services, and schools, in fact there will be less access. And because democratic society rests on a bedrock of freely exchanged public information, Connecting Canadians will undermine democracy.

Carleton University communication scholar Vincent Mosco defines

democracy as "the fullest possible public participation in the decisions that affect our lives."[16] Not only must people participate in
decision-making, he explains, but everyone must be able to participate
equally. And Mosco does not mean mere political participation. He
includes economic, social, and cultural dimensions: what to produce
and how to produce it; how to ensure that all citizens receive the bare
necessities of food, shelter, and health care; how to engage in local,
regional, and national forums that discuss and monitor the actions of
decision-makers. Finally, Mosco claims, democracy must be public –
marking your ballot in the privacy of the voting booth every three or
four years is not enough. People need to assemble in community and
union meetings, in both small and large public gatherings, to debate
and discuss issues and decide what should be done about them.

Participation in the institutions of a democratic society is not possible without adequate information about how those institutions
operate and other issues of significance. Such information can be
thought of as the collection of facts and knowledge needed so people
can be responsible and effective citizens, workers, consumers, and
members of communities. Public information is generated largely by
funding from local, provincial, and federal taxes; produced by government agencies and federally funded research institutes and university
researchers; stored in publicly accessible libraries, museums, and
archives; transmitted to this generation through publicly supported
film, video, and broadcast media, and to the next generation through
the public-education system. While public information derives from a
variety of institutions established for a variety of reasons, in sum we
can think of it as an information commons: information "owned" in
common by society, supported by taxpayers, and made freely available to all citizens.

Public information came to prominence in the late nineteenth and
early twentieth centuries to support the expansion of democratic
rights that occurred at that time, especially the extension of voting
rights and the growth of trade unions.

- Publicly supported libraries and information services were
  established in North America and Europe during the nineteenth

century to ensure that people had access to essential information, and that their opportunities to participate in political, social, and economic activities were not determined by their ability to pay for books and other information media. Anybody who could read could find books of interest to them, helping them participate in society and the economy.

- Taxpayer-supported public education was established around the same time to ensure that future industrial workers could read, write, and add. Social-studies curriculum provided students with an understanding of larger forces in the world. The result was the world's first widely educated, literate workforce and electorate, which gave Canada its economic advantage throughout most of the twentieth century.

- Open, responsible government was encouraged by mandating information-disclosure requirements in some government statutes. Information was made available through government archives, depository-services programs, and statistics-producing agencies such as Statistics Canada, Environment Canada, and Agriculture Canada. Governments conducted research into potential hazards in the workplace and marketplace, and made the results available to citizens. Later, in the 1980s and 1990s, governments passed freedom-of-information laws, giving citizens a right of access to information in government files.

- Public broadcasting was established in the 1930s as a taxpayer-supported service meant to resist the flood of private American programs beamed at the country, ensuring that radio service would be extended to all Canadians and would consist primarily of Canadian programs of high standard.

- With the establishment of medical health insurance in the 1960s, taxpayers ensured that all citizens would have reasonable access to treatment, to information about prevention, and to good health care from family doctors, specialists, hospitals, and clinics. Taxpayer-supported doctors dispensed information and advice, along with prescriptions and referrals.

- Public information was greatly expanded in the post–Second World War era by increased spending on colleges and universities, institutions where students learned marketable as well as critical-thinking skills. By producing research essays, they acquired the ability to find the information they would need in their later lives.

- In the 1960s, taxpayer-funded science research became an important tool in social and economic development. Along with maintaining support for research in government labs, the federal government established new institutions to coordinate science activities and new agencies to award scholarships and research grants to university researchers. This produced a growing store of basic and applied knowledge that was published in academic journals and made available to citizens in university libraries.

The era from the 1960s to the 1980s may have been the golden age of public information in Canada. And for a while, with the development of the Internet, which in its first half decade promised to usher in bountiful information resources and expanded democracy, it seemed that the era would continue into the 1990s and beyond. But governments were already turning away from expanded public access. The Trudeau government's budget-containment exercises of the 1970s became budget cuts and user-pay under Mulroney in the 1980s, and budget slashing under Chrétien in the 1990s. Every public-sector institution – including those that provide public information, such as libraries and archives, public schools, universities and colleges, government labs and agencies, public broadcasters, public health, even freedom-of-information programs – felt the sting.

Not only did the Mulroney and Chrétien governments slash spending on public information resources, they also encouraged the growth of a private information industry, following the lead of the Nixon and Reagan administrations in the U.S. Information companies would package computer-generated government and other information into databases and sell access to users. The information industry grew by exploiting public information resources. How convenient that budget cuts made public information vulnerable just when the industry was ready to exploit it.

Information was increasingly viewed by the industry and its supporters in government as a marketable commodity. During the 1970s and 1980s, information products, such as full-text medical journals and newspaper files, were delivered to users in offices and homes over expensive dial-up telephone connections or in libraries through proprietary machines and platforms. The Internet is tailor-made for the information industry and will make it that much easier to commercialize information, delivering, "for a fee, specific bundles of information to target audiences."[17]

Oakville-based information industry researcher Graham Norgate argues that the only information that should be free or inexpensive is what he calls "low-grade browsing information," such as advertising, graffiti, bulletin boards, and listservs. Electronic newspapers and magazines – what he calls "secondary browsing information for mass consumption" – may also be free, since they are paid for largely by advertising. All other information, Norgate argues, especially "high-grade browsing information" – well-researched and carefully edited articles in journals, for instance – should be relatively expensive.[18] Norgate's point is important. If it costs nothing for Web surfers to download well-written, well-researched articles, the quality of such work will decline. Writers and researchers (as well as photographers and animators) must be paid for their works so they will continue to produce them. We've always paid for this kind of information when we purchase newspapers, books, and magazines. If we couldn't afford these, we could still read them in the library, which did purchase them. In addition, some publishing activities have traditionally been supported by taxpayers, who fund universities and institutions that support research, individual researchers who do the work and write the articles, libraries that purchase journal subscriptions, and even the journals themselves. If government support is withdrawn, the whole system breaks down and such articles will not get written or read, unless readers are prepared to pay hefty fees. There will be such readers – namely, the well-off and corporate executives. A corporate-controlled Internet is pushing the dividing line between free and fee back down to where it was in the nineteenth century – near the bottom. The tragic result will be that many will not be able to afford to access the high-quality information necessary to their lives.

whose information networks?

Does it matter whether the Internet is public or private? After all, some may argue, Canada developed one of the best telephone systems in the world under mixed public-private ownership. Bell Canada in Ontario and Quebec, BC Telephone in British Columbia, and the phone companies of the Atlantic provinces were privately owned, while those serving the Prairie provinces were owned by provincial governments. With 98.7 percent of Canadian households connected to the telephone system, Canadians enjoy virtually universal access at affordable rates. Why would information networks need to be publicly owned?

There are two reasons. The telephone system is mainly privately owned, but it is publicly regulated − at least for most of the century. In return for being allowed to operate as monopolies, telephone companies agreed to meet social goals established by government. Profits earned from long-distance were used to subsidize rural and local service to lower rates enough that everyone could have access (although vast regions of the North still remain without phone service). Today, however, business is making a concerted effort to reduce government regulation and let companies regulate themselves. Business claims that regulation is no longer possible because technology is changing too rapidly for regulators to keep up. Regulation will slow the pace of change, and that is bad.

But what if the unregulated market cannot produce the results desired by Canadians, such as universal access? In a 1996 discussion paper, Industry Canada did allow that "where market forces fail to provide this level of access, the government is prepared to step in ensure affordable access to essential information highway services for all Canadians. . . ."[19] How would this affordable access be assured? The document presents no proposals for how to achieve such a goal in an unregulated economy. Nor did the Information Highway Advisory Council have any bright ideas. IHAC devoted an entire chapter of its second report to issues of Internet access, but presented few concrete proposals.[20] Its recommendations urged the government and the Canadian Radio-television and Telecommunications Commission

(CRTC) to "monitor the way in which the market for Internet access develops" (Rec. 4.4), and "monitor the deployment of high-speed access" (Rec. 4.5). What if all this monitoring uncovers a growing access imbalance? Silence. The conclusion is inescapable: to ensure that the century-old goal of universal access at affordable prices can continue to be met, information networks need to be publicly owned or, if privately owned, tightly regulated.

A second reason for public ownership or tight regulation of information networks is that they are more like broadcasting than telecommunications. The network is not just an infrastructure of copper wire and fibre-optic lines, satellites, switches, and routers, but is intimately tied to the type of content transmitted. Full-motion video, for instance, requires much more bandwidth than simple voice or data messages. Bandwidth is the range of frequencies required to transmit a signal; or, more simply, the capacity of a network. More complex signals require more bandwidth. An eight-letter word such as "business" might be eight bytes transmitted over a network. (A byte is a string of eight binary digits, or bits – zeros or ones – that a computer processes as a unit.) A one-square-inch colour photo would be about 4,000 bytes, while one second of colour video with sound consists of one million bytes. Building a high-bandwidth network for multimedia applications – called broadband – costs orders of magnitude more than a simpler narrowband network that is normally used for a single purpose such as voice transmission, and could provide basic voice or data services, which is perhaps all that most people need. A privately controlled network will inevitably favour broadband applications because that's where profits lie for global corporations and media and entertainment industries. Such a network, once again, excludes those Canadians who cannot afford computers, high-speed modem connections, and commercial services.

One way to understand the difference between a privately owned, unregulated network and a public, regulated one is to reflect on the phrase "information highway." In the early 1990s, a proposition gained currency, first in the U.S. and then in Canada, that the complex web of networks that was being built to span the globe was like an information highway. It is true, as Joshua Meyrowitz suggests, that physical and material changes such as ageing, industrialization, or war are easy to understand because they are concrete and imaginable, while informational changes, such as the development of a new communication technology, are difficult to understand because they seem abstract and mystical. The image of the information highway was one anyone could comprehend, even if it was not that accurate ("a plate of spaghetti that works like trains in a switchyard" is the way Reed Hundt, former chairman of the U.S. Federal Communications Commission, describes the network).

The information highway image was a product of political spin-doctoring by the ethically challenged team of Bill Clinton and Al Gore during their 1992 U.S. presidential election campaign. Gore claims to have invented the term in 1979, and it harks back to the building of the interstate highway system, which, along with the space race, sparked the economic boom that entrenched the U.S. as the world's superpower. Clinton and Gore promised renewed greatness with spending on the information highway. The phrase had a particular resonance for Gore because his father, Albert Gore Sr., was the senator from Tennessee who spearheaded the interstate highway system in the 1960s. Gore's friend Bill Gates, along with countless others, later used the information highway as a marketing strategy. Gates's paean to himself and his company is titled *The Road Ahead*, and the cover pictures him standing on an arrow-straight highway leading to the horizon and beyond. Microsoft asks its customers, "Where do you want to go today?"

The information highway metaphor was scrutinized by U.S. college professors Herbert Dordick and Dale Lehman, who compared it with the multi-billion-dollar interstate freeway system, which was a triumph of the American political system of trade-offs.[21] There was something for everybody, they note — costs were widely shared and all political constituencies contributed support. All segments of society can use the interstate system, although some — carmakers and -dealers, oil companies, asphalt-paving and construction companies, rubber and tire companies, and the trucking industry — benefit the most. Subsidized freeways led to the rise and eventual political dominance of middle-class, mainly Republican, suburban municipalities, along with shopping malls, Wal-Marts, land-dependent industry, strip cities, and huge fortunes based on suburban real estate. But there were losers too. In the U.S., freeways drained inner-city neighbourhoods of their vitality, harmed the urban poor, devastated rural towns, killed smaller retailers, and brought the once-mighty railway system to its knees. Freeways also contributed to smog, congestion, and global warming.

A second type of transportation investment could have been made, Dordick and Lehman argue. Instead of spending hundreds of billions of dollars on freeways, government could have invested similar amounts in public transit, which would have benefited the poor by giving them better access to jobs and housing, thus making them more productive. Improved transit would have reduced education inadequacy, crime, and inequitable health-care delivery (because inner cities would not have been deserted by the middle class). There would certainly have been less environmental destruction. Cities would be more compact, giving everyone more mobility, saving millions of acres of prime farmland from destruction, and even reducing global warming. The cost-effective railway system would have remained an essential part of the overall transportation system, and rural America would have retained its vitality.

It's clear that major investments in public transit would have yielded greater social, economic, and environmental benefits for America than the interstate. So why didn't they happen? Dordick and Lehman answer this question by proposing two types of infrastructure investment. Interstate investment is an example of "trickle-down" infrastructure. "The most successful firms, industries and households were the primary beneficiaries of the interstate. . . . While poorer households, firms and industries did not benefit to the same extent, some of the benefits . . . trickled down to these groups as well."[22] The interstate was supported by the already well-off, since they received the lion's share of benefits. And it was not opposed by the poor, since they received benefits too, albeit at a much reduced level. Investment in public transit, they argue, illustrates an alternative infrastructure theory – one they call weak link – which focuses on the idea that "improving the efficiency of the weakest link in the economic structure would provide greater benefits than enabling the most able segments."[23] Such an approach would eliminate many of the negative consequences of the interstate and add the benefits noted. But weak-link proposals have traditionally had a rough ride, since the wealthy do not support them and the poor do not have the political clout needed to make them happen.

There are similarities between the Canadian and U.S. political and transportation systems. In Canada, trade-offs occur within political parties, so they're not as transparent as they are in the U.S. But they do exist, and a party's position – say, on transportation or information technology – represents the results of horse-trading behind closed doors. So even though Canadian inner cities never suffered the devastation and depopulation that characterized American ones, freeways and trucking still replaced rail transportation, urban sprawl is just as bad, and poverty and the lack of educational opportunity is as widespread. Most important, economic thinking in the two countries is very similar. Ever since the Mulroney era, the trickle-down theory has been official dogma. Improving the weakest link is not an option, although most Canadians would probably support this alternative if ever given an opportunity to express their views on the subject. But because the Americans were leading the way into the information economy, Canadians were simply left to follow along behind.

When trickle-down and weak-link approaches are applied to information networks in the U.S. and Canada, it's clear that the phrase "information highway" limits the terms of debate. Yes, there could be on-ramps and off-ramps and even a public-access lane, but the network really exists for the already well-off – private individuals and corporations with their modems, browsers, and virtual private networks. Where do you, the individual consumer with your personal browser, want to go today? If the information highway had been promoted as a "public information network," this would have engendered a different attitude towards the possibilities of the new technologies. Think of the CBC and non-profit radio, community cable-TV, telephone access to government and non-profit information services, the National Film Board, public libraries, public archives, art galleries, and museums all mixed together, with their contents (not just their catalogues) made available to every Canadian through inexpensive, easy-to-use terminals installed in every public building and community meeting place and perhaps in every home. Instead of Bill Gates's "Where do *you* want to go today?" question, we would ask, "Where do we, *as a society*, want to go?"

Trickle-down theory is the name of the game in information networks, say Dordick and Lehman. "The need for advanced services, new network capabilities, and greater bandwidth can be traced to those segments of the information age economy that have been most successful," in particular the telecommunications giants building the networks, the computing giants providing access, and the video and broadcasting giants providing programming.[24] Increased bandwidth addresses the needs of educated, computer-literate, up-to-date, well-off users like lawyers, investment bankers, consultants, scientists, technicians, academics, and business people. It enables massive volumes of data to flow between far-flung outposts of corporate empires; broadcast-quality video clips to fly over the Internet to win multi-million-dollar contracts; corporate annual reports (now no longer simple low-bandwidth text, but full-blown multimedia presentations) to entice potential investors; video-on-demand services for pay-per-view subscribers; and pictorial advertising of products.

Bandwidth will confer its benefits disproportionately on large computer-using organizations like global corporations, law offices, banks, universities, and the information and entertainment industries. Bandwidth will not inspire people to upgrade their skills, nor will it help people without university degrees get out of their lower-paying service-industry jobs. In fact, it will erase millions of such jobs. Instead of pumping billions of dollars into fibre-optic wiring, high-speed switches, and routers, we should be investing an equivalent amount in literacy and training, in providing user-friendly, intelligent terminals on a universal basis, and in enhancing access to existing and new services. Get everyone on the bus first, Dordick and Lehman argue, then determine, democratically, which network improvements should be made. This is the strategy of a public information network.

literacy training

Literacy upgrading is clearly an investment worth making if the goal is to get everyone on the bus. A 1997 Conference Board of Canada study concluded that people with higher literacy skills were more likely to be employed, to earn more, and to be better at finding full-time jobs. A female employee with high literacy skills can expect to earn an additional $683,000 over her lifetime more than a woman with low literacy skills. A man with higher literacy skills can make an extra $585,000 over his lifetime.[25] The findings are clear, yet Canada is doing very little to increase literacy. A 1994 Statistics Canada study concluded that 22 percent of Canadian adults had serious difficulty reading and another 26 percent could handle only simple material.[26] They read, but not well. The study tested respondents' abilities to read news stories and labels, decode job applications and maps, and calculate chequebook balances and restaurant tips. The results were similar to those recorded in a 1989 survey. Little had changed over five years, despite the fact that 1990 was the International Year of Literacy, and that the federal government had vowed to wipe out illiteracy by the turn of the century. Canadians over sixty-five scored worst and the nation's youngest adults, those aged sixteen to twenty-five, fared best. This difference in literacy according to age suggests that literacy rates are improving, but there were significant differences among younger Canadians: 37 percent of young Westerners exhibited "document literacy" at the highest level, compared with 32 percent in Ontario, percent in Quebec, and only 18 percent in the Atlantic provinces. Why do Atlantic Canadians score so poorly? They get less schooling, Statistics Canada notes. Differences in literacy correlate strongly, almost perfectly, with educational attainment – more education equals higher literacy. Since most jobs in the information age require higher levels of literacy, the conclusion is clear: put resources into education and literacy training. That's why the reluctance of federal and provincial governments to do just that is so troubling.

Manley's IHAC told him that "an estimated 38 percent of Canadians lack the basic literacy skills required in today's workplace. Even more lack computer literacy skills. In spite of the development of audio-visual and multimedia tools, including voice-recognition technology, the acquisition of basic literacy and computational skills is more important than ever. . . ."[27] Literacy was clearly the number-one challenge facing public education in Canada, yet IHAC offered not one word in its recommendations to address the problem. Instead, it focused relentlessly on building a privately controlled, high-bandwidth information highway. Could this be because most IHAC members came from the telecommunications, computing, and cable industries, and would profit not from a public information network that promoted literacy training but from a high-bandwidth information highway that hyped multimedia applications?

Connecting Canadians is not about literacy upgrading, nor will it provide the network needed by most Canadians. It assumes and encourages — in fact, mandates — the development of trickle-down infrastructure. CANARIE, as the Chrétien government's designated agency for Internet developments, is building the "fastest network in the world" for university researchers and business, proof that Connecting Canadians reflects corporate, not societal, priorities. Only public enterprise, or an effectively regulated private enterprise, can foster the creation of a public information network, and only such a network can ensure the continued survival of a healthy and growing democracy. Citizens themselves, not John Manley and his corporate allies, must be in charge of connecting Canadians.

the information industry
targets the public library

*If we don't maintain the public library, we risk a future
that mirrors the past. A future in which the affluent have an
electronic, modern equivalent of the gentleman's private library:
home access to the Internet and commercial databases. One in
which the middle-class pay to use a fee-laden public library,
which will grow more and more to resemble a subscription or
circulating library. One in which the poor, as was the case
until the mid-19th century, have no place at all.*

— Peter F. McNally, associate professor in the graduate school
of library and information studies at McGill University

If Canadians ever set up a public information network, libraries will
be the homepage. For more than one hundred years, the public library
has operated on two core values: it is free and can be used by anyone
regardless of ability to pay; and its mandate is to provide materials
of all kinds, on all sides of an issue. Some of the best information
required by citizens is kept in libraries: newspapers from other times
and places; current directories on subjects as diverse as business,
health, employment, and technology; basic information from ency-
clopedias, handbooks, and other reference sources; government

studies and reports; extensive collections of magazines on a wide variety of topics; and up-to-date information in books. By combining their collections through inter-library loan programs, libraries formed the first public information network long before "network" became an overused word. They're local knowledge centres that help people inform themselves on their own terms, as Ottawa writer and activist Heather Menzies observes.[1] Librarians provide direct, personal, knowledgeable service that helps patrons answer their information questions. As Herbert Schiller and Anita Schiller see it, "The public library has long been regarded, justifiably, as one of the most impressive achievements, and steadfast institutions, of the . . . democratic experience."[2]

But the rise of the information industry and the commodification of information threatened the library's traditional role as custodian and interpreter of public information. A process of colonization began quietly in the 1960s with the automation of library cataloguing operations, accelerated in the 1970s and 1980s with on-line database searching, and threatens to overwhelm the public interest with a one-two punch of government cuts to library funding and the establishment of corporate-sponsored, for-profit digital libraries, a combination that may not be entirely coincidental.

The problem for librarians is that their view of information as a public good is incompatible with the information industry's view of information as a commodity. Paul Zurkowski, of the Information Industry Association, was true to his industry's Cold War roots when he accused libraries of "imposing 'an iron curtain of free information' over the land."[3] Indeed, public-service-minded librarians pose a challenge to the information industry that needs to be neutralized, just as the Soviet Union was. For their part, librarians fear they may become irrelevant in the information age as corporate-controlled technologies bypass libraries. Increasingly, Canadians can do their research from home using industry products and services and rarely needing to set foot in a library. When librarians insist on free and untrammelled access to information, "unrestricted by administrative barriers, geography, ability to pay or format," they are treated by information privatizers as backward-looking, if not obsolete, irrelevant, and unrealistic, says American communication scholar Herbert Schiller.[4] The inescapable conclusion is that libraries must embrace not only information technology, but also corporate control of the technology. If libraries surrender their traditional role, then democracy will have lost a key foundation stone. And as libraries go, so go other information institutions.

Many librarians have done a good job of incorporating new technologies and providing access to a wider array of information sources while attempting to remain faithful to their principles. At the same time, some librarians have been swept up by the rhetoric of the information industry, calling themselves information brokers, their patrons customers, and their teaching institutions schools of information management. They've honed their business and financing skills and think of themselves as part of the information industry, not as representatives of the public interest. They organize conferences where industry problems are discussed in relative seclusion. The annual Access conferences, hosted by university libraries and provincial library agencies, focus narrowly on "innovative technology in libraries" and discuss topics such as user authentication, electronic payment systems, and the like. Ironically, they are really conferences on how to *limit* or control access to information, not on how to *provide* access. When librarians focus on technology and information management, they forget their bedrock principles and play, wittingly or unwittingly, into industry hands. Corporate interests and government supporters in Industry Canada and elsewhere are working hard to turn information into a commodity and to create an information market, undermining the good works of librarians. But libraries can remain relevant and continue to operate within a funding-reduced environment. The challenge is to provide free and untrammelled access to information using the new technology. Their failure to maintain free services may result in a return to an era of libraries for the few, since even as more Canadians acquire access to the Internet, they may find that access restricted because of user charges.

beware bureaucrats bearing gifts

The Science Promotion and Academic Affairs branch of Industry Canada brought a small group of librarians to Ottawa in 1996 to explore ways that the ministry could help them. Alarm bells should have sounded the instant an agency responsible for industrial development asked how it could help professionals responsible for protecting public information, which was rapidly escalating in economic value. But a half decade of budget cuts made the librarians at least prepared to listen. And besides, as Industry Canada officials pointed out, they had already been helping schools, a story we will take up in Chapter 7. So why not libraries?

The librarians were interested in finding ways to "plug learners into the world" and develop community networks; Doug Hull, the Science Promotion director general, suggested instead that libraries should become agents of economic development, a startling departure from their traditional functions.[5] Surprisingly, the librarians agreed to participate in this venture, which would be delivered by a new program called LibraryNet, whose details had yet to be formulated. Just as there are two models for information networks – the information highway and the public information network – there are two models of community economic development (CED). One utilizes all the resources in a community to develop economic options that promote local business, provide well-paid jobs, and expand the role of non-profit organizations while protecting the local ecosystem. Libraries already play a major role in this model. Their business, government, technology, and other reference collections and services are an invaluable resource for local people. The second model of CED is centralized and top-down, allowing large multinational corporations such as IBM and Microsoft to extend their tentacles further into local communities. Libraries would play a subservient role in this model, serving as public-access points to mainly American commercial services rather than the homepage for the local community.

To explain what community economic development might mean to LibraryNet, Industry Canada turned to two ex-librarians. Stan Skrzeszewski and Maureen Cubberley had left the profession to form a consulting company, ASM Advanced Strategic Management Consultants, whose name probably says it all. ASM prepared a concept paper that made the amazing claim that LibraryNet would "facilitate the transformation of Canada into a knowledge society."[6] These are code words for a society in which most jobs are temporary, and laid-off workers have to upgrade their skills for the next temporary job by taking on-line training courses delivered for a fee by private or public "learning institutions." Presumably such courses could be accessed through Internet connections in libraries. The paper also stated that industry should be a partner in LibraryNet. It drew a picture of libraries as economic development sites, business incubators, distribution points for government information, providers of cultural and recreational services, and supporters of community networks.

ASM's principals had close ties to the Ontario library establishment. Skrzeszewski was the former deputy CEO of Southern Ontario Library Services in London, Ontario, and had chaired the Ontario Library Association's task force on information policy. Cubberley was manager of the Information Resource Management Division of the former Ontario Ministry of Culture and Communication. As well as setting up ASM, Skrzeszewski and Cubberley helped form the Coalition for Public Information (CPI), which sounds about as public as you can get but is actually a public–private coalition of librarians and information-industry representatives. CPI adopted a top-down approach to public information rather than a grassroots one, which is what's required; librarians need to create public support for their goals if they are going to succeed, a theme taken up in the final chapter. Instead, CPI threw its lot in with Industry Canada, CANARIE, and the information industry, attempting to influence policy from the inside, an impossible task. As a result, CPI never became a champion of the public interest.

Industry Canada helped ASM organize a conference called "Libraries as Leaders in Community Economic Development," held in conjunction with the Canadian Library Association (CLA) annual conference in Victoria in 1998. Having a conference on a controversial subject in a place where many rank-and-file librarians are congregating is a good example of "strategic management." Librarians will become used to hearing the words "library" and "economic develop-ment" in the same sentence, and will even come to believe this is acceptable, since there is an implied endorsement of the concept by the profession's leadership.

Few sessions or presentations at the conference addressed the impact of economic development on the environment, the workplace, or even the community.[7] No sessions addressed issues of concern to employees who would bear the brunt of new technologies in the workplace, and no worker representatives presented papers. A few presentations dealt constructively with the development of co-operative ventures in impoverished rural areas, but the focus was relentlessly on how libraries could provide information support ser-vices for business. The CLA's new executive director, Vicki Whitmell, is a keen advocate of fee-based information services, and she publishes a magazine called *Fee for Service.* She wrote a paper for the confer-ence which argued that fee-based services raise money for the library and also raise its profile in the local community. Since fee-based ser-vices are a source of competitive and timely information – and provide information not available to non-fee-paying library patrons, presum-ably – they will help community officials and businesses make the best choices for economic growth, Whitmell argues, in what seems to be a perversion of free-market rhetoric.[8]

The conference went so well that ASM held a second conference in 1999, in conjunction with the CLA conference in Toronto. The title of this one incorporated even more Industry Canada buzzwords – selected, no doubt, to please the bureaucrats: "Community Economic Development in a Connected Canada: Libraries and Smart Communities 1999."

Eventually, LibraryNet was folded into Connecting Canadians and given a mandate to assist in connecting all 3,400 public libraries to the Internet. Industry Canada uses its Community Access Program (CAP), in partnership with provincial agencies, to provide funding for this. CAP's first goal was to help residents in small communities (urban sites were added later) by providing up to $30,000 to help cover the costs of equipment, connections, staff training, and tech-nical support. Libraries will be unrecognizable once Industry Canada finishes with them. The LibraryNet Web site informs visitors that libraries are "defining new roles for themselves as economic incubators, community development agents, distributors of electronic information, and centres for life-long learning. The purpose of LibraryNet is to encourage the growth of these new roles. . . ."[9]

Two roles outlined by librarians at the first LibraryNet meeting are conspicuously absent from this mandate — providing cultural and recreational services, and supporting community networks. And these new roles are not supported by library users. A 1998 public opinion survey on library usage, conducted by Ekos Research Associates on behalf of the CLA, a group of library organizations, and Industry Canada, found that the "overwhelming majority of respondents agree that public libraries should be involved in . . . promoting literacy and recreational reading, providing information to citizens and helping Canadians to learn. Closely related, the notion of equitable access is also a strong belief held by the majority."[10] There was considerable support for libraries to play a role in life-long learning, evidently the only one from the survey that Industry Canada considers worthy. Promoting literacy received the highest rating in the survey, yet, surprisingly, is not considered an appropriate activity for libraries, at least not in the narrow view of LibraryNet.

A greater priority is Network 2000 in Ontario. Led by Avita Technologies of Oakville, Ontario, this pilot project will provide electronic-commerce services for libraries, allowing users to make municipal licence payments, access fee-paying provincial government services, and pay for library services. Corporate vendors in the project are Microsoft Canada, Hewlett-Packard, and Bay Networks (since taken over by Northern Telecom), all of which have made major forays into electronic commerce. Once the Ontario pilot project has been completed, Avita will launch an e-commerce secretariat for public libraries across Canada. According to Avita president C.K. Tan, the technology will allow libraries in the future to make money through service charges. "We are giving [libraries] the tools to bring them into the new millennium," he said at the opening of the first Network 2000 library in Oakville in April 1998. And Ontario's then-minister of citizenship, culture, and recreation, Isabel Bassett, told guests, "There's no stopping where this is taking us."[11] Says Lesley Ellen Harris, the author of *Digital Property: Currency of the 21st Century* and a keen advocate of electronic commerce, "Simple e-commerce solutions like micropayments will help shape the library and museum of the future."[12] And the person doing most of the shaping is Bill Gates, who is breaking into the electronic-commerce market in myriad ways, including participating in Network 2000 and ensuring that libraries access the Internet and e-commerce applications using Microsoft products.

bill gates's trojan horse

Bill Gates can't stop making money even when he gives it away. Of course, he may plan it that way. In June 1997, he and his wife set up the Gates Library Foundation with $200 million from Gates's personal fortune, which was to be matched by $200 million worth of software from Microsoft. It was a gift whose magnitude far outstripped other corporate donations, but it actually represented a minuscule amount (0.22 percent) of his net worth that year. The foundation says its purpose is to partner with public libraries to bring access to computers, the Internet, and digital information for patrons in low-income communities in the U.S. and Canada, and to provide training to staff members in every library.[13] It may well do that, but the foundation is a Trojan horse, which once inside the library spreads Internet Explorer, Microsoft Windows, and Microsoft Office and BackOffice into every nook and cranny of North America. Eventually, libraries will become dependent on Microsoft products, and once programs like Network 2000 are up and running Gates and Microsoft will benefit handsomely from his minimal largesse.

Gates tries hard to be compared favourably with Andrew Carnegie, the great benefactor of the public library, even appointing Carnegie Corporation president Vartan Gregorian to his foundation board. "Gates to Aid Libraries, in Footsteps of Carnegie," proclaimed the *New York Times* headline. "This is Bill Gates becoming the twenty-first century's Andrew Carnegie," echoed Elizabeth Martinez, the American Library Association's executive director. "His foundation's impact on the library world will be enormous," she said.[14] No question about that, but what kind of impact would it be? ALA rhetoric aside, there is a vast chasm between Gates and Carnegie, not in their ruthlessness and single-minded dedication to creating monopoly control in their industries, but in their impact on the library. In his determination to give away his fortune before he died, Carnegie created the public library; in his obsessive quest to conquer new markets, Gates may destroy it.

Gates started his library contributions small. Just months after the obscene spectacle of the $130-million launch of Windows 95 and Internet Explorer, Microsoft teamed up with ALA for Libraries Online!, a one-year, $3-million initiative to test ways to provide public access to the Internet for low-income people living in rural areas and inner cities. Librarians were thrilled. The program would "help to extend the benefits of new information technology to all people, not just those who can afford it," Martinez effused.[15] Nine U.S. libraries, including Gates's home-town library in Seattle, received a package of cash grants, Microsoft software, computer hardware, training, and technical support. It was actually a solid program based on the principle that training (a five-day training course in Seattle for library professionals) and ongoing support were critical to its success. Computer-only donation programs usually fail – too many ageing computers sit unused in school libraries because librarians aren't trained to use them properly and little ongoing support is provided.

The pilot project was a big success. The ALA found that the installations were being used at maximum capacity and were "positively impacting the lives of library patrons," who, in hour-long sessions, could access information provided by host libraries on a local network; search global information resources through the World Wide Web; and make use of PCs for word-processing, spreadsheets, presentation and graphics design, CD-ROM titles, multimedia, and other software.[16] The success was due in part to the requirement that librarians had to be trained to use the technology so they could then offer workshops for users.

Eventually, Microsoft expanded its philanthropic initiative to forty-one libraries and later to more than two hundred, including three in Canada (which were coordinated with the Canadian Library

Association). Public library branches in Toronto and Ottawa were the first in Canada to receive the Microsoft packages.[17]

Gates, his wife, and his father, William, visited many of the libraries personally, and were so impressed with the results that they took the project away from Microsoft and set up the foundation. Unlike Carnegie's, Gates's scheme succeeds as both philanthropic gesture and market development. In announcing a donation to a Vancouver Public Library branch in an affluent neighbourhood, far removed from the disadvantaged inner-city neighbourhoods the program was supposed to support, B.C. regional manager David Willis demonstrated the intimate connection between philanthropy and business expansion. "B.C. is one of our fastest-growing regions for the information technology market in general. There's a strong development community and a strong Internet community here," he said.[18] Philanthropy spurs business expansion and provides publicity a company just can't buy (but Microsoft hired PR giant Hill & Knowlton to publicize Gates's largesse anyway). Gates's philanthropic donations encourage the use of the technology that made him rich. The fact that the network was inaugurated just after Windows 95, Internet Explorer, and Microsoft Network hit the market was a boost. Of course, any expansion in the use of technology helps Microsoft, and will inevitably give the company's software more exposure, since that is what's being given away. It boosts Internet Explorer in Microsoft's titanic battle with Netscape for browser domination. The donations also provided both the company and Gates himself with hefty tax deductions, so U.S. and Canadian taxpayers actually foot much of the bill for supplying Microsoft products to libraries.

Libraries Online! was successful for library partners too. Ottawa Library Board chair Elizabeth Buckingham put it well when she said, "The budget situation of the city of Ottawa and the library is making the further expansion of our electronic networked services more difficult. By providing resources and support, Microsoft is enabling the library to reach out and make a real impact, especially in areas of the city where the gap between the information rich and information poor is particularly high."[19] But as library board member Alayne McGregor pointed out, "Free money isn't always free." Microsoft most

likely chose Ottawa as a Canadian beneficiary to garner some publicity in rival Corel Corp.'s home town (Corel's WordPerfect is used in
many government offices in Ottawa).[20]

Providing access to the Internet may be a pyrrhic victory for the
library community if the costs of supplying ongoing support for users
of library computers are so high – because many patrons require basic
help using the equipment – that the library must cut its budget for
books. The library in Demopolis, Alabama, received $33,000 (U.S.) from
the Gates Foundation to install eight PCs. Support for the machines,
though, required the equivalent of 1.5 full-time persons on a staff of
only four. Moreover, the library had to allocate at least $20,000 a year
to support and maintain the computers from a total annual budget of
$155,000. Within one year, the library spent more than the total
amount of Gates's one-time gift. And the city of Palo Alto, California,
had to close three branch libraries, partly because of the increased
expense of maintaining and improving electronic services.[21] How will
it benefit the information poor if they gain access through Gates's
generosity, only to find that, owing to electronic-commerce strategies
such as Network 2000, they must pay for the best resources or else be
satisfied with low-quality but free information? Such a situation will
return the library to the past and the era of private libraries.

private libraries

Libraries have existed since the fourth century B.C. in the West and
somewhat later in China, but the idea of a public library, open to all
citizens equally, was not conceived until the nineteenth century in
North America and Europe, with the expansion of democratic rights.
The first libraries in Canada were private collections. New France's
educated elite – priests, government officials, and other well-schooled
members of the community – possessed libraries for their own use,
and in Western Canada fur-trading companies provided a few books
in their trading posts. Eventually, though, these private collections
were superseded by a second type of library, the social or subscription
library, which was supported by member fees. This type of library was
formed to serve the growing merchant class, whose members needed

books but could not afford to acquire large private collections. In 1731, Benjamin Franklin was one of fifty co-signers of the Charter of the Philadelphia Library Company, North America's first subscription library. The first Canadian social library was founded in Quebec City in 1779 by the governor of Quebec, Sir Frederick Haldemand, who noted that the ignorance of the people "must be conquered to make them acquainted with their duties and their own interest,"[22] hardly a democratic urge. It had high fees and catered to the wealthy. The first subscription library in Upper Canada, in Niagara, was more democratic, having been established by townspeople who were convinced that "nothing would be of more use to diffuse knowledge amongst us and our offspring than a library supported by subscription in this town."[23] By 1830, thirty-three social libraries had been established in Canada.

A variation of the social library was the mechanics' institute, brought to North America from Great Britain in the early nineteenth century to provide lectures and a reference and circulating library for the growing population of urban workers who could not afford the high subscription rates of social libraries. Because of the educational purpose of mechanics' institutes, provincial grants were available to them, and institutes spread rapidly. By 1850 there were forty-five, but even these charged fees that excluded many working people, and grants varied widely from year to year and from province to province. Something more was needed.

The public library is supported by funds raised for municipal purposes. It is meant to provide free access for all, and materials of all kinds on all points of view. The public library in Peterborough, New Hampshire, founded in 1833, is the oldest public library in the world to be supported by taxation. Ontario's Free Libraries Act, passed in 1882, provided for free public libraries governed by boards of citizen-trustees with prescribed duties and responsibilities, and financed by a special tax that had to be approved by a majority vote of ratepayers. The next year, mechanics' institutes in Toronto and Guelph transferred their assets and library collections to their respective municipalities and became the first free tax-supported libraries in Canada.[24] By the turn of the century, tax-supported public libraries had become the dominant form of public information service in the country.

andrew carnegie's legacy

The success of the public library is a result of taxpayer support and the great contributions of steel magnate Andrew Carnegie (1835–1919), who built the largest steel company in the world by forcing other companies out of business and ruthlessly crushing attempts by his workers to organize for better pay and working conditions. He supported local management at his Homestead plant, which used Pinkerton guards to bust the Amalgamated Association of Iron, Steel and Tin Workers during its bloody 1892 strike.

Carnegie believed it was his prerogative, and not his workers', to set the conditions of work. He would raise the standards of the working man not through higher wages, but through his philanthropy, calling this "the stewardship of wealth." He wrote an article in 1889 declaring it a disgrace to die rich; funding libraries would be his ticket to heaven.[25] He believed, as a result of his own experiences, that most workers, if given an opportunity to educate themselves through access to books, could become successful, productive members of society, overcoming poverty and ignorance. Carnegie started his program in his native Scotland, moved next to his adopted U.S., and finally to Canada and other countries around the world. "The sun never sets on Carnegie libraries," the saying went. Carnegie – and after he died, his foundation – provided a grant for a library building of two dollars per capita to any municipality that applied; the municipality, in turn, had to pledge continuing annual support for its collections, and operating costs of at least 10 percent of the cost of construction. Between 1887 and 1911, Carnegie gave more than $41 million to erect 1,679 public library buildings, including 125 in Canada. He nevertheless had difficulty giving money away faster than he earned it. In 1900 alone, his share of profits from Carnegie Steel was $25 million. The next year he sold out to J.P. Morgan's U.S. Steel Corp. for $250 million, yet he was still earning $15 million a year in interest payments. Carnegie did not die disgraced, though; he eventually gave away a total of $350 million.

the era of budget cuts

In its September 1996 issue, *Quill & Quire*, the magazine of the book trade in Canada, contained two short items about libraries on adjacent pages. On page 19, the magazine reported that two of the five library branches in St. John's, Newfoundland, were closing as a result of a 17 percent cut – about $1 million – to the public library system contained in the May 1996 provincial budget. One branch in the Gould's, a rural suburb of St. John's, would continue to offer a limited selection of books through donations and volunteer help from the Friends of the Library. On page 18, *Q&Q* reported that in July, Bill Gates was at the Toronto Public Library's Lillian H. Smith Branch for the Canadian launch of Libraries Online!, and that he had donated $1 million worth of cash, hardware, software, training, and support to Toronto and Ottawa libraries. One million dollars cut from public, taxpayer funds; one million dollars contributed by a company with a business interest in what libraries do. It's a pattern that has been repeated with increasing frequency across Canada in recent years.

Today's library funding crisis began in the summer of 1978 with the passage of California's Proposition 13, which sliced in half property-tax support for local government and required most local tax measures to be approved by a two-thirds majority of voters. Public libraries and schools in that state took a big hit. Eventually, the California public library epidemic spread into Canada, where the Metro Toronto Reference Library, Canada's only public reference library, was a high-profile victim first of the Bob Rae government's "Social Contract" and then of the Mike Harris government's "Common Sense Revolution" (you don't need information, just use your common sense). Metro Toronto Council cut its grant to the library from $25.3 million in 1991 to $19 million in 1996, a reduction of 25 percent, with half the hit coming the first year of the Harris regime. Virtually every library in Canada faced cuts. Even when budgets were frozen or actually rose, as was the case with the Winnipeg Public Library, whose budget increased by 1.3 percent between 1990 and 1995, funding was actually down because inflation rose 17 percent during that same period.

Cuts to libraries, schools, health care, and other social programs were sold to Canadians as the antidote to our having lived beyond our means, as I'll discuss in Chapter 8. We were told incessantly that our high deficits were a consequence of out-of-control spending on these programs. But thanks to the work of Linda McQuaig and others, it has been made clear that these claims were fraudulent. McQuaig demonstrates that the major cause of high deficits and growing debt was not spending on libraries and social programs, but the zero-inflation campaign run by the Bank of Canada during the late 1980s and early 1990s to protect the wealth of bondholders. The bank's high interest rates caused Canada's recession to be deeper and longer than those experienced in other industrialized countries; more people were thrown out of work and government revenues were wiped out.

So while spending on social programs did not cause the deficit, these programs would bear the cost of eliminating it. In effect, library funding was cut so that the affluent, those who could afford to buy their own books and pay for their own information services, could continue to receive a greater proportion of the national wealth. The irony is that the cuts came at a time when citizens placed public libraries near or at the top of the priority list of all local government services. Yet even when the recession ended and government coffers began to refill, funding to libraries was not fully restored. The propaganda machine began churning out a steady stream of studies calling for tax cuts, which would make permanent the underfunding of public libraries.

Faced with reduced public funding, library boards and administrators had a number of options: they could campaign to restore funding; they could cut programs and services; they could look for alternative sources of funding, such as user fees and corporate contributions; or they could replace expensive professional staff members with less highly paid para-professionals and with information technology, which was already making its presence felt through the actions of the industry. Boards and administrators did all of these except the most important: rally the public to their cause.

In November 1990, just before his government started to slice away at public services through his "Social Contract," Ontario premier

Bob Rae warned librarians that "nothing will happen until librarians and trustees speak and speak strongly. But you are going to have to shout much, much louder if you are going to be heard."[26] (Rae was referring to a threat to eliminate library boards, but his words apply equally to funding cuts.) This should have been a relatively easy endeavour, given the strong public support for libraries and the fact that, on average, the public library's share of local tax revenues is quite small – less than 5 percent. But librarians and trustees did not heed Rae's words, and a promising avenue of action was closed. Why? For one thing, library board trustees are appointed by municipal councils and are not likely to go public with protests about council cuts to their budgets. Many belong to the same political organizations as the councillors, and may even have their own political ambitions. They are appointed quietly, have little public profile, and a limited constituency. Citizens do not know who their library trustees are, or what they do. And while the board form of governance buffers library staff from political council, librarians are still municipal employees and thus have great difficulty opposing council decisions. And librarian associations have not done much better in marshalling public support, which perhaps isn't surprising. Given the public library's tradition of providing materials on all sides of an issue, how could librarians advocate for one position only?

cutting staff, imposing fees

Reducing costs was the route taken by most libraries. Because libraries are service oriented and labour intensive, staff costs consume the largest portion of their budgets. The Edmonton Public Library is typical; about 65 percent of its budget is allocated for salaries, 12 percent for books and other library materials, 8 percent for supplies, and the rest for rental and maintenance of library properties. Obviously, cutting staff would be the most effective way of reducing costs. But providing direct, personal, knowledgeable service to patrons is the library's most significant long-term investment and in some ways its raison d'être. Nevertheless, to lessen the severity of the cuts from above, administrators slashed away below. The Metro Toronto Reference

Library's cuts translated into a reduction of its entire staff by almost 25 percent through voluntary separation, early retirement, reducing the hours of service, and reorganizing library departments into centres that require fewer staff to operate. And the worst wasn't over. In the summer of 1996, Metro Council let the library know that it had in mind a further large cut of as much as 12.5 percent. Furious lobbying by trustees, management, and the librarians' union led to this being scaled back to 4.6 percent, but that still meant laying off thirty-seven more staff members and closing the library for one week in August. And there was still more: when the Harris regime amalgamated the Metro Toronto municipalities, the six regional library systems became one library board, and the reference library was hit yet again.

For some libraries, raising funds through user fees was preferable to cutting staff, hours, and services, even if it seemed like a return to the subscription libraries of the nineteenth century. Alberta, the Reform heartland of Canada, is the only province where it wasn't illegal for public libraries to charge an annual membership fee, and now most municipalities have them. In 1994 the Edmonton Public Library imposed a twelve-dollar user fee for adult library-card renewals. (Users under eighteen and low-income earners receive free cards.) Edmonton city councillor Tooker Gomberg, who sat on the library board, was concerned that the fee could "end up being a barrier to the widespread use of the library." But library director Penelope McKee dismissed this concern, believing user fees were essential. "I see it as the survival of the public library. It's a reasonable direction to take."[27] User fees as a way to save the *free* public library!

Today, fee-based services are being introduced in libraries across Canada – to save them, presumably. Metro Toronto, for example, set up Intellisearch. For fees ranging from twenty-five to sixty dollars, plus extras for full-text articles and documents, Intellisearch provides basic information on companies; market research; database searches for journal articles, patents, and trademarks; and price and volume histories of stocks traded on North American exchanges. The Vancouver Public Library's InfoAction charges eighty dollars an hour for information on small businesses, industry profiles, or market research. For $350 a month, subscribers can be kept current on any topic from both print and Internet sources. Library users who cannot afford these services can still do their own research for the cost of photocopying, but they do not have access to the full range of resources available to fee-paying "customers." Of course, since fee-paying services are still money-losers, taxpayers are subsidizing them. Worse yet, if Intellisearch and InfoAction are successful, more resources will be structured this way, with fewer remaining for free use.

business lends a hand

Once Edmonton library users pay their twelve dollars, they can borrow books from the Stanley A. Milner Library, formerly known as the Centennial, the city's main downtown branch. For a laughably low $250,000 (how much did taxpayers invest in the facility without receiving recognition?), Milner, who is one of the city's corporate elite – president of Chieftain International Oil and a director of Canadian Pacific, the Canadian Imperial Bank of Commerce, Alberta Energy Co., and other corporations – gets his name enshrined for all time above the library entrance. Milner was a chair of the Edmonton Public Library Board in the 1960s and headed the library's capital fund-raising campaign in the 1990s. His donation set the benchmark – anyone who wants a library branch named after himself or his company can write a similarly-sized cheque and the board will consider it. Of course, this largesse can go only so far. With thirteen library branches, $250,000 each will yield only $3.25 million. Given that the city cut its grant to the library by $500,000, that sum will cover about six years' worth of cuts. What will the board sell next?

Well, the Metro Toronto board threatened to sell its most treasured collection – John James Audubon's lavish *Birds of America*, 435 hand-coloured, life-size illustrations published in England between 1827 and 1838, one of only five copies in Canada. The threat worked to bring in a corporate sponsor. Canada Trust, which is owned by Imperial Tobacco Co., put up $1.2 million to keep the collection in the library and make it available for public viewing. The board then searched for other corporate sponsors who would help underwrite operations; in return, these sponsors would get parts of the building, computer terminals, the photographic image library, the consumer health-information centre, or the newspaper and periodical centre named after them. They could even set up centres to meet their own needs. The library leased 3,200 square feet in its basement to Smart Toronto, a public-private consortium that acts like the PR arm of the information technology industry, for a centre to promote the use of communications and IT products and services. In 1998, Atomic Energy of Canada Ltd. paid the library $350,000 to create a Web site that would provide access to authoritative science information on the Internet. Presumably the site will also provide unbiased information on the hazards of atomic energy. At the other end of the country, General Motors of Canada leased the Vancouver Public Library's plazas and concourse to create GM World Plaza, a showcase for seventeen cars and trucks.[28] Needless to say, the library did not set up a display outlining the dangers of global warming from increased automobile usage. Libraries even rented out their roofs. In 1997, the Canadian Library Association signed a deal with Clearnet Communications, a digital wireless company, to allow it to locate antennas on library roofs in exchange for high-speed Internet access or a cash payment.

hijacking the library

Many Carnegie libraries wear their names proudly, although Carnegie did not require municipal councils to name their buildings after him. These libraries epitomize nearly a century of uncompromising public service, with their reading rooms and book stacks accessible to all citizens. Their sanctity began to be debased when corporate logos and elite names were plastered on buildings, reading materials, and even library cards. But as long as library staff doesn't censor collections to placate donor sensitivities, there is little infringement on the library's fundamental mission. No one has ever suggested that the Stanley A. Milner Library should screen from its collection materials critical of the Alberta oil industry, for example. But there is a problem when the corporate donor is Bill Gates, who has a business interest in what libraries do.

Libraries were early adopters of automation, and their purchases of computers and systems helped establish many IT companies in the 1960s and 1970s. And libraries today continue to be big purchasers and users of the most up-to-date products and services. So it's no surprise that they targeted IT companies as donors and partners. And it's also not surprising that the industry has long considered libraries a key market. The library's role was to familiarize the public with new information products and services, sometimes for a fee. But expanding the role of the information industry in libraries blurs the line between the two, and turns the library into another distribution channel for the producers and vendors of information and technology. Libraries are becoming adjuncts of the information industry, especially if library management sees acting more like a business and less like a public service as its mission.

The dismal prospect of libraries becoming adjuncts to the information industry is the culmination of thirty years of industry activism. Robin Alston, a British professor of library studies, reportedly says of this era that "the community of librarians was 'hijacked' . . . by the merchandisers of electronic goods in one of the most wonderful conspiracies in the history of librarianship."[29] From the moment it arose in the 1960s, the information industry, whose firms "produce, distribute, retail, manage and process information products and services,"[30] was a threat to the public library and its philosophy of free public access. The industry was created from massive U.S. government spending on defence and the computer. Lockheed Aircraft, for instance, developed Dialog, one of the first major database services. Firms capitalized on publicly funded inventions and discoveries; exploited the contents of government files; and turned to libraries to develop their markets, test new software, hardware, and databases, and train new generations of potential users.

In the 1970s and 1980s, services like Dialog, Bibliographic Retrieval Services (BRS), and others mounted hundreds of databases on remote computers, which were accessed through regular telephone lines and incurred long-distance charges. On-line searching was attractive to librarians and users because of its fundamental superiority to searching a printed index. It is faster, more comprehensive, provides more points of access, and allows results to be transmitted to other locations. And perhaps most important, many databases provide full-text records.

But such accessibility came with a high price. Searches were usually undertaken by librarians trained in search procedures to minimize fees and search times. Libraries paid a fee based on elapsed time and number of records captured from a search, and then passed all or part of the cost on to the patron. Librarians disliked acting as the intermediary between database and patron, but were compelled to follow this practice because on-line searching was expensive and the final cost could not be predicted and budgeted for. Although on-line searching gave users access to previously unavailable information resources, it made libraries more dependent on information providers.[31] And by subscribing to on-line search services, librarians were approving, albeit reluctantly, the division of their users into two classes – those who could afford to pay for searches and those who could not.

Because of the cost factor, this market was limited. Starting in 1990 many of the same databases moved from remote mainframe to local high-powered microcomputers; libraries could provide unlimited searching by buying the computer on which the database resides or licensing the database on an annual basis. Databases that had previously been accessed on a cost-per-minute basis could now be purchased as a CD-ROM and made available for unlimited searching for a reasonable fixed cost. With the declining cost of computing power, libraries could afford to purchase more powerful machines that could support more users and larger databases. Libraries also connected their computers into local networks to allow users to access a cluster of CD-ROM databases from inside the library or from locations around the university campus. During the 1990s, libraries were able to move from databases that provided indexed and abstracted information to those that provided full text and had powerful search tools.

Unlike books and journals, electronic databases are leased to the library under licence agreements that spell out who may use the database, how many can use it at one time, and how much the library will pay. Libraries are being pushed out of their traditional role as owners of materials and are now simply owners of equipment that can access materials. But if a library decides not to renew a licence, it must in some cases return all tapes or CD-ROMs from previous years to the vendor, leaving it with nothing for future users. Once again, libraries became further dependent on the information industry. Reference librarians quickly discovered that computerized catalogues and databases required lengthy and frequent interactions with patrons. New databases were continuously being created, which required protracted training sessions for staff. And computer hardware, software, and networks, which became obsolete at an ever-accelerating pace, had to be continually upgraded or replaced.

With the explosion in the popularity of the World Wide Web, libraries faced their biggest challenge yet: irrelevance. Historically, they had been intermediaries between producers and vendors of information, whose interests are economic, and users of information, whose interests are social and educational. Libraries purchase books, serials, newspapers, videos, and photographs and lease databases from corporations that own rights to information and will sell to anyone who can pay the price. But with the Internet, information owners and distributors can bypass libraries altogether and distribute materials directly to PC users in their homes and offices. Each rise in home PC use may lead to fewer users for libraries, which are scrambling to make themselves part of the new distribution equation. Ironically, some librarians see Bill Gates and other information vendors as their saviours from irrelevancy. Once again, though, the information industry may be creating a market by initially providing Internet access at low cost, with plans to raise prices later. And if attempts to create digital libraries are successful, users, whether in the library or elsewhere, might have to pay each time they access a document, or even a page or an image from a document.

digital libraries

The digital library, one goal of Connecting Canadians, is the ultimate threat to the free public library. Having built networks with huge bandwidth capacity, the information industry needed profitable applications to take advantage of what it had created — a build-it-and-they-will-come theme we will take up in the next chapter. Soon the industry alighted on digital libraries, where the entire contents of libraries are digitized and mounted on computer servers as a "killer application." The idea of a digital library has gained momentum since the early 1980s, when reporters first switched from typewriters to computers and newspapers started saving the day's stories in electronic databases, which were then offered to subscribers through services like Dialog. Over the next decade, most magazines and periodicals moved to the same format: preparation and storage electronically but distribution in print. About 1990, a new medium appeared on the scene, the e-zine, produced in electronic format only, with no print version. Electronic-format-only publishing took off with a vengeance with the emergence of the World Wide Web. By the mid-1990s, a plethora of e-zines, on-line newspapers, government documents, and other types of electronic information was readily available on the Internet. With the advent of rudimentary search engines to locate and retrieve documents, digital libraries were born. But this production is a drop in the bucket compared with all the books and journals already in existence in print format, to say nothing of videotapes, audiotapes, photographs, maps, drawings, historical records, and sound recordings. The digital library transforms the holdings of libraries, archives, museums, even art galleries into electronic documents that can be stored in computers and sent anywhere in the world on global information networks.

A digital library need not be contained in one library or mounted on one computer. Different items, even different parts of the same item (each a separate "object," in the language of distributed networks), may be stored in geographically dispersed locations. A multimedia record might have an audio clip stored on a computer in one location, a video clip in another computer on a different continent, and the text somewhere else. When the record is called up, its parts are quickly located and sent to the requester, where they are presented as one integrated piece in the correct sequence without any indication that the elements were ever separate.

On its own merits, the digital library is neither positive nor negative, enabling nor restricting, a blessing nor curse, to use Neil

Postman's words. But the question is, Who is creating the library and for what purpose? Do public and academic librarians and other researchers want to develop digital libraries so they can provide free public access for all citizens to an expanded storehouse of public information? Or do corporate interests want to create new streams of revenue for cash-hungry information corporations? Given the resources available to each camp, and the direction of government information policy, corporate interests will likely prevail.

Librarians become involved in digital library projects because they see the digital library as a logical extension of their role in creating collections and providing access services. Referring to the immense and invaluable collections of the U.S. Library of Congress, Guy Lamolinara, editor of the *Library of Congress Information Bulletin*, argued that "such treasures, many in fragile condition, were previously available only to visitors to Washington, on a limited basis. But digital versions will make it possible for citizens anywhere to see and hear this record of the American experience."[32] Libraries have an "obligation to share . . . resources with as many people as possible," said Librarian of Congress James Billington on announcing the library's ambitious National Digital Library Program.[33] Librarians can protect rare and fragile objects without denying access to people who want to study them. Researchers can scrutinize national treasures over the Internet without handling the originals. Digital materials can be accessed quickly, at least in theory (given the current painfully slow speeds of accessing Web sites over the Internet). And more than one person can use the same record at the same time. Most important, users unable to visit in person can read, view, or listen to the materials at remote locations. Electronic records occupy much less space – millimetres on magnetic disks, as opposed to metres on bookshelves – and they don't need to be reshelved after use.

But digitization merely provides expanded access to materials; it doesn't preserve the materials. Says Canada's acting national archivist, Lee McDonald, there's "no guarantee we can send that digitized version down the road. For sure, the medium itself is going to deteriorate and the key will be making sure we can move the software and the content forward generation to generation."[34] Given the industry's penchant for planned and rapid obsolescence, archivists worry that the hardware, operating platforms, software, mark-up language, and document format they selected so carefully might not even exist one hundred years from now. They also worry about the instability of computer tapes and disks, which are not effective for long-term storage without regular refreshing. Will our grandchildren be able to access and read today's digital documents?

And then there's the stupendous cost involved. Digitizing the collection of the Library of Congress ("the world's largest repository of human achievement," as it unabashedly calls itself) – 20 million books, 4 million maps and atlases, 14 million prints and photographs, 600,000 films and videotapes – would be an impossible task of incalculable cost. But the political payoffs of such a high-profile venture are irresistible, and politicians from former Speaker of the House Newt Gingrich – "a public-private partnership for learning," he called it – to Vice-President Al Gore lined up to back the National Digital Library Program, providing a congressional appropriation in 1996 to get the ball rolling. It's worth noting that the project was sparked by a group from Bell Atlantic, the Disney Channel, and other major corporations. It would digitize Revolutionary War maps, hand-written drafts of the Declaration of Independence and the Gettysburg Address, the personal papers of the first twenty-three U.S. presidents, Civil War photographs, full-motion videos of the earliest American documentary films, and sound recordings of historical events. Most financial support would come from the sponsoring corporations, which began raising private capital for the digital conversion of the library's holdings.[35]

The Library of Congress estimates its conversion costs at two to six dollars per page of text, but expects prices to decline as the project proceeds. Scanning pages into digital images of text, pictures, and drawings is the cheapest and most frequently used method, having fallen to one to two dollars a page. This is satisfactory for preserving fragile historical records, because it can capture the look and feel of a document. But it produces huge files – a legible image of a map measuring 15 by 31 inches with printing only 0.05 inches high would create a 125-megabyte file, "large enough to choke a desktop computer," notes Michael Lesk.[36] His solution is more powerful machines and new image formats. Further problems could be created by these bulky files zinging around the Internet eating up huge gobs of bandwidth – in fact, just the kind of application foreseen by Connecting Canadians. And scanning produces images that can be viewed but not manipulated. As Lesk notes, there is as yet no easy way to find specific words or passages in the text, no easy way to e-mail the image, and no way to cut and paste it into a document.

Converting print materials into electronic text solves these problems, but creates others. The cheapest conversion technique is optical character recognition (OCR), which uses pattern-matching techniques to extract words from scanned images. Although relatively cheap, it is inaccurate: 99 percent accuracy translates into a dozen or more errors per page, errors that must be corrected by hand, which is an expensive, labour-intensive procedure. Another way to convert print to electronic text – the most expensive – is to type it in. Even with companies in Asia that employ thousands of low-wage typists, a typical 300-page document can cost $600 (U.S.) to convert.

Of the $60 million required by the Library of Congress to get digitization under way, $45 million would come from the private sector and $15 million from congressional appropriations.[37] The Library of Congress would enter into joint ventures with private companies to digitize some collections, but says it will "grant no exclusive rights to our materials to anyone." Presumably, non-exclusive licences, the option often preferred by information vendors anyway, will be allowed. The Library of Congress also sparked the creation of additional digital collections through a partnership with Ameritech Corp., which provides local telecommunications services in the American Midwest (and owns Ameritech Library Services, one of the largest suppliers of information technology to libraries in the U.S. and Canada). Ameritech provided $2 million to the library to sponsor a competition that enables public, academic, and research libraries, museums, historical societies, and archives to digitize their primary materials.

The Library of Congress effort ensures that there will be public involvement in the digital world, but the main direction of digital library development, as set by the Clinton-Gore National Information Infrastructure (NII) – the model for Canada's information highway –

is relentlessly private. As NII's considerable rhetoric put it, the program is to "transform the lives of the American people – ameliorating the constraints of geography, disability, and economic status – giving all Americans a fair opportunity to go as far as their talents and ambitions will take them."[38]

In September 1993, the Clinton administration released its Agenda for Action, the government's blueprint for creating an American information highway. Digital libraries were seen as a potential killer application of the NII – but within the context of the Clinton-Gore initiative, the digital library was far removed from the notion of traditional public libraries. Digital library development was to follow nine principles of the NII. One principle did address access – it was a call to "ensure that information resources are available to all at affordable prices" – but affordable prices are a far cry from free access. The other principles were aimed at the private sector. In fact, the number-one priority for the NII was to promote private-sector investment, and Gore took this message with him wherever he went. Other principles he espoused were the protection of intellectual-property rights, and the commitment of government research programs and grants to help the private sector develop and demonstrate technologies needed for the NII. In the digital library projects that flowed from these principles, scant attention was paid to access and affordability and a great deal to the needs of private investors. In their search for a national economic strategy, the Clintonites were attracted by the considerable commercial development already taking place, presaging the future economic importance of digital library technology to the U.S. A vast number of projects got underway almost simultaneously, as everyone scrambled to get a piece of the action.

Canada was left at the starting gate in this race to capitalize on public information resources. The federally funded National Library has a mandate to collect all Canadian publications, as well as foreign publications with Canadian content, and make them available for study. It wasn't until March 1997, about four years after the Clinton administration targeted digital libraries as a growth area, that the National Library finally invited a number of academic and public libraries to a conference in Ottawa to establish a Canadian Initiative on Digital Libraries (CIDL). Most representatives were from university libraries, though several came from public libraries that had their own digital projects underway. The Leamington, Ontario, public library had a digital local-history database, and the North York Public Library had a collection of recorded children's stories. CIDL's goals were limited to sharing information, reviewing best practices, defining roles and responsibilities, raising awareness, and discussing issues. There was no program and little money. CIDL did, however, decide to form a partnership with CANARIE, and the two bodies signed a memorandum of agreement during the summer of 1998 to work together to develop digital libraries and related "services and industries in Canada."[39]

The National Library took a big hit under the Liberals, who cut its funding by 30 percent between 1993 and 1999. But instead of restoring its budget once the deficit monster had been slain, the Liberals established a commission of one person, a former Liberal MP and professor of history, to assess the library's role in the electronic era. Was this the Connecting Canadians agenda again? Some Liberal insiders claimed privately that the purpose of the review was to digitize library holdings for use on the Internet as part of the e-commerce initiative. National librarian Marianne Scott says, "We want to be sure that . . . we are properly positioned to deal with this electronic age. And also the role we can play in fostering Canadian content for the Internet."[40]

Canadian activities notwithstanding, digital libraries are turning into a private-sector American effort, repeating a pattern that has occurred many times in the history of computers and the Internet. Public and non-profit sectors put up the money, take the risks, make the discoveries, and develop the potential. Then the private sector takes over and reaps the benefits. The Clinton-Gore administration set up the multi-agency Digital Library Initiative (DLI), with financial backing from the three largest federal sponsors of U.S. scientific research: the National Science Foundation (NSF), the Department of Defense Advanced Research Projects Agency (DARPA), and the National Aeronautics and Space Administration (NASA). These agencies have a long history of initiating major projects that were subsequently commercialized. The initiative granted about $4 million to each of six projects selected from a large number of applications. Each was led by a major American university, together with a consortium of public- and private-sector organizations. Some projects positioned librarians front and centre. The University of Michigan's Digital Libraries Research Project, for example, proposed a multimedia digital library of earth and space science that would involve university, public, and school libraries, as well as companies such as Elsevier Science and IBM. Other projects framed libraries as merely one market for the information industry's services and products. If these succeed, and if micropayment systems are implemented, free universal access to library materials may become a fond memory.

micropayments – the key to commercialization

Carnegie-Mellon University in Pittsburgh received a $4.8-million DLI grant for its Informedia Digital Library Project, which allows users to retrieve science and mathematical materials from video archives. There is a touch of irony in Carnegie-Mellon's participation in the DLI. The university was founded in 1900 by Andrew Carnegie, the benefactor of the free library. Yet his namesake institution is developing technologies that could help write *finis* to the free public library system. The problem isn't entirely with Informedia, though. This project licensed one thousand hours of video from the archives of the public television station in Pittsburgh, videos created by the local public school system, and video course material produced by the BBC for the Open University in the United Kingdom. The technology Informedia uses partitions video into small-sized video and audio segments that can be retrieved and manipulated by the user. Informedia will use commercial servers to distribute its segments. "The partnerships we have established for resources, field testing and productization will enable us to achieve a more pervasive impact and potential commercial realization," noted project leader Howard Wactlar.[41]

The "commercial realization" of Informedia may depend on a project called NetBill, which shares Informedia's grant and claims to be "a dependable, secure and economical payment method for purchasing digital goods and services through the Internet."[42] NetBill is an electronic-commerce project headquartered at Carnegie-Mellon's Information Networking Institute, an organization that brings together the schools of engineering, computer science, and business to study commerce over the Internet and private networks. NetBill is led by CMU professors Marvin Sirbu and Doug Tygar, who worry that since most information on the Internet is free, "intellectual property owners have little incentive to make valuable information accessible through the network." There are many providers who could sell information on the Internet, and many potential customers for that information. "What is missing," they argue, "is an electronic-commerce mechanism that links the merchants and the customers." NetBill, they hope, will be that mechanism;[43] they claim it solves three problems facing electronic commerce on the Internet.

A typical digital library interaction is the purchase of something as small as a page from a journal article, a photograph, a portion of a map, or a video or audio clip, the cost of which could be as low as ten to twenty cents, hence the label "micropayments." VISA and MasterCard impose a minimum purchase limit of thirty cents, because the cost of processing smaller transactions would be more than the value of the transaction. NetBill, however, has a very low transaction cost, about one cent for a ten-cent item, and thus could succeed in this market. For those worried that NetBill would spell the end of free public access, it has an answer, sort of – just think of "free" as "a marginal price of zero." "The transaction begins when the customer requests a formal price quote for a product. The price may be different than the standard list price because, for example, the customer may be part of a site license group, and thus be entitled to a marginal price of zero."[44]

The second problem facing e-commerce is how to ensure secure transmission of information goods and payments over the open Internet. If libraries charge customers for accessing their digital collections, then they need a secure and economical transaction-processing system. NetBill authenticates users, manages their accounts, processes their transactions, bills them, and issues reports to clients and users. "With a NetBill account and client software, users can buy information, software, CPU cycles, or other services from NetBill-authorized service providers, under a variety of payment schemes. Its delivery mechanism will deliver the goods only if the customer has paid for them."[45]

The third concern is how to prevent users from redistributing information when they have purchased only one copy. NetBill, like other e-commerce initiatives, embeds a unique watermark in each copy sold, so that "illegal" copies can be traced to their source. Digital watermarking is one of the technologies designed to distribute images of valuable documents and works of art securely, while also protecting ownership rights.

The NetBill-Informedia projects took a giant step towards commercialization in April 1997 when NetBill signed an agreement with CyberCash Inc., a leader in developing software for secure financial transactions over the Internet. For $2.2 million (U.S.), CyberCash acquired worldwide rights for the commercial use and sub-license of NetBill's e-commerce technology. CyberCash already had a number of Internet payment systems in the works, but this acquisition positioned the company well for the expected explosion in the sale of multimedia and digital information requiring small payments and assured delivery. A third partner was Mellon Bank, Pittsburgh's third-largest financial institution and one of the original participants in the design of the NetBill system. Mellon's role would be to electronically store money put aside by NetBill users.

It might seem that in this world of high finance and big business, libraries are not part of the picture, that NetBill's intended market is business. It's worth noting, then, that NetBill's project manager, Chris Deephouse, was an invited speaker at the Access 96 conference in Vancouver (sponsored by the libraries of the province's three major universities and the provincial electronic-library network). Many speakers touched on digital library issues with topics like encryption systems and user authentication. Deephouse told a roomful of librarians and information-system vendors about NetBill's network-security and electronic-payment systems and about its Library Card, a credential issued by a local or school library that allows authenticated access from any home or campus computer and offers "efficient cost-recovery for reserve books, interlibrary loan, database searches, overdue charges, printing and copying." Extracting revenues from libraries is very much part of the Informedia/NetBill/CyberCash/ Mellon Bank business plan. There will be exceptions, such as NetBill's "marginal cost of zero." But the world's treasures might soon be accessible only to those who can afford it – unless librarians fight to retain their core values of making information on all sides of an issue freely available to all citizens, especially in the digital era.

whither libraries?

Librarians do not present a united front in resisting the colonization of public information resources, as I've suggested several times in this chapter. In fact, the profession is deeply split over corporate funding. At the 1995 annual general meeting of the Canadian Library Association, delegates narrowly voted down a resolution to oppose corporate advertising on library cards. The issue had been prompted by the decision of the Vancouver Public Library board to accept advertising on the commemorative card issued to everyone who donated twenty-five dollars or more to the library's campaign for a new building. The successful bidder was Concord Pacific Development Corp., the city's largest developer and owner of most of the land around the new $30-million, nine-storey structure, which resembles the Roman Coliseum. Concord paid $500,000 to have its name on the card for seven years. On the day the library opened, Concord took out full-page ads in local newspapers welcoming the library and touting its own proposed convention centre, which would be three blocks away. Many librarians were upset by this deal. "It's prostitution," said one central branch librarian, who spoke on condition on anonymity. "I don't know what's happening with us in Vancouver." Still, several delegates argued that this was an issue for individual library boards, and that it would be inappropriate for the CLA to "instruct member libraries in corporate decision-making." Others said that it was just a local issue and not one in which CLA should get involved.[46]

Making libraries more business-like is another trend that began in California, where some library directors began to think of their institutions not as departments of local government, but as non-profit corporations that receive tax funds as part of their revenue mix. "Public librarians must begin to think of their customers not as a totality but as an aggregate of market segments, each of which needs targeted resources, services, and appropriate public relations techniques," argues Brian Reynolds, director of the San Luis–Obispo City-County Library.[47] Such thinking, which may be the real California library disease, quickly spread across the U.S. and into Alberta. To sell its twelve-dollar memberships, the Edmonton Public Library mounted an aggressive marketing campaign that included free rock concerts and T-shirts for those who signed up. Library communications manager Iolani Domingo said the library was targeting eighteen- to thirty-five-year-olds. The next event after the rock concert was a billiards tournament. "We used to call people who use the library a patron," said Domingo. "Now we think of what the customer wants. Libraries are like any other business. You have to market to your customer. . . . You have to catch them where they play."[48]

Across the country, librarians have adopted the business model in varying degrees. In Ontario, head librarians are called chief executive officers, implying that librarians have been, or will soon be, replaced by business managers. In Vancouver, the library board abolished the position of deputy library director and replaced it with two others, unrelated to direct library service – marketing and strategic planning. But VPL computer services librarian Brian Campbell, for one, decries the adoption of the business model. "An occasional visitor to CLA conferences could be forgiven for thinking they had wandered into an MBA seminar on marketing and neo-conservative economic theory," he wrote just before the information highway exploded into public consciousness. At the same time, he noted, "There [was] an almost total absence of critical analysis of the threat to library service in Canada."[49]

Campbell is one of many librarians working to preserve the public sphere in library services and create a public space on the Internet. He was the founding president and one of a number of activist librarians in the group that helped create Vancouver's community network, which, in wanting to provide access to information as a right of citizenship, had goals that were more overtly political than most community networks.

I'll argue in the last chapter that a key objective to accomplish in our efforts to reclaim public information is to establish, in law, the right of everyone to have equal access to information and advice services, one of a new set of human rights that citizens must have if they are to function effectively in a so-called information society. With so much information available, how do we find what we need to function as effective citizens? How do we interpret and analyze the information, once found? Citizens need a network of easily accessible and inexpensive information services to help them perform these tasks. There are important roles for librarians to play as guides to information resources, interpreters of results, and tutors in how to use resources, search engines, and databases.[50]

The public library faces daunting challenges as Canada enters the digital era, and each challenge seems designed to restrict free access to information. Once NetBill and others have perfected micropayment systems, there will be a vast scale-up in the use of fee for service, and many citizens will be locked out of the information equation. Even if they can afford access, citizens will not likely find all the information they need because of something called market censorship. Information on social issues will be dropped while legal and business information will proliferate, because vendors deem that the market doesn't want the former and has an insatiable appetite for the latter. Increasingly, restrictions will be placed on the use of information in databases because of expanded copyright and intellectual-property laws. Libraries will be forced to use databases under increasingly onerous licence conditions. They're pressured to become enforcers of intellectual-property rights for multinational electronic-publishing firms, undermining their traditional allegiance to their local communities. Finally, libraries face restrictions in the quantity of documents they can receive under the government's Depository Services Program because electronic documents are not always included. As these examples illustrate, librarians and library supporters can do only so much to protect public information, since defining decisions are being made outside the library by a private government of cyberspace.

the private government
···◀
# of connected canada

···

You have maintained the viability of a Canada-wide Internet
during the early years of this new industry, and in so doing you
have laid the groundwork for the commercial Internet of Canada.
— Bell Advanced Communications president John MacDonald
to Internet pioneers, June 23, 1997

In the 1989 Universal Studios film *Field of Dreams*, a voice whispers to Ray Kinsella (Kevin Costner), as he works his Iowa cornfield, "If you build it, he will come." "Build what? Who will come?" the startled Kinsella asks, and the answers unfold over the course of the film. "Build what?" is easy: the thirty-six-year-old Kinsella ploughs up a large chunk of his acreage and puts in a baseball field, complete with bleachers and lights, nearly going bankrupt and losing his farm to his brother-in-law's syndicate. "Who will come?" is not as evident. Kinsella has to travel back in time to recruit long-gone baseball greats like Shoeless Joe Jackson, who died the year before he was born. Kinsella ends up with two teams of dead baseball stars playing ball on his diamond, but only he and his family can see them. Just as he is about to sign away the farm, his daughter abruptly exclaims, "You don't have to sell the farm." "Why?" he asks. "People will come from all over," she says. "They'll decide to take a vacation and come to Iowa City and think it is really boring. So they will drive up and want to pay us, like buying a ticket . . . to watch the game. It'll be just like when they were little kids, a long time ago and they will watch the game and remember what it was like – people will come." Then the 1960s counter-culture hero Terence Mann (played by James Earl Jones) weighs in with his explanation of why the daughter is right. "The one constant through all the years, Ray, has been baseball. America is ruled by it like an army of steamrollers. . . . Baseball has marked the time. This field, this game, is a part of our past, Ray. It reminds us of all that once was good and it could be again. People will most definitely come!" The movie ends with Kinsella playing catch with his dead father – he did come – under the lights; the camera cuts away to show an endless line of cars snaking towards the farm. They are coming, and he will be rich.

But author W.P. Kinsella was wrong about one thing. America is ruled not by baseball and the past, but by technology and the future. New technology and the progress and prosperity it will bring, not baseball, are the one constant through the years – "the American dream of the mechanical sublime," in American communication scholar James Carey's apt phrase. In the nineteenth century, technology meant steam engines, electric lights, and telephones; in the twentieth, it means satellites, spaceships, computers, and now the Internet. But the dream remains the same: a better future through technology. Today's futurology, as practised by seers like John Naisbett, Alvin Toffler, and Nicholas Negroponte, is merely the dream commercialized. We can have perfect democracy, a clean environment, two chickens in every pot, and much more if we only believe in what computers and information technology can, and will, accomplish. Have no fear – the benefits will come.

We Canadians too have a love affair with technology, though our obsession is communication. One of our most enduring beliefs is that Canada has survived as a nation and resisted the expansionist urges of our neighbour to the south by building east-west communication links. Our motto might as well be Build It and We Exist, or else Build It and They Won't Come from the South. These notions can be found everywhere in official Canadian government thinking over many decades. An important 1987 Department of Communications report, for example, which kicked off discussions about advanced computer-communications networks, said this:

> Communications have always played a central role in Canada's history. From the fur trade of the seventeenth and eighteenth centuries to the canals and railways of the nineteenth, from the broadcasting networks, airlines and highways to the telephone and satellite systems of the twentieth, communications technologies have helped Canadians reach new frontiers, settle and develop the wilderness, and build both a society and culture that are unique in the world for the degree to which they depend on good communications systems.[1]

The report's conclusion was clear: if we want to continue to exist as a nation, we'd better get on with the job of building information networks. University of Ottawa communication professor Robert Babe says this argument is based on the myth of technological nationalism.[2] It's a myth, he argues, because many of our communications links go north-south, not east-west. "It may be fairly said that Canada as a nation persists despite, not because of, communication media."[3] Telegraph lines linked Canadian centres with U.S. metropolises, often precluding connections to other Canadian communities. And newer technologies, like satellite communications and cable-TV, Babe argues, help "efface local culture by facilitating the spread of 'global consciousness.' Likewise, computer networks extend the hegemony of transnational corporations, speeding instructions from headquarters to distant localities and then facilitating data retrieval and processing."[4] If anything, new communication technologies have fragmented, not cemented, our country. And even when communication networks did run east and west, it's not clear they were meant to bind the country together. In 1988, when high-speed network discussions first began, Prime Minister Brian Mulroney pushed through the Canada-U.S. Free Trade Agreement and won re-election even though most Canadians opposed the deal. An east-west Canadian information highway and a

Free Trade Agreement with an undeniable north-south pull were clearly at odds with each other. Was the Mulroney government using the Canadian information highway as a smokescreen to hide its real purpose: the promotion of north-south communications?

Technological nationalism is Canada's brand of technological determinism – the belief that developments in technology cause changes in society, changes we cannot resist. Read the Electronic Highway Accord, published by British Columbia's Information and Technology Access Office. "The convergence of computer and telecommunications technology is transforming the way people live, work, learn and play," it insists.[5] Explore the views of David Johnston, who chaired the Information Highway Advisory Council and co-authored a book called *Getting Canada OnLine*, which purported to explain the workings of the information highway. He wrote that "digitization and the convergence of technologies are structurally transforming our economy, with three results: privatization, deregulation and globalization. . . . Traditional telecommunications monopolies and quasi-monopolies are crumbling while enterpreneurialism and competition are flourishing. This is largely a product of technological progress."[6] Or read John Manley's speaking notes for his Board of Trade address in December 1998: "Why connect Canadians? Essentially, connectedness builds a stronger society and a stronger economy."[7] With connectedness we are strong; without it we fail.

Field of Dreams extols the same kind of determinism. Building the stadium causes Ray Kinsella's father to come – indeed, he has no choice but to come. Similarly, converging technologies will cause us to change the way we live; Connecting Canadians will cause us to be strong. This is a dangerous proposition that leads to fatalism among citizens. We cannot resist the changes new technologies bring, so we might as well adapt to them. Our attention is diverted from the fact that new technologies are introduced and developed not as a consequence of some magical property of technology, but because they suit corporate profit strategies and government policy agendas. Technologies can do nothing without human agency. What usually happens is that business decides which technologies go forward (usually the ones under tight corporate control) and which ones wither and die. Certain technologies are encouraged, supported, and financed, while others are ignored and rejected. The explosion of big-screen Hollywood movies in the 1950s is a good illustration of this. The advent of wide-screen technology in the 1930s (Cinerama, Cinemascope) did not cause the studios to adopt its use. In fact, the technologies languished in their inventors' basements because studios had no interest in them. But with the challenge of television in the late 1940s, studios dusted them off and pressed them into the task of demonstrating the superiority of movies over the box – big screen, big sound, big stars, big budgets.

The myth of technological determinism is used to justify nearly everything corporations and governments are foisting on Canadians in the course of connecting us. Fortunately, we can rely on Babe to be our detector of technological determinism. He found one particularly troubling example in the opening remarks of Canadian Radio-television and Telecommunications Commission (CRTC) chairman Keith Spicer at the CRTC's show hearings on the information highway in 1995: "Within a very short period of time, we've witnessed the virtual explosion of information technologies that will someday no doubt reshape our lives in ways that even the richest and wisest entrepreneurs haven't begun to dream of."[8] Spicer's remarks provoked the usually restrained Babe to exclaim, "Such an unadulterated, if not indeed blind, faith in the inevitable beneficence of technological outcomes can only be described as technological determinism."[9] Yet Spicer's remarks merely reflect the framing of the hearings. Telephone and broadcasting technologies were converging whether we liked it or not, we were told. We'd better start to work immediately to accommodate convergence; otherwise, we'll be left behind or, worse, disappear from the world stage. None of this is true, of course. What really happened was that about a decade earlier, telephone companies, or telcos, decided they wanted to be able to provide content services such as broadcasting, and then they set out with a single-minded determination to do so. In retrospect, it's clear that the CRTC hearings merely rubber-stamped telco strategies.

Discussions about building a high-speed Canadian research network that would parallel the emerging public CA*net, began the same year *Field of Dreams* was released. The film must have been on everyone's mind. Andrew Bjerring, a research networking pioneer who went on to become president of CANARIE, recalled in 1992 that the "*Field of Dreams* argument (i.e., build the network and the applications will come to fill it) has not yet had much effect in Canada, largely because our research networks are coping with tariffs for communication links that are seven to ten times those in the United States."[10] Bjerring believed, correctly as it turned out, that a breakthrough − CANARIE − was near. CANARIE would be the Ray Kinsella of Canadian information networks, but with one big difference. It wouldn't merely build an information highway and wait for applications to appear magically, like the cars snaking to Kinsella's cornfield from Iowa City. What if they didn't come? What if the wrong kind of applications, such as community-oriented ones with little profit potential, came? To forestall these undesirable possibilities, CANARIE decided it would build the highest-bandwidth, fastest network it could muster resources for, and then fund developers and researchers to come up with applications to make profitable use of the bandwidth. Such a strategy would cast in stone the direction of Canada's Internet, limiting, perhaps even eliminating, the possibilities of non-commercial uses. With CANARIE in the driver's seat, there would be no public information network.

public policy, private decisions

Why did the Mulroney and Chrétien governments turn so much power over to CANARIE's private-sector interests, which would benefit financially from high-speed networks? To some extent, they were responding to the propaganda of the day − get government off the backs of industry and let markets work their "magic," whatever that meant. In a previous era, government might have set up a new regulatory body or extended the mandate of an existing one, such as the CRTC, which already regulates broadcasting and telecommunications. Or it might have established a Crown corporation or other government agency to develop and run the network, as it did with Canadian National Railway and the CBC. Chanting the mantra of "less government, deregulate, privatize," the right-wing-dominated Ottawa of the eighties and nineties had little enthusiasm or support for these approaches. Instead, Ottawa brought the private sector into the policy process to ensure that whatever government decided would be acceptable to business. In CANARIE's case, government even let business decide what the policy should be, and then gave its stamp of approval.

Public and private interests traditionally congregated around each major policy area in informal private governments. These were groupings of federal and provincial government agencies, corporate and (rarely) public-interest pressure groups, major corporations, members of the media, and others who attempted, over a long period of time, to influence policy in a particular field.[11] They worked together as a closed community; the public, even most back-bench MPs, were locked out. Decisions made in a particular policy field were always couched in terms of their benefits to Canada and Canadians. This was a wilful and (for the private government) necessary deceit. Usually, the major benefits actually accrued to private government members: an agency's clout was increased; an industry received a subsidy or tax benefit; news reporters who covered the beat enjoyed enhanced reputations and commanded larger salaries. Of course, benefits from the decisions made and endorsed by private governments did "trickle down" to the general population. Governments needed to justify their spending to taxpayers, so there had to be some pay-off to citizens. A tax benefit for the IT industry, for instance, might be framed as a policy to increase employment in the industry, which it might or might not do, and which regardless was not the real intent.

Private governments for information technology, broadcasting, and telecommunications were already well established, but the convergence of the three industries put everything up for grabs. The stakes were enormous, the interests powerful, and the issues difficult. Who would dominate – telephone, cable, or high-tech companies? Which technologies would be selected (and which companies would profit)? What were the appropriate roles for the federal and provincial governments? There was also a sense of urgency, at least among government bureaucrats. They feared that Canada would be left behind, a fear that corporate executives encouraged. Companies like IBM were engaged in similar exercises in the U.S., Japan, and the European Community, engendering the same sense of urgency there and creating a whipsaw effect around the world. A decision was made early on to bestow more power than usual on the private-sector side of the private government. Let CANARIE work it out. Government, which hesitated to enter the business of picking winners, would be the referee and the banker.

the barons of bandwidth

The information highway wasn't exactly a focus of Jean Chrétien's first Speech from the Throne on January 18, 1994 — it merited just twelve words in all — but his vow to implement a Canadian strategy for the information highway became an integral component of the Liberals' first government and was fleshed out as the Connecting Canadians strategy in the second.

Chrétien didn't use the word "Canadian" as it is commonly understood. Normally, "Canadian" would have meant mixed public and private enterprise, as had been the case with most major projects for more than 150 years. Rather, this would be a private-sector-dominated initiative, although taxpayers would pick up some of the tab. "Canadian" could also have meant wide consultation among citizens from all walks of life to arrive at a consensus as to the shape and direction of information networks. Chrétien didn't mean that either. Instead, he was officially sanctioning the emerging private government and signalling that it get on with the tasks of sorting out power relations and building the network. Bureaucrats in Industry Canada and several provincial ministries; senior corporate executives from telecommunications, cable, and computer-networking firms and their lobbyists; academic researchers; administrators; and computing officials — all were coalescing into groups like CANARIE and regional research institutes like OCRInet in Ottawa, WURCnet on the Prairies, and Rnet in British Columbia. They were men and women who knew about switches, routers, and networks, and the technical decisions they made about bandwidth and transmission technologies became policy decisions about ownership and content. There was little room for public-interest considerations.

A similar situation in the U.S. worried Gary Chapman, who is the director of the Twenty-First Century Project at the University of Texas at Austin and writes a column called "Digital Nation" for the *Los Angeles Times*. In one column he wrote that "no other industry is as self-absorbed, arrogant, insular or in love with itself and its products as high tech." On the few occasions when the industry has taken an interest in public issues, he continued, "[Its] leaders have limited their focus to what is good for their bottom lines."[12] In Canada, policy decisions were being made based on narrow technical and industrial considerations; once made and implemented, no other options would be possible.

industry canada's role

The private government received a major boost during the brief prime ministership of Kim Campbell. The Department of Communications was eliminated and its responsibilities carved up between a new Department of Canadian Heritage, which would deal with culture and broadcast policy, and Industry Canada, which inherited telecommunications and spectrum management. When these latter responsibilities were combined with Industry Canada's pre-existing mandate for science and technology policy, regional economic development, and services to business, it became the super-ministry for the information highway and Internet. And with the election of the Chrétien government, John Manley became the information highway czar, if anyone can be said to hold this position. That he was acceptable to industry was confirmed by his re-appointment in the second Chrétien government. His work in strengthening patent protection for the multinational pharmaceutical corporations (costing Canadian consumers millions of dollars) is believed to have helped him keep the prized portfolio.[13]

Manley was more like the representative of industry in government than the MP from Ottawa-South. (The blurring of public and private domains under Manley was evident in a small way on his department's Strategis Web site, which was operated jointly with the

Information Technology Association of Canada and showcased the activities and publications of both organizations with little differentiation.) Indeed, he was attuned to information industry issues even before he entered politics in 1988. He was a tax lawyer, the president of the Ottawa Board of Trade, and a director of the Ottawa-Carleton Research Institute, which later sponsored, along with CANARIE, a regional high-bandwidth network that became a building block in CANARIE's CA*net II. Manley was one of the "4 M's" in the first Chrétien government — four conservatives who formed the collective force that dominated Chrétien's first term (Finance Minister Paul Martin, former Intergovernmental Affairs Minister Marcel Masse, and Trade Minister Roy McLaren were the other three). Southam News columnist Giles Gherson, who did a stint in the first Chrétien government himself, wrote that "together they ensured that the left-of-centre, more traditional Liberal *Red Book* election platform took a back seat to the over-riding objective of conquering the deficit."

Manley's job was to oversee "the dissemination of technology throughout the economy,"[14] and he accomplished this on a number of fronts. Through its SchoolNet program, for instance, Industry Canada extended its industrial-development mandate into education and provincial jurisdiction by providing Internet access for schools. It's doing the same for libraries and in health care, other areas of provincial jurisdiction, through LibraryNet and telehealth initiatives. The agency also operates on the increasingly important international stage, where treaties with significant consequences for Canadians are hammered out, usually in secret. Is copyright an aspect of culture or industrial development? Industry Canada's job is to promote the latter, and it was Manley's agency and not Sheila Copps's heritage department that headed the Canadian delegation to the 1996 World Intellectual Property Organization in Geneva, where Internet copyright treaties were approved. Industry Canada also expanded into other areas of cultural activity, establishing a New Media and Entertainment Industries Directorate, for example, to extend information technology and industrial development into areas of film and video, publishing, music, and learning (not "education," which is a provincial responsibility).

manley sells his strategy

Connecting Canadians is the ultimate expression of Manley's mandate to extend technology throughout Canadian society. To package and sell the program, he turned to Earnscliffe Strategy Group, a powerful Ottawa lobbying firm that helps smooth relations between industry and government. By teaching Paul Martin how to spice up his budgets, Earnscliffe earned its reputation as a saviour of government agencies that were trying to put a winning spin on their policies. The firm's chief operatives in the Martin effort were Elly Alboim, former Ottawa bureau chief for CBC-TV, and David Herle, former president of the Young Liberals and a Paul Martin campaigner in the 1990 leadership race. Their enormous triumph, according to Ottawa parliamentary reporters Edward Greenspon and Anthony Wilson-Smith, was to introduce Martin to PowerPoint and videotaped visual presentations.[15] This gave normally dry, boring financial stories visual appeal and helped Martin convey his message – cutting the deficit is good for people – to a television audience, which is the only one that counts in politics. Industry Canada was another department with a difficult message to sell – that benefits for all will flow from connecting Canadians. Manley wanted to impress his Cabinet colleagues with a key report on converging voice, data, and video communications, so he turned to Alboim and Herle for help.

Earnscliffe and other lobbyists, like all members of the private government, prefer to work behind closed doors, out of the sight of citizens and even back-bench MPs. Rarely does the unwelcome glare of the public spotlight illuminate their usually secret activities. But Earnscliffe's work for Manley became the only lobbying controversy to blow up since the Chrétien Liberals took over in 1993. Ethical questions were raised over revelations in the fall of 1995 that Earnscliffe, which had high-level Liberal connections, was lobbying Industry Canada on behalf of information-industry clients, while at the same time advising the department on how to sell its information highway policies.[16]

The firm's partners also include Harry Near, a staunch Tory who served as director of campaign operations for the federal Conservative Party in 1979, 1984, and 1988. He worked at Imperial Oil for nine years before becoming chief of staff to Pat Carney, former federal minister of energy, mines and resources, and then joined Earnscliffe. Michael Robinson is close to Paul Martin, having served as his campaign manager in the 1990 leadership campaign. He became part of a Chrétien kitchen cabinet and was the Liberal Party's chief financial officer in 1991. In the late 1990s, Robinson and Near continue to be active in their respective political parties.

Joe Thornley, a competitor with impeccable Liberal connections, objected to Earnscliffe's Industry Canada contract because of the conflict of interest. In response, Robinson took the high road. There could be no conflict, he intoned, because he operated "with a code of conduct and a standard of ethical behaviour."[17] Indeed, where Thornley saw a conflict, Industry Canada saw an advantage. In fact, one reason Earnscliffe won the competition, said Francine Charbot-Plante, Industry Canada's director general of information, was because it had a superior understanding of the field and the policy environment within which the department wanted to make its impact. This was private government at its finest. Where most Canadians see conflicting interests, insiders see a fusion of interests – what is good for industry is good for government, and that is good, ultimately, for all Canadians.

The plum was a $100,000-a-year contract to advise Manley, write his speeches, make videos for him, and even travel with him to peddle the Connecting Canadians strategy. Nothing exceptional about that, except that Robinson and Near were already lobbying Manley and his officials on behalf of powerful corporate interests that wanted Industry Canada to enact Internet policies from which they would benefit. For example, the Canadian Alliance Against Software Theft, a Microsoft front group, wanted Industry Canada to push for changes to the Copyright Act that would make it more difficult for people to gain access to Internet resources without paying Microsoft. Lanser Wireless was pushing for a wireless telecommunications licence, B.C.-based Western International Communications was watching information highway developments, AT&T Long Distance Canada wanted to crack into the long-distance market, Microcell wanted into the local telephone market, and Astral Communications was concerned about policy issues affecting the pay-per-view industry.[18]

In the end, Chrétien's ethics commissioner concluded that the public interest was fully protected, but he dealt only with narrow technical questions and ignored the broader issue: can one firm work both sides of the street? Earnscliffe thought yes. Alboim and Herle took an oath of secrecy and promised not to tell anyone else in Earnscliffe what they had found out from the Industry Canada contract. They set up separate support staffs and computer systems and worked in a different part of the office, far from Near and Robinson. Industry Minister Manley did raise concerns for a few days, but he was quickly persuaded by his officials that they needed the advice and there was no conflict of interest.[19] When the flurry of attention dissipated, the contract was signed and it was business as usual for the private government.

canarie rules

While Earnscliffe helped Manley spread the good news about Connecting Canadians, CANARIE was working in relative obscurity extending information technology and marketplace ideology into areas of Canadian social life, such as education and health care, that had been relatively insulated from such activity before. The quest to build a network that could achieve these goals got underway earlier, in September 1990, the same month CA*net was launched as a public network. More than sixty leaders from industry, education, research institutes, and federal and provincial governments met in Ottawa to discuss the strategy for achieving a high-speed network and the rules for how they would participate. They made two key decisions: the network would be a co-operative private-public venture and it would evolve from CA*net. The next year, Industry, Science and Technology Canada (Industry Canada before the Kim Campbell reorganization) sponsored a Network Organizing Conference to initiate work on the network.[20] At that stage, discussions were broad and democratic, a major exercise in consensus-building. Scores of people from across Canada – representing all levels of government; dozens of universities, colleges, and research institutes; and numerous large and small corporations – participated in the conference. They established an executive committee and four working groups that were dominated by public-sector representatives – only six of twenty-two executive committee members came from the private sector.

But the public interest got left behind when a new group was formed to put the plan into effect. CANARIE Associates was established in November 1992, and its members pledged funds to complete the business plan and bring CANARIE to incorporation. Twelve of fifteen members of CANARIE Associates came from the private sector. They included Stentor Resource Centre (representing the major telcos); Unitel Communications (telecom successor to CP Telegraph and precursor to AT&T Canada); Northern Telecom; major multinational IT firms such as IBM Canada, Digital Equipment Canada, Hewlett-Packard (Canada), and Unisys Canada; and two Canadian-based companies, Newbridge Networks and Gandalf Technologies. Several associates were, or would be, chairs of the Information Technology Association of Canada, the leading lobby group for the IT industry, which represented more than 1,200 firms in computing and communications. One major financial institution, Canada Trust, was also present, as were several smaller high-tech companies and consulting firms. The private sector couldn't help swamping the three public-sector representatives: the University of British Columbia's Jack Leigh, CA*net's Andrew Bjerring (who went on to become CANARIE's second president), and Gerry Miller from the University of Manitoba. CANARIE Associates' plan was approved by the Mulroney government in December 1992, and the organization received $26 million from the government for its first phase. (It received an additional $80 million for phase 2 in 1995, and $55 million in phase 3 in 1998.) The private sector contributed several times these amounts in cash and services, mostly from the telcos, which would receive the greatest benefits from the networks.

CANARIE set out to accomplish three tasks.[21] The first was to upgrade and privatize CA*net. This was completed in 1997, when Bell Advanced Communications took over both the ownership and the management of the network, ending the decade-long era of the public Internet in Canada. CANARIE's second goal was to build a high-speed research and development network that would parallel CA*net and connect universities, companies, and regional test networks across the country to each other and to American and European networks. This network would be designed for use by the Canadian information industry. It went through several stages. It was known first as National Test Network in 1995; CA*net II, Canada's "next generation" Internet in 1997; and in 1998, CA*net 3, promoted in the Connecting Canadians strategy as "the fastest network in the world." As described in Chapter 6, CA*net II and CA*net 3 would have serious consequences for the direction of university research in Canada, tying researchers ever closer to the requirements of industry, rather than to the more fundamental social and public-interest needs of society. It was as if there was an electronic assembly line leading from university research labs to corporate marketing divisions.

The third goal was to develop commercially viable high-speed applications that could be tested on the network and quickly commercialized. Evidently, the corporate executives and university computing officials who ran CANARIE didn't trust the *Field of Dreams* scenario – merely building the network was not enough. A market had to be created for the bandwidth. That meant encouraging potential users of the network to develop commercially viable applications using taxpayer subsidies. The goal of CANARIE's applications program was to "stimulate innovative early commercialization-stage R&D projects that lead to advanced networking, technologies and applications for the marketplace."[22] Citizen groups wanting to develop non-profit applications to benefit their communities were out of luck. This would be 100 percent trickle-down; no weak link allowed. "All projects are expected to lead to commercially successful product development." By the late 1990s, CANARIE had narrowed its focus to three areas: life-long learning, electronic business, and health.

To get this ambitious program underway, CANARIE turned to IBM for its first president. Carmelo Tillona had a seventeen-year career with IBM Canada, serving most recently as the national industry manager of telecom market development, where he worked on projects with key players like Rogers Communications, NBTel, Bell Canada, and Northern Telecom. He also had extensive dealings with the Department of Communications. He was an ideal president, someone connected to telecommunications, broadcasting, the computer industry, government, the research community, and funding sources. But he lasted only two months before being lured away by the Montreal-based Groupe Videotron. Evidently, his expertise in computer telecommunications projects was just what Canada's third-largest cable operator needed for its interactive television trials.

Tillona's replacement was not quite as ideal – he didn't have the industry connections – but he met other qualifications. Andrew Bjerring came from the public-sector side of CANARIE. He had been the senior director of IT services at the University of Western Ontario and had been involved in network development for nearly a decade – first as chair of Onet, the Ontario regional network, then as treasurer of CA*net, as a member of CANARIE's steering committee, and as a CANARIE associate. Bjerring's appointment could be read as a statement that in CANARIE, at least, there would be few differences between public and private, university research and corporate, interests.

By 1999, CANARIE had a membership of more than one hundred universities, information companies, government departments and agencies, research institutes, consultants, libraries, major industry associations, and, of course, telephone and cable companies. A board of twenty-two members is selected each year (in 1998 twenty-four were selected).[23] CANARIE stresses that there should be a balance between public and private interests, or institutional and industrial sectors, as CANARIE refers to them, but the arithmetic was always questionable. The make-up of the board changed over the years, reflecting changing priorities, yet there were some constants. Bell Canada and the Stentor companies were always represented, reflecting the centrality of the telcos in all network developments (in fact, Bell had two representatives on the board between 1995 and 1998), as were Unitel (later AT&T Canada) and Rogers Communications, reflecting the government's determination to not show favouritism between telephone and cable companies, or between incumbent and alternative carriers. Teleglobe was a 1997 addition, as links to the U.S. and overseas became a concern with CA*net II developments. IBM, along with a variety of computer and smaller high-tech companies, completed the private-sector contingent.

As for the public sector, a school board was usually represented. For the first few years, there was someone from the Centre de recherche informatique de Montreal, or Computer Research Institute of Montreal (CRIM), which has more than sixty members. CRIM was designated an institutional (i.e., public) organization; in fact, it is a non-profit corporation with about three-quarters of its members coming from the private sector. The same problem applied to other research organizations with membership on the CANARIE board, such as TR Labs from Western Canada and OCRInet from Ottawa. These were already mixed public-private organizations and should not have been classified as institutional or public. Researcher Gerri Sinclair, of Simon Fraser University's Excite Lab, was a CANARIE director for three years (she was also a member of Manley's Information Highway Advisory Council). She was designated an institutional (i.e., public) board member, even though she had taken leave from her university post to start a company that developed intranet publishing and content systems. Similarly, Montreal's Hubert Manseau was designated institutional although his career spans the academic and private sectors. Even the Coalition for Public Information, which had a seat on the CANARIE board as a public representative, had a significant minority of private-sector members. When the public-private balance is recalibrated, the private sector truly dominates.

After industry, post-secondary institutions constitute the second-largest grouping in CANARIE: twenty-eight universities and colleges are members, and over the years seventeen out of a total of fifty-five board members have represented post-secondary institutions, as computer facilities executives, university researchers, and, more recently, administrators. University computing officials had a strong presence from the beginning and were the only public-sector representatives in CANARIE Associates. Their expertise created CA*net in 1990 and contributed to CA*net II, the high-speed network. Researchers were also prominent. Most universities have been recipients of CANARIE grants, albeit in collaboration with corporate applicants (all projects are expected to lead to "commercially successful product development"). A typical example is SFU's Excite Centre, a co-applicant with "CTV National News" in a project called Schoolsite, which received

CANARIE funding in 1997 to create a Web site where high-school students can use CTV resources to create their own news stories.[24] There are two problems with public participation in this project. Private-sector news media like CTV are too positive towards business and too negative towards government, creating a serious distortion in the material with which the students must work. Further, the project must lead to a commercial product, and students will inevitably be guided in that direction rather than towards a more useful media-literacy service to help debunk commercial media.

CANARIE's 1998–99 chair and vice-chair illustrate the seamless connection between public and private. Chair Jocelyne Ghent Mallett represents the industrial or private sector, but she spent fifteen years in the federal government and in 1990 was appointed director general of Industry, Science and Technology's information technology industry branch, where she helped stick-handle to fruition the project that was to become CANARIE. She left the government in 1995, set up a consulting firm, and became associated with Terry Matthews and Newbridge Networks, a CANARIE founder. She's a member of Matthews's executive council, whose job in 1997 was to promote Newbridge technology as the "platform for broadband networks into the new millennium"[25] and, less controversially, in 1998 was to "promote the company's vision."[26]

Vice-chair Jacquelyn Scott, on the other hand, is an institutional representative, but she seems closer to the private sector. She is a new type of post-secondary participant in CANARIE, the university administrator, and as such broadens representation from computing officials and researchers to entire institutions. Scott is the president of Nova Scotia's University College of Cape Breton, and is one of only nine women presidents in Canada's ninety-two colleges and universities. She brings some interesting connections to the enterprise,[27] connections that both extend information technology into education and open education to greater corporate influence. Among many other activities, she sits on the board of the Corporate Higher Education Forum, a fifteen-year-old association of university presidents and corporate executives whose goal is to forge stronger links between business and universities by considering topics such as how to support university-business collaboration in research and how to better integrate university teaching into working life. She is also a director of the Atlantic Institute for Market Studies (AIMS), the East Coast's equivalent to the Fraser Institute, which applies "market-based solutions" to Atlantic Canada's problems. These are code words in the right-wing campaign to convince Canadians that government created all our problems and only business can get us out of the mess. AIMS targets the public-education system and promotes charter schools. One major AIMS publication claims that "universities will have to . . . operate like private businesses working to satisfy the needs of their customers."[28] Scott also chairs the 21st Century Learning Initiative Canadian Working Group, which is striving to reduce the role of public education ("formal institutions do fewer things better") and downgrade its authority ("there is no distinction between work, school and living as sources of learning" and "learners achieve credentials and get credit for their experience without artificial barriers"[29]). She has won Conference Board of Canada awards for business-education partnerships. (CANARIE's role in colonizing education is described in Chapter 7.)

difficult questions about ca*net's demise

Scott had not yet joined the CANARIE board when the decade-long flowering of public information networks in Canada came to an abrupt halt. On April 1, 1997, CANARIE turned over ownership of CA*net, the public Internet in Canada, to Bell Advanced Communications, the data-networking arm of the Bell empire. CA*net president Ken Fockler called it "an historic, perhaps sad, but honourable day" in a mailing list posting the day before. "After approximately 2,500 days of operation, CA*net Networking Inc. is ceasing operation at midnight tonight."[30] For an undisclosed sum, Bell acquired the leading Internet backbone in Canada and immediately renamed it Bell Internet Transit Service, removing all trace of its public roots. An important, perhaps critical, decision was made about the kind of information networks Canadians would enjoy in the future, yet they had heard nothing about it, unless they were among the two hundred subscribers to the e-mail list on which Fockler's note was posted.

Meanwhile, during the years CA*net was developed as a leading taxpayer-supported, public-sector enterprise, Canadians were drowned in a torrent of coverage about trivial networking developments. First came the $130-million launch of Microsoft's Windows 95 operating system, touted as offering "more power, more freedom, more fun." The company sponsored an entire edition of Rupert Murdoch's *Times* of London, while a banner that unfurled from Toronto's CN Tower made the front page of the *Globe and Mail*. CEO Bill Gates was sent out to visit political leaders, including Prime Minister Jean Chrétien, and that made the front pages too. The weeks of media coverage, first anticipating the release of Windows 95 and then documenting the release when customers lined up at midnight to be first into stores the next morning, constituted free advertising. Windows 95 was followed by the irrelevancy of the so-called browser wars. Who would control access to the Internet, Microsoft's Explorer or Netscape Navigator? Between 1995 and 1997, Internet Explorer was mentioned 733 times in major Canadian newspapers and Netscape Navigator 405 times, while CA*net appeared 29 times, 1/25 Explorer's frequency and 1/14 that of Navigator.[31]

The disparity in coverage is instructive. The threats to public access to information networks that could result from the privatization of the Internet were largely ignored. But if big business controlled every megabit of cyberspace, how free and unbiased could information be? The news media were mainly silent, but the implications were ominous. Canadians deserved to know more about CA*net, CANARIE, and the privatization of cyberspace. They would certainly want to know if the cost of accessing the Internet was going to rise. They might fear that profit-making would take precedence over the needs of ordinary citizens. If everything was focused on making money, what would happen to libraries, freenets, and other community networks, especially in a time of declining financial resources? Would they be squeezed out? Would the range of available public information be narrowed?

Canadians would also want to know about the role of the telephone companies. Ma Bell and her brood are so big and powerful that they seem able to do whatever they want, especially in these days of deregulation. Would they be able to remonopolize telecommunications to the detriment of all but the strongest corporate interests? Canadians would almost certainly want to know why a network that was established through the hard work, risk, and financial participation of public-sector universities and government research labs should be turned over to the private sector once the network had become successful. Who would be the gatekeepers for public access to the technologies and services being developed on the privatized highway? Would only those services that are profitable be developed, while others, ones that are significant to people as citizens and not as customers, are ignored?

And Canadians would certainly want to know who really needed the higher bandwidth – the reason cited for privatizing CA*net. If the private sector wanted higher-speed bandwidth capabilities for multimedia applications, for instance, then why shouldn't it develop and build its own network to its own specifications and leave the public Internet for current users? Was this merely an exercise in inflating demand and then appropriating the resources to satisfy that demand? By preoccupying itself with bandwidth, and by shutting out other potential users, CANARIE ensured that CA*net could never develop a mandate to provide all Canadians with access to networking facilities and services. Yet these questions did not receive the public discussion and debate they required because the decision-making process was in the hands of the private government and was closed to the general public. In fact, most Canadians were unaware that major decisions were being made.

ca*net becomes the internet in canada

Between 1990 and 1995, CA*net was the Internet in Canada. Universities and research institutes across the country were the original users, and they were joined later by community colleges, government agencies, industry groups, public schools, and freenets. CA*net did not provide direct Internet access to these users. Rather, it was the backbone network for ten provincial networks that actually provided access to member institutions, which in turn provided access to end users. CA*net was the culmination of a half decade of computer-networking development across Canada. It was publicly financed and supported, and was based on open principles of association, providing access mainly to non-commercial users.

In the early 1980s, most large universities in Canada installed high-speed computer networks and connected their campuses together, although these early networks were not based on the Internet Protocol (IP). The first IP-based provincial network was developed by CRIM in Quebec in 1986, and was replaced three years later by RISQ, a Quebec regional network connecting about ten universities, research institutes, and Hydro-Québec. In 1987, BCnet linked the University of British Columbia and Simon Fraser University to the American NSFNet via the University of Washington in Seattle. In Ontario, Onet was formed in 1988 to connect that province's universities and institutes. The University of Toronto established a link to NSFNet at Cornell University. By 1990, networks had been established in most other provinces, with links to the U.S. through Onet, RISQ, and BCnet. They were Canada's access to the worldwide Internet. The provincial organizations varied in origin and structure, but with the exception of Nova Scotia Technology Network (NSTN) were governed by a common philosophy of exclusive public and non-profit use.[32]

The other organization that played a key role in implementing the Internet in Canada was the National Research Council (NRC), the federal government's research arm. It hosted a meeting in Ottawa in 1987 to design a national research network for Canada, and in 1988 produced a paper describing its plans. The network was called variously NRCNet, NRNet, and finally, in January 1990, just months before the launch, CA*net, a name suggested by the NRC's John Curley at an NRNet board meeting. The NRC established a committee to oversee a competitive request for proposals to provide a national backbone to link the provincial networks. The successful bidder was a consortium of public-private interests that included the University of Toronto. In late 1989, the University of Toronto hosted a conference to create an organization that could manage the kind of network that U of T had defined in its proposal to the NRC. From that meeting came the agreements and principles that underlie CA*net. In June

1990, formal documents creating CA*net Networking Inc. were signed. A $2-million contribution from the NRC was a key factor in the birth. Official opening ceremonies were held on October 25, 1990. The contract would run until March 1993.

CA*net, an exercise in massive co-operation, was managed by U of T's Computing Services Department. Integrated Network Services Inc. (Insinc) was a Canadian network reseller that provided the network by leasing circuits on long-term contracts from Stentor carriers and Unitel at tariffed rates with high-volume discounts, and then re-leasing a portion of the circuits, along with support services, to CA*net. IBM Canada was part of the consortium too; it provided the technology that routed messages around the network. CA*net then resold its leased capacity to the ten regional member networks so they could connect with each other and with the outside Internet. Each regional network in turn provided access to end users, such as computer centres at universities and community colleges, which acted as nodes on the regional networks. Individual users connected to a local node through dedicated connections or through dial-up lines to the university's central computer or network server. To access the global Internet, users of the provincial networks first connected to CA*net and then to one of three direct links to NSFNet. These links were established through Montreal, Toronto, and Vancouver as part of an arrangement for reciprocal carriage.

Insinc was also required, as part of the agreement, to increase the bandwidth available to CA*net. Along with the increased bandwidth went an increased base of users. CA*net started as a university and research consortium, but it diversified right from the beginning by bringing in other public-sector users and, in some provinces (Nova Scotia was one), commercial and individual users. With the financial support of the NRC and strict guidelines for extending its lines and services, CA*net was able to achieve its goal of being a viable, self-sustaining network, able to increase its capacity as usage rose. However, NRC funding was scheduled to end in March 1993. Where would the money come from to support expansion? The answer was: From the same source as before — the taxpayers of Canada. But there would be a difference. Instead of the money being directed through the research-oriented NRC, it would flow through the business-dominated CANARIE board. This was a peculiar way to implement public policy, but was in keeping with the neo-conservative direction of the Mulroney and Chrétien governments.

Insinc and U of T would continue to operate and manage CA*net, but with the guiding hand of CANARIE. The first task was to upgrade CA*net's leased backbone network to T-1 speed (1.54 megabits a second – a bit is one binary digit, while a megabit is a million bits, about the size of a telephone directory). Funding for the upgrade would come from the federal government via CANARIE ($5 million), from CA*net member networks ($15 million), and from user fees ($3 million). Industry would contribute little, yet would end up controlling the direction of the network. In December 1993, CA*net and CANARIE signed a memorandum of understanding that included an intention to work towards a merger of the two organizations.

CANARIE supporters argued that CA*net would require government funding during the network upgrades. They believed, though, that in the long run, CA*net should cover costs by finding more users, which would reduce the expense of leased circuits, thus lessening costs for member networks. More users meant more revenue, which would allow CA*net to become increasingly self-sustaining. The largest component of CA*net's costs was the rates paid to telcos to lease circuits. These rates were passed on to regional members as usage fees. The general principle – according to the schedule of fees established by the Canadian Radio-television and Telecommunications Commission, the federal regulator – was the higher the traffic, the lower the rates. Elizabeth Angus, a telecommunications consultant who did a 1994 study for Industry Canada, pointed out a basic fact of life for telecommunication charges: a user with enough volume of traffic to fill a T-3 circuit (43 megabits per second) paid about one-third as much as if the equivalent carrying capacity was composed of individual T-1 circuits (1.54 megabits per second).[33] Angus argued that CA*net didn't have enough traffic to justify leasing T-3 circuits. If it did have sufficient traffic, CA*net's unit costs would drop dramatically, and it would be able to provide much less expensive connectivity to regional member networks. To reach that point, CA*net would have to multiply its total volume of traffic, and probably revenue, by ten or fifteen times. This would not completely fill a T-3 circuit, but would fill it sufficiently to justify its cost relative to multiple T-1s.

In CANARIE and Industry Canada, the consensus was that once CA*net had enough traffic, public funding should cease. There was a minority view that CA*net was a national network and therefore should be provided to Canadians free of charge, paid for on an ongoing basis from general government revenues. CA*net was like the Trans-Canada Highway, they argued – a public highway, not a private toll road. But most claimed that the government could not afford the cost, and besides there was no need to subsidize the Internet, since many kinds of infrastructure, such as the telephone system, were paid for by users without subsidies. Why should Internet users receive special treatment? They pointed to the burgeoning growth in Internet use during the mid-1990s, after Netscape had commercialized the publicly created Web browser Mosaic and business and home-computer users discovered the Web. Public schools, hospitals, and government agencies were lining up to get on-line. Dozens of small- and medium-sized Internet service providers (ISPs) had sprung up, often overnight, to provide access to the Internet for a fee or, in the case of freenets, for free or an annual membership fee. They saw that CA*net and its member networks were competing with them for business from customers whose traffic they wanted to carry. Some larger ISPs already had sufficient traffic to make their per-circuit cost lower than CA*net's, even after the subsidy. They questioned the fairness of directing taxpayers' funds to an organization that competes with them for traffic and customers, which was the same argument put forward by private broadcasters in their crusade against the CBC. This would be a valid argument if the public-sector ISP merely replicated services offered by private-sector service providers. But if the mandate was to create a public information network, then these criticisms would be irrelevant.

These issues were never debated on their merits, at least not in public. The reason may have been that some major ISPs were participants in CANARIE and thus had a conflict of interest when it came to making decisions about CA*net. Would the public interest get left behind? NSTN, for instance, was an original CA*net provincial network and was one of the few established as a commercial operation (it provided Internet access to individuals, businesses, and institutions in Nova Scotia). In 1995, NSTN merged with i*internet, another large commercial ISP. The merged entity became I*star Internet, one of the largest Internet-access companies operating in Canada. Consequently, I*star was competing with CA*net and many of its provincial network affiliates.

Michael Martineau, general manager and later president of NSTN, had been a member of the CANARIE executive committee in 1991–92, as well as a member of the CA*net board of directors. Martineau was also a 1994 member of CANARIE's Operational Network Products and Services Committee. This group had been set up by CANARIE to fund possible Internet applications (creating uses for the bandwidth CANARIE was building). NSTN had received a CANARIE grant, although not when Martineau was on the board, for its CyberMall, a project described by CANARIE as "one of North America's first on-line Internet-accessible shopping centres." Funding would help transform the mall "into a long-term, revenue-producing service. Key elements of the project include migration to WWW, development of mall navigation tools, redesign of the CyberMall 'look and feel,' and development of a new process to load merchant information into the CyberMall Server."³⁴ CANARIE's support for such purely commercial enterprises stood in sharp contrast to its lack of interest in the notion of a public network with non-profit uses.

After the merger, I*star went on a spending spree, buying up smaller ISPs across Canada. In two years, the company:

- bought Vancouver's Mindlink Communications for $3.5 million;
- went public with a stock issue that raised $33.7 million and was followed by a frenzied day of trading on the Toronto Stock Exchange that saw the company's shares soar from $12 to $22 (and later slide to less than $5);
- snapped up Toronto-based InfoRamp for $4.3 million;
- paid $3.5 million for Wimsey Information Services and AuroraNet, both of Vancouver;
- bought Ottawa's Magi Data Consulting for $3.4 million;

- entered into a strategic alliance with the CTV Television network to provide Internet access to television programs;
- cut its workforce by 20 percent;
- teamed up with Fonorola and Clearnet Communications to bid for a wireless licence;
- signed an agreement with Microsoft to offer its services through Internet Explorer;
- built its own national backbone with a high-capacity link to the U.S.;
- sold a 10 percent interest to the Bank of Nova Scotia for about $10 million; and
- raised an additional $15.5 million to finance its move into e-commerce.

By the end of this two-year flurry of activity, I*star had moved from being one of CA*net's regional networks to a company that served primarily business customers with lucrative Internet services such as e-commerce and intranets. It also held onto its dial-up customers, becoming the third-largest ISP in Canada. But by 1997, the company had overextended itself and lacked the cash for further expansion. Later that year, the shareholders sold out to PSINet, one of the largest American ISPs. PSINet continued I*star's policy of buying smaller Canadian-owned companies, such as Interlog Internet Services and its 50,000 subscribers. In 1999, PSINet said it would be spending $100 million to assemble a high-speed network to carry voice and data across Canada. Ominously, though, the first purchase – for $12 million – was the right to use twenty lines of fibre-optic cable running between Vancouver and Seattle. It looked like the strategy was to offer cross-Canada service by going through the U.S., in effect betraying ten years of Canadian Internet developments.[35]

Other CANARIE insiders also had vested interests in CA*net's future. Big computer companies such as IBM Canada, a key player in CANARIE, were racing to shift their corporate strategies from desktop and company network computing to the Internet. In fact, IBM was developing its own network, Advantis Canada, which would provide Internet access for Canadians to hundreds of cities around the world. But the telcos had the greatest conflicts. They owned the lines leased by CA*net and by the CANARIE test network. At the same time, they had established their own Internet services, such as Sympatico, which competed with CA*net. Corporate interests infiltrated the regional networks as well, transforming those bodies too. The result was that the predominantly not-for-profit member organizations changed over the years to eleven out of fourteen being for profit, notes Worth Johnson, SFU's director of operations and technical support and a participant in BCnet since 1990.[36] In such a conflict-ridden situation, we must ask to what extent were public information and the public interest sacrificed in the name of corporate profit?

Meanwhile, in December 1994, Insinc was scooped up by Sprint Canada, the third-largest long-distance carrier in the U.S., which was busy building its own Internet network that would connect Canadian nodes not with each other, but with the Sprint network in the U.S. E-mail from Vancouver to Toronto would be routed over Sprintlink to Sacramento, California, across the U.S. and back into Canada. Also in December 1994, John Manley approved another $80 million for CANARIE. With the Insinc–U of T contract up for renewal in April 1995, quiet, intensive negotiations were changing the nature and pur-pose of CA*net.

The resulting plan was a two-stage operation. The first stage kicked off at Centennial College's "fabulous" – according to the col-lege's Web site – Bell Centre for Creative Communications, Canada's "largest interactive multimedia centre." (The college's president, Catherine Henderson, would become a CANARIE director.) The launch took place November 23, 1995, three weeks later than originally planned because of the Quebec referendum. On-stage were Industry Minister John Manley; CA*net president Ken Fockler; CANARIE pres-ident Andrew Bjerring; Ginny Dybenko, then-CEO of Bell Advanced Communications; and George Harvey, vice-chairman of Unitel Communications. They outlined two related developments. One was the launch of CA*net II, "a new national infrastructure for Canada," as the PR spin put it. This would be the next stage of the National Test Network, a high-speed research and development network owned by CANARIE, operated by Bell, and intended for universities and researchers only. (It is discussed in Chapter 6.)

The second development was the transfer of CA*net's operations from U of T–Sprint to Bell Advanced Communications (BAC), which would supply coast-to-coast fibre links for both the private research network and the public CA*net network. Unitel Communications (on the way to becoming AT&T Long Distance Canada) would provide linkages to its own network and to points south of the border. At the same time, Newbridge Networks would supply asynchronous transfer mode (ATM) backbone switches to move the signals around the network, while Cisco Systems Canada would provide the high-speed routers for each node on the system. The University of Toronto would manage the network, as it had since 1990, for another six months, at which time Bell Sygma would take over. CA*net would be the main tenant. Bell would upgrade the network from T-1 speed to ten megabits a second, and eventually up to 100 megabits a second, if the capacity was needed. Bell estimated its commitment to the two networks at nearly $100 million, although the rate at which system upgrades occurred would depend on network traffic volume. CA*net would obtain higher bandwidth capability, but would lose its identity as a separate entity.

History seemed to be repeating itself. As had been the case in the U.S. with AM radio in the 1920s and FM radio and UHF television in the 1950s, new technologies were being pioneered by the government and non-profit organizations when they were not yet profitable. And once profitable, these technologies were handed over to private interests with little compensation to taxpayers.[37] By the end of 1996, CA*net had been turned into just another Internet-access provider in a crowded communications landscape. So there was little surprise when the second shoe dropped and the CA*net board transferred ownership of the network to BAC on April 1, 1997 ("No, it's not an April Fool's joke," CA*net president Ken Fockler also wrote in his distribution-list posting the day before), and ceased operations when the contract expired. On June 23, 1997, the board voted itself out of existence. Two days later, the board and other "pioneers" of public networking in Canada assembled in Ottawa to celebrate the official launch of CA*net II, and to receive commemorative plaques and congratulatory letters from Prime Minister Chrétien, who echoed, once again, the myth of technological rationalism:

Over the past decade, you and your colleagues have been building a
new kind of Canadian infrastructure for a new age – the information
age. I believe CA*net and the Canadian Internet that you started in
the late 1980s will prove to be as central to this new age as the
development of the canals and railroads were to the country's
manufacturing capability more than a century ago.[38]

BAC president John MacDonald, a CANARIE board member, was
more to the point. "You have maintained the viability of a Canada-
wide Internet during the early years of this new industry," he said,
"and in so doing you have laid the groundwork for the commercial
Internet of Canada."[39]

The Internet was built. But it was not the Internet some pioneers
had envisioned a decade earlier. CANARIE, Bell, and Industry Canada
made sure of that. And while Bell was consolidating its hold on a
high-speed, coast-to-coast network for business users, it was also
busy on a more important front – transforming itself from a simple
carrier of telecommunications messages into a participant in the creation, storage, and distribution of those messages. For more than a
decade, Bell had been driven by the belief that in the future, its profits
would derive from content, not carriage.

telephone companies
enter the content business

> *Our future doesn't lie in bandwidth, it lies in value-added*
> *services.*
>
> — Brian Milton, Stentor's national director of social policy

The Halifax-based Atlantic Institute for Market Studies (AIMS) delivers a simple message: Determine "whether and to what extent market-based solutions" can be successfully applied to Atlantic Canada's problems.[1] This is the propaganda message that only business can get us out of the mess caused by government, a message I analyze in Chapter 8. AIMS uses the same formula as the Fraser Institute and other right-wing think-tanks:

1. Establish yourself as a non-profit corporation with charitable status (received in 1994) so that taxpayers subsidize your controversial activities.

2. Solicit tax-deductible funding from corporate Canada. (All five major chartered banks; many brokerage houses and corporate law firms; Atlantic Canada's largest corporations; a clutch of right-wing foundations, including the Atlas Economic Research Foundation,

based in Fairfax, Virginia, which has helped more than one hundred right-wing groups set up so-called policy institutes in locations around the world; and the foundations of the McCain, Pirie, Sobey, and Weston families have contributed.)

3. Use funding to pay for work by Canadian and American academics who support your conservative goals, although on occasion fund a more liberal academic so that you can claim to have a balanced program.

4. Focus on right-wing targets such as privatizing the Atlantic fishery, airports, local government, and public education; reforming taxes; cutting government spending and unemployment insurance; and deregulating the economy.

Once studies with academic credibility are produced, the next step is to ensure that they receive wide media attention. Like the Fraser Institute, AIMS is preoccupied with its media presence; it strives to take "the AIMS message to new readers," and to reinforce the message with old ones. "Calls from the regional and national media seeking comments on current issues continue to come in at a rate of approximately one a day, giving AIMS a substantial presence is [sic] printed and broadcast reports," reports AIMS president Don Cayo in the institute's 1997 annual report.[2] Cayo and senior policy analyst Fred McMahon are "published regularly in five influential Atlantic dailies, one Western paper and the *Globe and Mail*." Cayo understands the media well. He was managing editor and editorial page editor of the *Telegraph Journal*, New Brunswick's leading provincial paper, before taking a two-year leave of absence to head AIMS.[3] Cayo's predecessor, Brian Crowley, who founded the institute, was president of the Atlantic Provinces Economic Council and a professor at Dalhousie University before joining AIMS. He became a frequent commentator on political and economic issues for the CBC and Radio-Canada, and then left AIMS to join the editorial board of the *Globe and Mail*, where he continued to promote his right-wing agenda.

Applying "market-based solutions" to the purported problems of public education is a recurring theme in AIMS studies. One AIMS publication argues that universities should "operate like private businesses."[4] Promoting charter schools is a priority, perhaps because charter schools are a priority with the Donner Foundation, which provided start-up funding for AIMS — $150,000 a year for three years. Donner is one of the country's top ten charitable foundations, with an endowment of more than $130 million. It is perhaps the largest donor in Canada to charter schools and other right-wing causes. Donner funded *The Next City*, a far-right Toronto-based quarterly magazine; the Fraser Institute; the C.D. Howe Institute; and a growing number of university researchers and organizations that are sympathetic to the foundation's views. Donner-funded organizations work on such issues as privatizing the Liquor Control Board of Ontario, the Canada Pension Plan, and Ontario's social housing; fighting so-called political correctness at universities and reinstating the authority of ageing white males; opposing child care; and undermining equity policies.

In 1996 AIMS published a "primer" on establishing charter schools in Atlantic Canada, with the claim that there is "accumulating evidence that charter schools are not only superior for their students, but also improve the rest of the school system by providing competition and new ideas."[5] The primer was written by Joe Freedman, a radiologist from Red Deer, Alberta, who, AIMS says, single-handedly launched the successful drive for charter schools in that province (AIMS neglected to point out that Freedman received $700,000 from Donner).

In charter schools, a non-profit group (often consisting of parents) and a granting authority (in Canada, the provincial department of education) prepare a charter, or written agreement, that spells out the goals of the school and the responsibilities of the parties to the agreement. The school receives public tax dollars but is run as a private institution, setting its own curriculum — usually one that promotes conservative values — and screening potential students — usually selecting the better-off ones. Advocates of charter schools say they introduce competition into a system that today is run like a monopoly (a puzzling claim, given the diversity of schools in any major urban area). In truth, schools would compete for students, and those left out would have to attend a declining number of financially strapped public schools. Charter schools would inevitably lead to a two-tier system and the demise of public education.

Given the organization's apparent hostility towards public education, it is surprising to note the presence on the AIMS board of two
leading Nova Scotia higher-education administrators: Jacquelyn Scott
of University College of Cape Breton (and CANARIE vice-chair), and
Tom Traves, president of Dalhousie University. But the AIMS–post-
secondary axis doesn't stop there. Also on the AIMS board are the
chancellors of Mount Allison University and Memorial University of
Newfoundland, the chairmen of Dalhousie University and Saint
Francis Xavier University Foundation, the vice-chairman of the Nova
Scotia College of Art and Design, and a director of Acadia University.

There's also an AIMS–telephone company axis. Joining Scott and
Traves on the AIMS board are four telco executives: Gerald Pond,
president of Bruncor in New Brunswick; Colin Latham, president of
Maritime Telephone and Telegraph in Nova Scotia (and chair of the
Stentor Alliance); James Palmer, chair of Telus (although it's in Alberta,
Palmer is a native son of Atlantic Canada); and Peter Nicholson, Paul
Martin's agenda-setter and Bell Canada's top strategist. Four AIMS
directors, including Latham, are directors of Maritime Telephone and
Telegraph (MT&T), Nova Scotia's dominant carrier.

In fact, AIMS provides a good illustration of the connection between
a weakened public role in education and a telephone industry seeking
to enter markets such as telelearning. Indeed, MT&T has made
distance education – called Campus Connect on its Web site – an
important area of growth. Already, MT&T provides a central link to
all Nova Scotia campuses and has developed with the department of
education a service called Ednet, which will connect 140 schools,
community colleges, and museums on a high-speed communication
network. MT&T also provides the telecommunications links for the
Acadia Advantage program at Acadia University in Wolfville, Nova
Scotia, where every student is required to have an IBM Thinkpad.
MT&T also worked with Scott's University College of Cape Breton to
set up learning centres in three communities so that rural students
could have access to a university education without the expense of
travel. This is an important use of education technology, but could be
the thin edge of the wedge in eliminating college campuses altogether
and replacing them with telephone-computer networks.

One indication of MT&T's direction is the telco's partnership with U.S.-based Jones Education Company (30 percent owned by Bell Canada, which also owns 35.3 percent of MT&T) to establish an on-line education initiative. Here "learning has never been so easy or convenient," the Web site tells us.[6] Virtual Learning Centre offers on-line education solutions for everyone – K-12, post-secondary, and professional. Mount St. Vincent University in Halifax is MT&T's first partner, and students can enrol and participate in accredited on-line university courses.

from carriage to content

To understand where MT&T and the other telcos are going – tele-learning, telehealth, e-commerce – it's useful to examine where they came from. Telcos have been central to the private government because they provide the bandwidth that makes all other activities possible. Their role in the late twentieth century parallels that of the railways in the nineteenth, when the strategy was to lay the track and then generate traffic by encouraging settlers to take up farming along the right of way and grow crops that could be shipped on the railway. Government's role in ensuring the success of the railways was to provide huge land grants backed with cash subsidies, and to change its immigration policies to entice millions of European settlers to populate the vast Prairies. Both policies made Canadian Pacific Railway (CPR) shareholders very wealthy.

Telcos are today's railways, building networks and participating in organizations like AIMS and CANARIE to generate traffic. But there's one difference. In the mid-1980s, the telcos decided that they should profit from the traffic as well as carry it, by participating in activities such as distance education. This meant that the telcos would enter broadcasting and offer the same services as cable companies, which would upset a regulatory regime that had lasted for decades. The telcos and cablecos both had a close connection to government and regulators, but the telcos were much larger, with a history extending back as far as 1905, when the Bell Telephone Company was able to head off a move to nationalize the telephone system.

Sir William Mulock was postmaster general in the government of Sir Wilfrid Laurier, and he chaired the House of Commons select committee's investigation of the telephone system. He told the opening session, "I cannot see why it is not as much the duty of the state to take charge of the telephone as it is to conduct the postal service."[7] His view was that long-distance lines should be taken over by the federal government and local lines by municipalities. His investigation documented Bell's high rates and predatory pricing practices, the inability of independent telephone companies to interconnect to Bell's long-distance lines, and Bell's lack of rural service. But after the evidence was accumulated, Mulock was mysteriously yanked from his position and replaced by a Bell apologist. The committee took no action. Mulock did not run in the next election, citing ill health (although Laurier soon appointed him chief justice of the exchequer division of the Supreme Court of Ontario, hardly a posting for a person at death's door). Replacing Mulock in his North York riding was A.B. Aylesworth, who had appeared before his committee as Bell's lawyer. Laurier won the election, and Aylesworth was soon installed as the new postmaster general. Thus ended any discussion of nationalization.

By getting rid of Mulock, buying off members of Parliament, and successfully lobbying the government, Bell was able to convince Laurier not to nationalize the company, which was at that time owned by National Bell in the U.S. Instead, Laurier's government passed legislation placing Bell under the supervision of the Board of Railway Commissioners for Canada, beginning an era of telephone regulation that lasted until the last decade of the twentieth century.[8] The U.S. and Canada became the only two countries where major telephone systems were not publicly owned. (Bell had refused to provide service to the sparsely settled Prairie provinces, so provincially owned systems were established in Alberta, Saskatchewan, and Manitoba.)

For most of the century, the theory of telephone regulation was based on the claim of "natural monopoly" – the cost of building a telephone system was so great that it made no economic sense to have more than one in a region. The government allowed telephone monopolies to exist – in violation of emerging anti-combines laws – as long as they were regulated. The telcos were assured of a "reasonable rate of return" on their investment, and in exchange had to meet standards of service, such as providing affordable, universal access. One principle underlying this system was that profits earned from long-distance service had to be used to cross-subsidize rural and basic local service (the assumption being that lower-income residents relied heavily on local service and made fewer long-distance calls). A second principle was that the telcos were treated as "common carriers" – anyone who paid the published tariffs was entitled to send messages over the network, messages that could not be altered by the carrier. The consequence was that the telcos were not allowed to enter the message-sending business – in other words, they could not own broadcasting or cable-TV licences.

From the beginning, this was a story of "regulatory capture," in which the industry being regulated controls its regulators. Industry executives are appointed to the regulatory board, and retiring board members find employment in the industry. Industry and board lawyers spend a large portion of their working lives in each other's company and become familiar with the other side's desires, strategies, and bottom lines. But since the industry is so much larger than the regulator – and has such vast resources at its command, while regulatory staffs are usually bare bones – the industry usually sets the agenda for regulatory action. Indeed, regulation and predictable, escalating rates of return suited Bell and the other telcos for the next seventy-five years. In return, Bell and the other telcos agreed to meet the social objective of universal access.

the revolving door

Regulators and regulated co-exist in the private government of telecommunications, and they routinely establish contact and reaffirm their status as a community through industry-sponsored conferences and government advisory boards. Here they can define solutions to current and anticipated problems that require government action of one kind or another. These forums probably also contribute to the "revolving door," which has government and industry officials moving back and forth between the CRTC, Industry Canada and other arms of government, and the telephone companies, further consolidating their interests. There's nothing conspiratorial about the revolving door, especially in Ottawa under Mulroney and Chrétien. In the past, hundreds of bright young Canadians set out to make their careers in the public service and contribute to the common good. But years of downsizing, right-wing attacks on government, and a widening salary gap between the public and private sectors have taken their toll. And the politicization of the public service has soured many senior government executives, who are more open to overtures from the private sector.

The telcos led the way through the revolving door, thanks to decades of regulation and necessarily close contact between regulator and regulated. As befits its status as the country's largest corporate empire, the Bell group has benefited significantly from government experience. Parent company BCE's biggest catch may be Peter Nicholson, son of a former Nova Scotia Liberal finance minister, who served one term as an MLA in the Nova Scotia legislature and then became a senior vice-president and executive assistant to Bank of Nova Scotia (BNS) chairman Cedric Ritchie. BCE chairman Red Wilson served briefly as a BNS vice-chairman in the late 1980s, which is when he met Nicholson. Nicholson caught Paul Martin's eye as a keynote speaker at the Liberal Party's Aylmer conference in the fall of 1991, when the business Liberals seized control of the party's policy direction from the social Liberals. Nicholson offered guidelines for the Chrétien government: cut government spending, overhaul social programs, balance the safety net with work retraining.[9] Next, he joined the department of finance in March 1994 as a visiting economist, eventually becoming a senior adviser to Martin. Nicholson was the architect of the government's deficit-reduction plan, the so-called purple book, which outlined the causes of the deficit and made deficit-fighting the government's number-one priority. Libraries, schools, universities, and health-care services are still reeling from Nicholson's ideas. And as we've seen in the case of libraries, spending cuts were tied to a vast expansion in the use of information technology and telecommunication services, a trend that greatly benefited the telcos. The link was made clear when, in 1995, Wilson wooed Nicholson to head up BCE's government-relations strategy. It was a short jump for the Nova Scotia native from there to the boards of MT&T and AIMS.

Another prominent BCE hire was Derek Burney, who was Mulroney's top political aide and Canada's ambassador to the U.S. prior to joining BCE in October 1992. Burney headed up BCE's international unit, and in his first year entered a partnership with the U.S. cable firm Jones Intercable to develop cable and telephone service in Britain. Burney later extended Bell's investment in the U.K. by buying a share of the third-largest cable company (since sold) and 30 percent of Jones. Burney also focused his investments in developing countries, particularly in Latin America (cellular phone operations in Colombia, a cable-TV network and a possible cellular phone network in Brazil) and Asia (cellular phones in India, a cellular radio system in China, a personal communication service in South Korea). Burney may have been following another guideline Nicholson offered at Aylmer: expand free trade into the rest of Latin America and Asia. With its increasing investment in Latin America, BCE is vitally interested in the Free Trade of the Americas Agreement (FTAA), which Canada and thirty-three other countries began negotiating in 1998. (The lucrative telecommunications markets are cited as one reason for wanting the treaty.)

Donald Johnston served on the BCE board in the early 1990s, while he was still president of the Liberal Party of Canada and before he moved on to become the American-backed secretary-general of the OECD in Paris. In their efforts to extend corporate rule over nations, Johnston and the Americans suffered a setback with OECD's inability to conclude the Multinational Agreement on Investment (MAI) by the self-imposed deadline of May 1998. But some critics suggest that the MAI charter of rights for corporate investment will be included in the FTAA, which should benefit Bell. In any case, Johnston and the OECD bounced back within a month of the MAI setback with some principles for corporate governance. The chief corporate objective, said an OECD report, should be to "maximize shareholder value,"[10] which meant that corporations should ignore environmental and safety concerns (unless they threaten the bottom line), pay workers as little as possible, and use any legal means available to maximize profits.

On the domestic level, former broadcasting executive Alain Gourde was a secretary to the federal Cabinet and deputy minister in the department of communications — which formulated satellite policy — before becoming president of Canadian Satellite Communications and chairman of ExpressVu, a fledgling direct-to-home satellite company. After Bell bought ExpressVu, BCE president Jean Monty offered Gourde the job of leading Bell Satellite, a new arm of BCE that would oversee the telco giant's vast satellite holdings. "You get an offer from Jean Monty only once in a lifetime," Gourde told the *Globe and Mail*'s telecommunications reporter, Lawrence Surtees.[11]

Telus, Canada's third-largest telecommunications company, made some interesting hires too. In 1998, Bud Sherman, previously vice-chairman for telecommunications for the CRTC and a former Manitoba Tory Cabinet minister, joined Telus as a consultant, and Lorna Higdon-Norrie, former deputy executive director of Industry Canada's Prairie and Northwest Territories region, joined the company as assistant vice-president of government affairs. But the biggest catch had been landed two years earlier, when the company appointed George Addy, retiring director of investigations and research at Industry Canada's Competition Bureau, as Telus's executive vice-president and chief general counsel. Addy was known in business circles for approving almost every major transaction he investigated during his three-year tenure, including the Rogers Communications takeover of Maclean Hunter, SmithBooks' merger with Coles (which led to the formation of the Chapters behemoth), and Canada Post's purchase of Purolator Courier. In response to numerous complaints from alternative phone companies that the Stentor consortium was acting like a "cartel," Addy undertook a three-year investigation but closed it without referring the matter to the competition tribunal for further action.[12] The Competition Bureau's *Backgrounder*, in its discussion of the review of Stentor, concluded with these curious words: "[The director] intends to continue to closely follow developments in the telecommunications industry."[13] Three months later Addy resigned, and the following month he joined Telus. The move was approved by the federal government's ethics commissioner, with the provision that Addy didn't contact the Competition Bureau for twelve months. Addy's boss, John Manley, had only glowing words for his director: "He's had a good run. We've worked well together and I'm quite sorry to see him go."[14] Addy would be leaving the public government, but as an important member of the private government he would have many occasions to renew his relationship with Manley.

stentor: the loudest voice

The revolving door probably led the telcos and the government to the same conclusion: that profits in the future would come not from operating telephone systems, but from providing content services over networks – selling rather than merely transmitting information (especially in broadcasting and electronic-publishing formats) – and the telcos wanted to ensure that they would be in on the action. Hudson Janisch, a communications law professor at the University of Toronto and a leading advocate for deregulation, argues that to "confine the telecommunications carriers to transmission only would be arbitrarily to block them almost entirely from the most important areas of growth."[15]

There was nothing arbitrary about seventy-five years of regulation and universal access, but the fact is that the telcos, used to reigning supreme in communications issues, wanted change. Their goal was to become full-service communication providers, offering telephone, cable, and all points in between. They agreed to permit limited competition in their traditional monopolies of local and long-distance service in exchange for being allowed to enter new fields and offer new services. They set up a new organization, Stentor (from the Greek, meaning "to speak with a strong voice"), in January 1992, to prepare for competition in the long-distance telephone market and to commence the move into content. Stentor was an alliance of provincial monopoly carriers – Bell Canada, BC Telephone Co., the Prairie companies (Alberta Government Telephones, on its way to becoming the privatized Telus Corp., SaskTel, Manitoba Tel), and the partially Bell-owned Maritime companies. This was not an assembly of equals. Through a system of weighted voting, Bell dominated. This was perhaps not surprising, given that more than 60 percent of Stentor's $300 million of funding came from Bell. The BCE group of companies, which includes Bell and Northern Telecom, is ten times the size of the next largest company, Anglo-Canadian (which includes BC Tel and Quebec Telephone), and fifteen times the size of AGT-Telus.

There were three arms to Stentor: a network-management organization that coordinated member company operations; a marketing, service-development, and network-engineering firm that accelerated the introduction of new services; and a lobbying and public-relations arm, Stentor Telecom Policy. This last arm was headed by Jocelyne Cote-O'Hara, who had worked in Prime Minister Brian Mulroney's office and at BC Tel before joining Stentor. Her vice-presidents all had experience working with the department of communications and the CRTC.

In October 1993, three months before Jean Chrétien mouthed the twelve words that officially launched Canada into the information age, Stentor Telecom Policy released a twenty-one-page "vision" document called "Information Highway: Canada's Road to Economic and Social Renewal," an attempt to catch the attention of the new government before it made any ill-considered moves. The document envisioned a national information highway that was capable of carrying "voice, text, data, graphics and video services to and from all Canadians."[16] Indeed, we can learn much from it. Yes, it was PR fluff – how could an alliance of corporations have a vision? – but the document did reveal Stentor's strategy to develop an information highway that "provides universal access to basic and advanced communications and information services through a network of many networks, *owned and operated by different service providers*"[17] (italics added). This was the first time the telcos admitted the possibility of competitors' providing services they had previously considered their exclusive turf. This door would be opened only partially, though; Stentor would still lead the way. And just like John Manley's Connecting Canadians strategy would five years later, the document imparted a sense of urgency: "Canada must act now or get left behind. It is a simple question of survival in this fast-changing world. Canadian industry will fall steadily behind, Canadian employment will suffer and Canadians' standard of living will fall."[18] Jean Chrétien and John Manley, are you listening? Finally, the document revealed Stentor's strategy for growth in the information age – to profit by partnering with public education, health, and government services organizations. Here are just a few of the alliances Stentor companies were forging:

- the Greater Victoria Hospital Society uses BC Tel's Ubiquity Service to transmit pathology slides and for voice and video consultation;
- MT&T partners with the government of Nova Scotia to implement the Distance Education Service for Knowledge (DESK), delivering educational material across the province;
- in New Brunswick, the provincial government, with the participation of NB Tel, carries out pilot programs to provide one-stop shopping for citizens looking for any provincial service.[19]

Stentor was positioning itself to move from carriage to content. "Our future doesn't lie in bandwidth, it lies in value-added services," said Brian Milton, Stentor's national director of social policy – a telephone company with a director of social policy! – in 1994.[20] Milton's job was to devise ways for the telcos to profit by providing services in those areas of public information most targeted for colonization by the private sector.

Stentor's vision statement was followed quickly by its so-called Beacon Initiative – the idea that telecommunications would be a beacon on the information highway. The Beacon Initiative put flesh on the bare bones of the vision, making home shopping and banking, virtual classrooms and courtrooms, remote diagnoses by doctors, and movies on demand a reality for most Canadians. Stentor would set up a company, codenamed Multimedia Inc., to produce multimedia software and content for Beacon. The telcos promised to spend $8 billion over ten years to upgrade their networks to provide broadband capability and another $500 million over six years to build a national switching network to route high-speed video signals based on a technology called asynchronous transfer mode (ATM). The money wasn't the significant part of the proposal, despite the fact that "$8 billion," or "nearly $10 billion," or in one case "up to $12 billion" became a standard feature of all media coverage. In fact, it came to only $800 million a year, and the companies were already spending half that amount annually upgrading their systems. What wasn't clearly spelled out was that the additional money would come from higher rates charged to telephone subscribers. In other words, consumers would subsidize Stentor's entry into broadcasting so the telcos could sell services that consumers might not want or need. Beacon was the carrot dangled before regulators – and the public – to ensure that Stentor was allowed into broadcasting. Later came the stick – Stentor threatened to cancel the entire project if it didn't get immediate entry into the broadcasting and cable-TV businesses.

the quest for broadcast licences

Broadcasting is the second area regulated by the CRTC. The private government of broadcasting was dominated by companies like Rogers Communications (whose real expertise, some say, lies not in providing cable services to Canadians, but in playing the CRTC like a Stradivarius violin), major industry associations such as the Canadian Cable Television Association and the Canadian Association of Broadcasters (radio and television industry), and a plethora of industry, arts, and cultural groups.

Regulating broadcasting was based on a theory different from that regulating telecommunications. The air waves were assumed to be a scarce resource with more potential users than available frequencies. Consequently, they were designated as public property and subject to licensing. In return for being granted exclusive access to this public property (which could earn them private profit), broadcasters agreed to be regulated by the CRTC, fulfil Canadian-content quotas, and meet other policy objectives.

The Beacon Initiative, a pre-emptive strike to ensure that people's connection to the information highway was via telephone, not television, was an attempt to muscle in on the traditional turf of cable companies and invade the broadcasting government. Long-time Ted

Rogers associate Phil Lind said, in response to Beacon, "I know they've been salivating to get into the TV business for some time." "This is scary stuff," added Ken Stein, president of the Canadian Cable Television Association, the voice of the cable companies and one of the most influential players in broadcasting.[21] Stein had been recruited by the cable companies in 1991, after eighteen years with the federal government (including a stint in the early 1970s in the department of communications, where he was responsible for developing the government's cable-TV policy). Stein later went to Shaw Communications, the second-largest cable company, and was replaced by Richard Stursberg, another department of communications expatriate (he was an assistant deputy minister for cultural affairs and broadcasting). Before he went to CCTA, Stursberg worked for Unitel Communications (later taken over by AT&T). In his role as a senior vice-president responsible for strategic planning and corporate development at Unitel, Stursberg was an early participant in CANARIE, as an associate before the organization was incorporated and later as a CANARIE director. Stein and Stursberg were consummate Ottawa insiders who knew all the nuances of decision-making in the nation's capital. They were worthy opponents to the telcos, but lacked the telephone companies' clout, since cable-TV industry revenues are about one-tenth those of the telecommunications industry.

Ted Rogers had his own problems with the telcos and the CRTC. In February 1994, Rogers bought Maclean Hunter, the country's fourth-largest cable-TV company, for $3.1 billion. If the purchase got CRTC approval, it would give him a virtual monopoly over the two most important cable markets in the country, Southern Ontario and Greater Vancouver, and a third of all subscribers across Canada – all of which would position him to be able to offer local telephone service when that day came. The takeover would also give him control over major content providers like *Maclean's* magazine, the Sun newspaper chain, and the *Financial Post*. Rogers would be first in Canada to merge content and communications and sprint past the telcos onto the information highway.

He quickly won CRTC approval, provoking another chorus of complaints that he had the regulator in his pocket. But his own bottom line did him in — he'd gone deeply into debt to do the deal. He was forced to sell off some non-cable Maclean Hunter assets, including the Sun newspapers and the *Financial Post*, and soon he didn't have quite the converged company he set out to create. Nor did he do well in his battle with the telcos, which erupted in Vancouver, where he attempted to fight off, unsuccessfully, BC Telecom's incursion into cable services. The telephone company had joined with Expo 86 site developer, and Vancouver Public Library commemorative card advertiser, Concord Pacific Developments to provide cable services to 13,000 condominiums in the development, which was located in the heart of Rogers's Vancouver licence area. Rogers mounted challenges in the B.C. Supreme Court and at the CRTC, but after a long, drawn-out series of hearings and rulings the CRTC allowed BC Telecom and Concord Pacific to continue offering cable services.

information highway advisory council

Stentor's lobbying efforts and Rogers's bold move in buying Maclean Hunter sparked the newly installed Chrétien government to take immediate action. Several months after Chrétien's 1994 throne speech, Industry Canada released a discussion paper and established the Information Highway Advisory Council (IHAC) to provide answers to fifteen questions that were posed in it.[22] Manley appointed David Johnston, former principal, vice-chancellor, and law professor at McGill University, to be IHAC's chairman.

Johnston was acceptable to players on all sides. "He's a dynamic leader who has tremendous credentials . . . without having any vested interests," commented Jocelyne Cote-O'Hara of Stentor.[23] He had been through the exercise before, as chair of the national round table on the environment and the economy under the Mulroney government, proof that he could play a neutral role in a forum of sharply divided interests. And he could understand business, since he had a couple of interesting corporate directorships under his belt. He was a director of Southam — resigning when Conrad Black took over — whose daily newspapers were a major source of information to Canadians about the information highway. And during IHAC's deliberations, Johnston was appointed to the board, and a year later to the position of lead director, of CGI, which develops computer systems for large companies, buys the data-processing units of others, and sells computer services back to them. Later, in 1998, CGI and BCE, Bell Canada's corporate parent, signed an agreement that saw CGI take over BCE's computer systems unit and BCE take over CGI. By then, Johnston was Manley's personal information highway adviser. He remained on the CGI board, acquiring even more influence as a middle man between BCE and Industry Canada spheres.

More than 2,000 people volunteered to sit on IHAC, but the thirty Manley chose included few surprises. Nine were, or became, directors of CANARIE. The private sector outnumbered the public eighteen to twelve. The largest contingent – eight members, or more than 25 percent – came from the telecommunications industry. There were two representatives from the cable industry, two from broadcasting, and two from computing. The pattern of CANARIE was repeated – the private sector would dominate, and telecommunications would be the first among equals. IHAC was to hold its meetings in secret, and originally Manley did not intend the group to release its final report to the public, an approach he tried often to repeat. The panel had to meet behind closed doors to be effective, Manley explained when announcing its formation. "We want to hear from them in a candid way. We want the flexibility of an in camera discussion."[24] Such an elitist approach didn't survive, and Manley was not able to keep IHAC's deliberations as secret as he would have liked. Some individuals and groups were invited to present briefs to working groups of the council. Minutes of IHAC's meetings were posted on its Web site and mailed to individuals who requested them, and preliminary reports and discussion papers were published. The council also published its first final report a month after submitting it to Manley.

The secretive, closely controlled, corporate-dominated machinations of Manley's IHAC contrasts starkly with the broad public debate that occurred in Canada in the late 1920s over the commercialization and Americanization of radio airwaves. To resolve that issue, the landmark Aird Commission (established by the Conservative government of the day) held public hearings in twenty-five cities across

Canada, and its recommendations were subject to further public debate before a final decision was made to create a public system – the Canadian Broadcasting Corporation. In contrast to Sir John Aird, Manley evidently believed the public was an impediment to the work of the private government, which was busy sorting out relations among competing powerful interests. Public input was neither wanted nor tolerated.

The report produced by the council a year and a half later was an astonishing document, a blueprint for a society in which most cultural, social, and economic activities are mediated by networks provided by the information industry. Government's role is to enable the private sector to take over the information highway, and to be a "model user" of private-sector services. The report contained more than 300 recommendations. A key recommendation was that "highway network and new infrastructure should be left to the private sector, and the risks and rewards of the investment should accrue to the shareholders,"[25] which ignores the fact that taxpayers had already invested large sums and taken great risks in developing the infrastructure. There was just one dissenting voice to this corporate agenda, even though twelve members of the council represented the public and not-for-profit sectors. Jean-Claude Parrot, a vice-president of the 2.3-million member Canadian Labour Congress, wrote a minority report about the impact of the information highway on employment and the workplace, topics IHAC studiously ignored.

While IHAC was in the midst of its secretive deliberations, the federal Cabinet ordered the CRTC to hold public hearings and issue a report on convergence. Appended to the Cabinet order was a ten-page schedule detailing questions the government wanted the CRTC to address. Canadians were very concerned about convergence. The commission received 1,085 written comments, and seventy-eight individuals and organizations presented briefs at the hearings, which lasted through most of March. But in the end, convergence came down to one key question: should telecommunications carriers be allowed to hold broadcast licences?

The CRTC said yes. Telephone companies should indeed be permitted to apply for broadcasting licences and cable companies be allowed to offer local telephone service. The recommendations were a signal that the CRTC would not resist the merger of telecommunication and broadcasting. IHAC's report, released several months later, also recommended that the telcos be allowed to hold broadcasting licences.

lobbyists − the private government's secret weapon

Two telephone companies − BC Telecom and Quebec Tel (which operates in eastern Quebec) − were not allowed to enter broadcasting because of their foreign ownership. They could enter the cable business, the CRTC said, only if their parent, U.S.-based GTE Corp., reduced its shareholding from 50.5 to 20 percent, the maximum allowed under CRTC broadcast rules. Given that BC Telecom was banking its future on entering the message-sending business, this was a setback. GTE had no inclination to reduce its holding in one of its most profitable cash cows. CRTC regulations also limit foreign ownership of telecommunications companies (to 33.3 percent), but BC Telecom had a long-standing "grandfathered" exemption to this rule. The company wanted a similar exemption for its future cable operations. Would the federal Cabinet let the company into cable even though it was foreign-owned? A "yes" would give it a regulatory windfall at the expense of Rogers and Shaw, the two major cable-TV firms in B.C. A "no" would bar the phone company from getting into the television business unless its American parent sold part of its stake.[26]

If BC Telecom and Stentor couldn't themselves convince the government to change its policies about foreign ownership, they could turn to Ottawa's lobby firms, another force in the private government. Converging the traditional governments of telecommunications, broadcasting, and information technology "opened up a gold-mine for Ottawa's lobbying community as powerful interested parties, massive financial stakes and dozens of issues have yet to be resolved."[27] They call themselves government-affairs consultants, not lobbyists, and they often say they rely on their expertise and skill in public-opinion polling, communications, and strategic planning, not on their connections. These may be valid qualifications, but they don't explain why so many government-affairs consultants come to the job fresh from experience in politics or government and loaded with connections. And some, like Harry Near and Mike Robinson of Earnscliffe Strategy Group, continue to be active political organizers even as they consult government.

Drawing on more than one hundred years of intimate relations with government – remember how Bell successfully conspired to get rid of Sir William Mulock in 1905? – the Stentor companies have an impressive capability to lobby government. As many as twenty Stentor employees are registered lobbyists in Ottawa, and the alliance employs Capital Hill Group for special projects, as do BC Telecom and Bell Canada. The telcos also use the Stikeman Elliott law firm (former finance minister Marc Lalonde is a lobbyist for the firm) and Ottawa powerhouse Ray Hession, a former deputy minister of public works and ex-president of Canada Mortgage and Housing Corp. Hession's partner is the dean of Ottawa lobbyists, Bill Neville, who had been executive assistant to Communications Minister Judy LaMarsh in the late 1960s and, according to John Sawatsky,[28] practically wrote the Broadcasting Act. He then became a professional lobbyist and snapped up the Canadian Association of Broadcasters (CAB), the lobbying arm of the radio and television broadcast industry, as a client. Over the next ten years, CAB twice tried to hire Neville as its chief executive officer, but both times events conspired to prevent the consummation of the relationship. Eventually, Neville became the leading voice for the tobacco industry in its fight against legislation curbing cigarette advertising.

Capital Hill Group is led by high-powered lobbyist Herb Metcalfe, who formed the firm in 1985 after the Liberals lost power; it has the largest stable of IT clients in Ottawa (including Andersen Consulting, Cancom, Compaq Canada, EDI Council of Canada, Lockheed Martin Electronic Systems Canada, Silicon Graphics, Sybase Canada and Tandem Computers Canada).[29] Metcalfe is a well-connected backroom Liberal, a former policy adviser and executive assistant to Marc Lalonde and to assorted ministers of environment, small business, and science and technology. Stentor engaged Capital Hill Group just before the 1993 federal election, and the lobbyists helped shape Stentor's vision statement and Beacon Initiative. At Capital Hill Group, every senior partner has political connections and experience. Of special note are David Angus, former caucus liaison to the prime minister and executive assistant and senior policy adviser to the minister of government services of Ontario; Jean-François Thibault, senior adviser to the federal ministers of international trade, communications, and the environment, and chief of staff to the Quebec minister of energy and resources; and David Dyer, chief of staff to the ministers of industry and consumer and corporate affairs, special assistant to the minister of federal-provincial relations, and executive director of the federal government transition team.[30] They would need all their political smarts and connections to persuade Ottawa to overturn one of the longest-standing planks in its cultural policy – limited foreign control of Canada's broadcasting industry – and grant a broadcast licence to foreign-owned BC Telecom.

Alex Carey, the Australian student of corporate power we shall meet in Chapter 8, would call it a classic grassroots and treetops propaganda campaign, albeit on a small scale. The purpose of grassroots propaganda is to reach a large number of people with the goal of making public opinion sympathetic to what business wants. A treetops campaign is more sophisticated, and its goal is to reach the leaders of society. The campaign is rightly called propaganda because it aims to manipulate people into changing their opinions until they hold the view desired by the originators of the messages, a view not necessarily in the best interests of the people who are the targets of the propaganda.[31]

BC Telecom took out full-page ads in every daily newspaper in the province, asking readers to mail their MPs coupons saying, "I want choice in the cable-TV market, and I support BC Telecom's right to apply for a broadcast distribution license."[32] Metcalfe and the phone company were able to harness the pent-up anger of cable-TV subscribers over Rogers' negative-billing option (in which subscribers were billed for new services unless they wrote in to say they didn't want them). More than 20,000 letters were sent to Ottawa. What likely wasn't clear to the letter writers was that granting a broadcast licence to BC Telecom could eventually mean that Canada would no longer support a policy of universal access to cable and basic telephone service. The company even lined up the support of its union, which was angry after having lost a Supreme Court of Canada case to bar cable employees from working on telephone facilities to install cable wiring. The union took out its own full-page ads and ran radio commercials warning British Columbians that unless Ottawa had a change of heart, consumers would remain captives of the cable industry. In a bizarre twist of logic, the ad claimed that the CRTC was "treating B.C. like a cultural backwater." The ads failed to mention BC Tel's foreign ownership and the CRTC rules regarding that. BC Tel also recruited support from B.C.'s New Democratic government (ironically, twenty-five years earlier a previous NDP administration had contemplated nationalizing BC Tel, for the same reasons Sir William Mulock had considered the possibility of nationalizing Bell Telephone).

Premier Mike Harcourt wrote to Prime Minister Chrétien, and Employment and Investment Minister Glen Clark wrote to John Manley and to Heritage Minister Michel Dupuy, both complaining that shutting out BC Tel would prevent the province from realizing the benefits of the information highway. BC Tel threatened to "reconsider" its share of Beacon Initiative spending of $1.8 billion. The company also complained of being treated as a "second-class corporate citizen," and promised federal Cabinet ministers that a BC Tel–cable-TV operation would be all-Canadian, with only Canadians on the board and in the ranks of senior management, and only Canadians making programming decisions. And BC Tel lined up the support of Transport Minister David Anderson and B.C.'s five other Liberal MPs, who met privately with Sheila Copps, Dupuy's replacement in the heritage ministry. With a federal election looming, political considerations weighed heavily in the Cabinet's deliberations – the party was hoping to increase Liberal representation in B.C.

The campaign was a major success. On August 6, 1996, the federal Cabinet ordered the CRTC to allow BC Tel (and Quebec Tel) to acquire cable-TV licences, along with the Canadian-owned companies, by "grandfathering" BC Tel's telecommunications exemption into broadcasting. It was a clear victory for the foreign-owned firm, and CEO

Brian Canfield, who announced his retirement soon after, basked in the glow of his victory. John Manley, Industry Canada, and the economics-first agenda were the other big winners. And Herb Metcalfe and Capital Hill Group saw their reputations enhanced by the outcome. But Heritage Canada and cultural interests suffered a stunning defeat. The cultural community had fractured, with prominent B.C. bureaucrats like Nini Baird, the province's representative on the board of governors of the Canadian Conference of the Arts, lining up with BC Tel. Other cultural leaders argued that a BC Tel broadcast licence would be the thin edge of the wedge, leading to foreign domination of Canadian broadcasting. In the end, it may well do just that.

the new world dawns

With Industry Canada's encouragement, and IHAC and CRTC approval, the telcos began exploring ways to enter the content business. Stentor started to disintegrate. Smaller companies bridled at Bell's control – it seemed decisions were being made to serve Bell's needs rather than theirs. Under Stentor, they had been prevented from expanding outside their provincial markets, but its purpose had been served: long-distance competition was firmly entrenched, and the telcos were moving, albeit slowly, into content.

The first overt blow to the Stentor alliance came with the audacious, but unsuccessful, bid by Telus Corp. to merge with Stentor arch-rival AT&T Canada. In response, Bell set out to establish its own $750-million coast-to-coast broadband company by buying fibre-optic lines from Fonorola Canada (which was gobbled up by Call-Net Enterprises, a major alternative carrier tied to U.S.-based Sprint).

These moves shattered one hundred years of provincial monopoly and inter-provincial co-operation. Telus responded by merging with BC Telecom, whose majority shareholder, GTE Corp., didn't oppose the bid. GTE itself was the target of a $54-billion (U.S.) takeover bid by Bell Atlantic Corp., which, if successful, would create a rival equal in size and reach to the U.S.'s largest telecommunications company, AT&T. AT&T's Canadian subsidiary was also busy. After the failed merger with Telus, it consolidated its position in Canada by taking over

MetroNet, an upstart company that was entering the local business-telephone market by wiring the downtown districts of major cities with fibre-optic cable. Bell Canada trumped its Canadian rivals by selling a 20 percent interest to Ameritech Corp., a U.S. "Baby Bell" based in the American Midwest, which was itself in the process of merging with yet another Baby Bell, SBC Corp. By 1999, the telecommunications landscape had changed dramatically, with the preliminary steps being taken towards the creation of one North American telecommunications market. The myth of technological nationalism was being rapidly replaced with a new myth of global competition.

These dramatic moves garnered headlines, but the telcos were also making important forays into content. With its new-found ability to enter the cable-TV business, Bell launched broadband content trials in London, Ontario, and Repentigny, Quebec; the company would provide pay-per-view movies, 160 digital channels, and Internet services to several thousand households. (Meanwhile, Telus was undertaking its own trials in Alberta.) Bell also acquired control of the direct-to-home satellite service, ExpressVu. But electronic commerce would be a priority. The company formed BCE Emergis, which started out as a joint venture with Netscape to develop and sell e-commerce software that runs on the Internet. Bell followed with a small investment in Digital Renaissance, a Toronto-based provider of new-media software and systems. Next, Bell developed for Industry Canada's Strategis site an e-commerce component, which would allow Industry Canada to charge an on-line fee for industrial and economic information. But the real e-commerce breakthrough occurred in early 1999, when Emergis won a bid for an Internet billing system for Canadian banks, beating out competitors like IBM. There's even more to come, as Bell makes plans to enter the U.S. market for e-commerce.[33]

Telus also entered the content market with Telus Geomatics, which uses digital mapping software to provide geographic information-systems products in Alberta. Its huge database includes geographical reference data and topographical map information for all of Alberta, aerial photos, and the addresses and postal codes for all 1.6 million lots in the province. Telus maps can be delivered electronically via e-mail, over the Internet, or on CD-ROMs.[34]

The telcos still earn most of their revenue as providers of local and long-distance, voice and data, wireless and wireline services. But their single-minded quest to acquire broadcasting licences and their increasing activity in content markets such as cable-TV and the Internet are evidence that they realize the future lies in content, not carriage. It's clear now that connecting Canadians is not the telcos' nor John Manley's ultimate goal; it's the content that's sold to Canadians once they're connected that will provide industry profits in the twenty-first century. And whoever owns the content will profit most.

enclosing the information commons

*Any exception or exemption [to copyright protection] is
essentially expropriation.*
> — Douglas Frith, President, Canadian Motion Picture Distributors
> Association and former Liberal Cabinet minister

Intellectual property is theft.
> — Pierre Joseph Prudhon, *What Is Property?*

*The growing trend towards copyright protection for purely
economic reasons seems to be in conflict with the original aims
of copyright to promote the progress of science and the arts.
Access to information and knowledge underpins society.*
> — International Federation of Library Associations

Heather Robertson is one of Canada's most successful writers,
author of scores of magazine articles and more than a dozen fiction
and non-fiction books, including three volumes on the life of William
Lyon Mackenzie King. In 1995 she wrote *Driving Force*, a history of
General Motors of Canada founder Sam McLaughlin and the influ-
ential McLaughlin family, for which she won the prestigious 1996
National Business Book Award. Robertson's publisher, McClelland &
Stewart, signed a contract with Thomson Corporation, owner of the

Globe and Mail, for a one-time right to publish an excerpt from the book in the *Globe*'s *Report on Business* magazine. After the excerpt appeared in October 1996, Robertson was shocked to discover that it was being distributed and sold on InfoGlobe, the *Globe*'s commercial electronic database. She did not authorize this subsequent "publication" of her work, nor did she receive additional payment for it.[1]

The *Globe* has published InfoGlobe since 1978, but freelance writers found out that their work was being sold on it only in the mid-1990s. Since they believed they owned their work, they demanded compensation for electronic publication. In September 1996, Robertson launched a landmark $100-million class-action lawsuit against Thomson on behalf of any freelance writers, artists, and photographers who had sold works to the company and wanted to retain control over their electronic-publishing rights. She sought $50 million in compensation, $50 million in punitive damages, and an injunction preventing unauthorized inclusion of freelancers' works on electronic databases. Robertson won her first victory in early 1999 when a judge in Ontario Court General Division gave her permission to launch the class-action suit.

For decades, informality governed the relationship between freelance writers and publishers. It was clear to writers that they owned their articles and had the exclusive right to license them to whomever they chose. They would normally assign first Canadian or North American serial rights – the right to publish the work for the first time in print form – and retain the right to resell the story to other publications. Publishers rarely bothered with assignment letters or formal contracts. Electronic rights were not an issue until freelancers started stumbling across their own works in electronic databases and, adding insult to injury, having to pay to read them.

The dispute between authors and publishers is one indicator that the content stored in databases and delivered over computer networks, and not the networks themselves, has great economic value. The media focus relentlessly on new technologies, hardware, software, and systems. But librarians, educators, academics, and others concerned about access to information as a right of democracy are discovering what freelance writers already know. The real change –

the real information revolution – is occurring behind the scenes, where corporate executives and intellectual-property lawyers plot to enclose and commercialize society's pool of information resources.

The term "intellectual property" refers to works of the mind in tangible form. It includes literary and artistic works, photographs, films, videos, recorded music, tapes or discs, architectural drawings, industrial designs and patterns, computer software, and database programs. Intellectual-property law – the entrenchment of legal rights to own and control the use of information – is the vehicle by which large corporations like Thomson Corp., the *New York Times*, Rupert Murdoch's News Corp., Microsoft, and Disney are amassing billions of dollars' worth of intellectual property. They are using their assets and corporate clout to extend their reach into every corner of individual and community life. In this revolution, intellectual-property lawyers are storm troopers who've been sent into recalcitrant countries and cultures as an advance guard to whip legal infrastructures into shape for the corporate invasion.

At stake in the Robertson–Thomson Corp. dispute is one aspect of intellectual property: the ownership of copyright. Copyright is granted to authors of original literary, dramatic, musical, and artistic works under the authority of the Canadian Copyright Act. It permits creators and other rights-holders to profit from their efforts by collecting royalty payments for the use and exploitation of protected creations. The theory of copyright is that a monopoly must be granted because without some system of reward, the incentive for creative expression and innovation would cease. Copyright usually lasts for the term of the author's life plus fifty years, beginning at the moment the work is created. The author is usually the first owner of copyright, unless he or she produced the work as an employee, in which case the employer is the owner. Copyright protects expression only, not the ideas that are expressed by the words (or images). When you buy a book, you can tell people what's in it, read it aloud to them, lend it to someone, mark it up, tear out pages, or even burn it. But you cannot copy it.

Copyright is supposed to balance society's need for ready and inexpensive access to a supply of new ideas with creators' needs to be rewarded for their work, which will stimulate them to further creative effort and hence keep society surviving and thriving. But the Robertson-Thomson dispute reveals the clout of a third party: publishers and distributors, those who transmit works from creators to society. Global book and periodical publishers; film, video, and music publishers and distributors; and radio and television broadcasters have appropriated most of the benefits of copyright at the expense of both creators and society. The same situation applies to two other forms of intellectual property – patents, which provide twenty-year protection for inventions, and trademarks, which protect corporate logos and marks. "However much the rhetoric of inventors, creators and innovators is employed, the [Copyright, Patent and Trademark] acts seem more designed by big business for big business. Smaller operations and the general public are left to the side as passive viewers – to be affected, but not themselves to affect anything," writes York University law professor David Vaver, one of Canada's leading copyright experts.[2] Most creators work for corporations as computer-game programmers, photographers, animators, script writers, reporters, and software developers. In these cases, it's the corporation that obtains and owns the copyright. But in the case of freelance writers, it should be they, not the corporation, who own the rights to reproduce their works.

Like Heather Robertson, Jim Carroll is a prolific Canadian writer, author of a half-dozen books about the Internet, including the best-selling *Canadian Internet Handbook* (co-authored with Rick Broadhead). Carroll was also a columnist for *Computing Canada* and wrote for major newspapers like the *Globe and Mail* and the *Toronto Star*. He recounted in *Media* magazine what happened to him when he was researching a project related to e-mail systems and searching through the Dialog database system, one of the largest electronic-database services in the world, then owned by Knight-Ridder newspapers:

[Y]ou can imagine my bewilderment when the search turned up a number of articles that I had written for my *Computing Canada* column. . . . 'Huh? what gives?' I thought. I didn't remember giving Dialog any permission to reproduce my articles in electronic form. Not only that, but I was paying serious money, a few bucks per article, to retrieve my own articles from some U.S.-based database service! Where did that money go? Why didn't I see any of it?[3]

Carroll discovered that his *Computing Canada* articles were being resold by InfoGlobe as well as Dialog. He had not given anyone – *Computing Canada*'s publisher, InfoGlobe, Dialog, Knight-Ridder, or anyone else – permission to resell his articles. He wondered how many people were downloading his articles at two to three dollars apiece, and how much money Thomson Corp. was making from them.

Robertson and Carroll are not alone. In the spring of 1995, a group of twelve (later eighteen) freelance writers at the Montreal *Gazette* served notice on the paper's owner, Southam, because of similar violations of electronic copyright. They charged that Southam had made unauthorized use of their articles on Infomart, the company's full-text electronic database. In fact, they were stunned to learn that their work had been offered on Infomart for eleven years without their knowledge or consent. Ann Diamond, one of the "Gazette 18," related how a search of UnCover, a Knight-Ridder magazine database, "turned up four obscure articles I'd published over the last four years in small Canadian magazines, including *Books in Canada* and the *Canadian Forum*. My pieces now sell for about $11.00 (U.S.) per download."[4] Presumably her piece about publisher rip-offs was also being offered by UnCover.

To preclude legal challenges from freelancers such as Robertson, publishers began imposing new contracts. The Periodical Writers Association of Canada (PWAC), an organization that represents freelance writers, maintains on its Web page a Hall of Shame, which claims that every major Canadian publisher is guilty of "copyright theft." However, given their low average annual income and dependence on a small number of publishers, most freelancers caved in to the unfair demands of publishers and signed these new contracts. The following are just a few of the deals that have been struck:

- Ted Rogers's Maclean Hunter, which publishes many leading national magazines, introduced a "take it or leave it" contract at *Chatelaine*, *Modern Woman*, and *Family Practices*. It requires writers to turn over, without payment, the right to publish articles in any electronic form, including databases accessible through the Internet.

- For one price, Conrad Black–owned Southam, publisher of many major Canadian dailies, demands the right to republish freelance articles prepared for one paper in *all* Southam newspapers, as well as in Southam's electronic databases, CD-ROMs, and Internet Web sites, and in Infomart.

- For no additional payment, Thomson Corp.'s contract with freelancers gives the company a "world-wide, perpetual, paid-up, non-exclusive licence to publish and republish the contracted material in original or edited form, and in all media and forms of reproduction and distribution now in existence or hereafter developed." As PWAC put it, "Thomson's appalling new contract is among the worst of a handful of greedy and abusive contracts issued by major publishing conglomerates since late 1995. In the past we could compensate for their low freelance rates by recycling our work, selling the same article to a variety of publications. Now they want to recycle it themselves, to pay for it once and use it repeatedly in various new electronic media."[5]

Freelancers fought back gamely in a number of ways: by challenging publishers in the courts as Heather Robertson did, by organizing their colleagues, and by lobbying for changes in their relationship with publishers. They even set up an electronic rights licensing agency (TERLA) to represent them and to act as a peacemaker in the bitter struggle between freelancers and the periodical publishing industry.[6]

The amassing of economic advantage by publishers is not new — it started almost as soon as the printing press was developed in the fifteenth century. In 1557, printers, bookbinders, and booksellers organized themselves into the Stationers' Company, a craft guild that lobbied Queen Mary for, and received, exclusive control over all printing and bookselling in England. Authors were marginal and the public played no role at all. Guild members bought manuscripts outright from authors and then had the exclusive right to print and sell them forever.[7] Worse yet, if an author allowed a manuscript to be publicly circulated, there was nothing to prevent a member of the

Stationers' Company from registering copyright himself and exploiting it. The author got nothing. Today, in the era of the Internet, the stakes are even higher. Information has been transformed into a commodity with great value. In the U.S., the intellectual-property industry is growing three times faster than the economy as a whole.

publishers gain control of copyright

In theory, copyright should be a despised activity. Everyone condemns monopolies, which lead to higher costs for consumers and excessive profits for monopolists, unless they are effectively regulated in the public interest. Copyright does create monopolies for copyright owners, but it differs from other forms. Society agrees to bestow a monopoly on a creator because the benefits to society supposedly outweigh the costs. Thomas Jefferson and the U.S. founders saw copyright as a minor evil needed to accomplish a larger good. Copyright seems to be the least objectionable way to ensure that new ideas will continue to be produced and that society will continue to benefit from them. "[P]roviding protection for the author against unauthorised publication for a limited period will encourage and promote learning and progress and thus act for the public good."[8]

The world's first copyright law was the Statute of Anne, which was passed in 1709 and broke the Stationers' 150-year monopoly on publishing. The act identified in its title the two groups with an interest in copyright: "An Act for the encouragement of learning" – society's interest – "by vesting the copies of printed books in the authors or purchasers of such copies, during the times therein mentioned" – author's interest. Publishers were not even mentioned. Parliament agreed that writers should be given control of their works for a limited time (fourteen years, with the option of renewing for another fourteen years).[9] The Copyright Clause of the American Constitution, framed eighty years later, reiterated the equal significance of authors and society. It provided that "the Congress shall have the power . . . to promote the progress of science and useful arts, by securing for limited time to authors and inventors the exclusive right to their respective writings and discoveries."[10] British statesman and author

Lord Thomas Macauley said it well in the nineteenth century: "The advantages arising from a system of copyright are obvious. It is desirable that we should have a supply of good books; we cannot have such a supply unless men of letters are liberally remunerated and the least objectionable way of remunerating them is by way of copyright."[11] The idea of a balance of rights continues in the twentieth century, and was expressed in the 1948 United Nations Universal Declaration of Human Rights:

> 27 (i) Everyone has the right freely to participate in the cultural life of the Community, to enjoy the arts and to share in scientific advancement and its benefits.
>
> 27 (ii) Everyone has the right to the protection of the moral and material interests resulting from any scientific, literary or artistic production of which he is an author.

But what started out as a balance between interests, a system to ensure that society benefits from the fruits of creative labour – and that still exists, at least in these constitutions and declarations – became distorted, even perverted, into a regime of firmly entrenched intellectual-property rights that takes precedence over all other interests and now reigns supreme at the millennium. The trend began during the nineteenth century, when the corporate form of organization was perfected by lawyers, judges, and legislators as a means of accumulating wealth, and when the public interest in copyright and other intellectual-property protections began its long slide into impotence. In the age of electronic publishing and distribution, intellectual-property rights are big business, and the public's right to information cannot be allowed to get in the way.

In Canada, the public's right to use copyrighted material is recognized as "fair dealing" (in the U.S., it's known as "fair use"). This covers private study, research, criticism, review, and newspaper summary. These rights came under considerable pressure in Bill C-32, which changed Canada's Copyright Act to incorporate electronic media. When the bill was tabled in the House of Commons in April 1996, the two sponsoring ministers, John Manley of industry and

Sheila Copps of Canadian heritage, wrote that "the Bill will achieve a fair balance between the rights of those [who] create works, and the needs of those who use them."[12] It was the usual rhetoric: corporate interests were bundled with those of creators, who had "rights"; society, which created the rights and bestowed them on authors, had "needs" only, not rights, and rights trump needs. The net result of this complex set of amendments was that corporate rights over information were further extended, the public interest was diminished, and creators received only a few benefits. An entirely new set of rights, called neighbouring rights, was established for record companies, performers, and broadcasters. As David Vaver writes, "Theoretically, none of these persons is an author, none does anything 'original,' none produces a 'work.' Performers interpret or execute works, record producers record them, broadcasters transmit them, so none is entitled to a traditional copyright."[13] Nevertheless, Bill C-32 extended traditional copyright protection "to these non-traditional subject matters."

extracting wealth from electronic information

Ken Thomson, owner of Thomson Corp. and Canada's richest person, and his senior managers discovered years ago what many are realizing today — "that information has taken on a new character, that it has passed from being an instrument through which we acquire and manage other assets to being a primary asset itself."[14] Thomson acquired ownership of copyrighted compilations of information — increasingly in electronic format — needed by lawyers, bankers, engineers, and accountants, who can pass the costs of access on to their customers and clients. He calls this the virtuous circle: acquire valuable products such as databases full of information that your competitors don't have and can't get; serve up this proprietary information in any form a customer wants, including as a CD-ROM, on-line, or in print; attract more customers and increase profits because these products are easier to use and more comprehensive; use the revenues to buy up more databases. Thomson abandoned its dominant position in the daily newspaper industry, where good profits could still be earned but the outlook for the future was uncertain, to become "one of the most clearly-focused specialized information and publishing groups in the world, rich in proprietary, differentiated and high added-value content."[15] As for where freelancers fit in the company's global vision, Thomson has this to say in its 1996 annual report: "Electronic services in specialized areas produce good operating margins and cash flows after an initial investment in computer hardware, software and the inputting of information."[16] The works of writers are considered to be little more than the "inputting of information," and they are to be contained within the "initial investment"; in other words, no ongoing royalty payments.

So far it has worked beautifully, at least from Thomson's point of view. "From negligible sums six years ago, the proportion of total specialized information and publishing sales from electronic products reached 38% in 1996, and by the year 2000 we expect this to approach 50%."[17] By then, even his newspapers will have actively moved into electronic media. Thomson's print and electronic publications include 45,000 books and directories, 250 multi-volume law libraries, nearly 600 loose-leaf services, 400 subscription-based journals, 400 newsletters, nearly 3,500 software and video/audio products, 2,000 CD-ROM products, and 350 on-line services, including Westlaw, which features more than 9,500 electronic databases. The company's balance sheet reflects the changed emphasis. The largest asset on the books is "publishing rights and circulation" (the estimated worth of the rights to publish its databases and of the circulation of its newspapers). These, in total, are valued at $5.1 billion (U.S.), or nearly 40 percent of all assets owned by the company. Computer hardware and software add another billion dollars. These two items dwarf the more traditional assets of newspaper companies: machinery, equipment, and newspaper presses, worth $1.5 billion; and land and buildings, worth $630 million.

The shift in Thomson's business reflects the growing economic importance of information. Since the 1970s, the information, culture, and high-tech industries have created some of the world's great global fortunes. The production, distribution, and sale of intellectual property is at the heart of this new wealth-generating machine.[18] Here are just a few of the beneficiaries:

- Bill Gates, of course, the world's wealthiest person, leads the pack. His net worth (what he owns minus what he owes) topped $80 billion (U.S.) in 1998 and approached $100 billion in 1999. Software became subject to copyright only in the 1980s. Without this protection, Gates would likely never have risen to global prominence and power. Separately from Microsoft, Gates purchased the 16 million images in the Bettman Archives, and adds to his "untold wealth by licensing electronic reproductions of the photographs of Ansel Adams."[19]

- Rupert Murdoch holds a vast array of intellectual property in his $20-billion empire: Twentieth Century-Fox's film library, 20 magazines (including *TV Guide*, the largest weekly publication in the U.S.), 128 newspapers (and their electronic databases), Fox Broadcasting, television stations, and HarperCollins publishing. Murdoch used his film library as collateral to secure an additional $1 billion in financing for the studio, which produced the splashiest hit of 1996, *Independence Day*. At the same time, he was busy signing deals with cable-franchise owners to distribute his programming. He excels in moving his content from one medium to another. Many of the Fox network prime-time series are produced by, or in association with, Fox's production arm, and the news division has access to overseas news coverage produced by Sky News, the twenty-four-hour news channel offered as part of the British Sky satellite-television service.

- Disney's crown jewels are its stable of film classics, which it repackages and reissues anew for each generation of young people. Disney was a key supporter of the 1998 Sonny Bono Copyright Term Extension Act, which extended copyright protection for an additional twenty years. Given that copyright protection for Mickey Mouse was due to expire in 2004, this law provided Disney with a bonanza of perhaps $1 billion. The company has used its IP assets for many purposes, including as financing for the takeover of Cap Cities/ABC, the third-largest broadcasting network.

- With his fortune established in drive-in theatres and Hollywood studios, Sumner Redstone, regularly in the top ten on the *Forbes* 400 list of the world's wealthiest people, initiated in 1987 a successful hostile takeover of Viacom, owner of Showtime, The Movie Channel, MTV, Nickelodeon, cable systems, and radio and television stations.

Redstone ended up knee-deep in intellectual property, with old television series, feature films, publisher Simon & Schuster, and rights to music videos. He expanded his empire enormously with his acquisition of Blockbuster Video and 50.1 percent of Paramount Pictures (and its huge film library). In 1996, he signed a licensing agreement for Viacom's movie and TV "products" with German media mogul Leo Kirch, a deal that should bring in $1 billion to $1.5 billion over the next decade. But Viacom's biggest money spinner is "Star Trek," which has achieved cult status among its millions of devoted, almost fanatical, fans. Before Christmas 1996, Viacom's lawyer sent a letter to a handful of the estimated 100,000 Internet Web sites devoted to Trek lore, ordering them to shut down. The letter caused a kerfuffle in cyberland. Fans were more than a little miffed and talked about a boycott. A plethora of resistance pages quickly appeared. *Home Computing & Entertainment* magazine reported that a company lawyer, whom Viacom asked not be identified (for fear she would be inundated with calls from irate cybernauts), explained that the offending Web sites were "depriving us of the opportunity to have control over how [our property] is used. Our intellectual property is the most valuable thing [we] own."[20]

- Ted Turner's $2-billion fortune lay in the broadcast rights to the 3,000-film MGM library, which he used to program his cable television network, Turner Network Television. He also owned Cable News Network, Headline News Network, and the Atlanta Braves baseball and Hawks basketball teams. In 1991, he bought Hanna-Barbera Productions and the rights to its library of 3,000 half-hour cartoons to show on the new Cartoon Network. He also used characters from the Hanna-Barbera library to create interactive games and CD-ROMs. In 1996, Turner sold his company to Time Warner for $6.5 billion (U.S.).

enclosing the commons

There are interesting parallels between the expansive IPR regime taking hold in the late twentieth century and the enclosure of the English village commons that took place in the seventeenth and eighteenth centuries. Until recently, the official consensus on enclosure was that the traditional, or "peasant," farms and open fields of the Middle Ages had stifled progress, and that enclosure and the creation of large farms was necessary for the technical revolution in agriculture to occur. Defenders of enclosure grant that it was unfair to the poor because it took away their farms and threw them off the land. But this was good in the end, they argue, because the dispossessed farmers became the new urban workforce that led to the first Industrial Revolution. Enclosure enabled the accumulation of capital, investment in machinery, and increased productivity. Eventually, everyone was better off, or so the argument goes. Similarly, it is argued today that strong IP laws are necessary to encourage new ideas from which everyone will benefit in time. People must be prevented from freely copying software programs, downloading magazine articles in electronic databases, or downloading CD-quality music from the Web if we are to create jobs, increase productivity, and compete in a global economy.

Both sets of assertions have been the subject of massive propaganda campaigns designed to change public attitudes regarding enclosure from hostility to approval. The argument is that enclosure, be it of the village or the information commons, which actually benefits only a privileged few, is in fact vital to the national interest. Yet such claims are false. Robert Allen's painstaking study of enclosure in the English midlands between the Middle Ages and the nineteenth century[21] pokes large holes in the received wisdom regarding the benefits of the system. Allen argues that productivity was already improving under the open-field system, which preceded enclosure. Open fields took their name from the practice of overnight pasturing of village sheep flocks on fallow fields. Family-owned strips of land were scattered across the fields surrounding a village. No one had the right to exclude village flocks from foraging on their strips when fields lay fallow. Not every resident of a village had the right to put animals on the common, of course; that right resided only with the owners of land in the fields. To prevent overgrazing, commons were frequently "stinted" (that is, restrictions were placed on the number and kinds of animals that could be pastured). Usually, a manorial court set the dates on which flocks could be pastured on particular fields; the court also enforced these rules. Winter flooding encouraged the growth of grass but often obliterated property boundaries and, on occasion, changed the shape of the meadow itself. Flexible and equitable management was essential to keep the system functioning smoothly.

Before the middle of the eighteenth century, land was fenced usually by agreement of all owners in a village. After owners registered their land they would swap with other owners so they could acquire neighbouring strips of land and thus create a bigger lot for themselves. In a few cases, successful farmers bought up all the land in the village and achieved enclosure. The sole owner could then bar common grazing and suspend collective decision-making. After 1750, most enclosures resulted from parliamentary act. Owners of three-quarters of the land in a village could petition Parliament for enclosure. Since land ownership had become concentrated by this time, parliamentary bills could proceed even with a majority of farmers – usually the small owners – opposed. Once a bill received royal assent, common grazing and collective control over cropping were abolished. Whichever way enclosure proceeded, the end result was the same: peasant ownership of small, scattered strips was replaced by large estates owned by absentee lords who leased the land to tenant farmers (who then hired local wage labour to work the fields). By the end of the eighteenth century, owner-occupiers had disappeared from the English countryside.

The English agricultural miracle meant a doubling of crop yields and labour productivity between the sixteenth and nineteenth centuries. But Allen shows that enclosure made only a minor contribution to this. Most gains in productivity – about 75 percent, he estimates – were achieved in the open-field villages. "It was small-scale farmers in the open fields – the English yeomen – who accomplished the biological revolution in grain growing."[22] But the yeoman farmers who were responsible for most of the productivity gains received few of the benefits, which, after enclosure, went to the absentee lords in the form of rent increases.[23] Agricultural prices went up, but wages didn't follow. In fact, enclosure played a large part in turning the last of the English peasantry into an insecure rural working class. Concludes

Allen: "[M]ost English men and women would have been better off had the landlords' revolution never occurred."[24]

There are obvious differences between enclosure of village fields and enclosure of public information, of course. If someone takes your farm, you can no longer enjoy its benefits. If someone takes your electronic publication, you still have it and can continue to benefit from it. A second difference is that the right to use village lands was held by a relatively small handful of landowners, while the right to use intellectual property, such as is allowed under fair-dealing or fair-use provisions in copyright laws, can extend to the entire world. But there are some clear parallels as well. In both cases, it's argued that enclosure was, or is, necessary for progress and prosperity. However, as Allen demonstrates, the reality of village enclosure was not only that most productivity gains occurred before enclosure, but also that the benefits of those gains accrued after enclosure only to a handful of powerful landlords. Similarly, new works borrow liberally from a common store of facts, information, and knowledge that exists in the public domain in reference books, libraries, schools, government documents, and the news media, as well as in society's stories, myths, and public talks. Disney, for instance, has taken *The Hunchback of Notre Dame*, *The Little Mermaid*, *Pocahontas*, and *Mulan* from the public domain and turned them into corporate-controlled intellectual property. The enclosure of the information commons leads to increases in global wealth, but like the yeoman farmers, individual creators and society as a whole receive few of the benefits. The huge gains in wealth accrue to the new intellectual-property lords, such as Disney, Bill Gates, and Ken Thomson.

the u.s. extends its hegemony

During the 1980s, the U.S. realized it was losing its economic clout in the traditional manufacturing industries. Emerging industrial power-houses like Japan and South Korea were capturing ever-greater shares of the markets for automobiles, televisions, and other industrial goods. What the U.S. was still good at, and led the world in, was information technology, entertainment, chemicals and pharmaceuticals – industries with high intellectual-property content. As a result, the country moved quickly to make the export of intellectual property a central plank in its economic strategy. Of course, the U.S. has exported Hollywood films and television programs for decades. What was new was the concerted effort on the part of industry and government to extend the reach of American information products and to ensure that IP rights were recognized and enforced in every corner of the world.

In 1984, President Ronald Reagan met with the CEOs of twelve major IP-producing corporations to identify their biggest trade concerns. They agreed on one: inadequate international intellectual-property protection. The members of this group formed a coalition called the Intellectual Property Committee (IPC), which became a leading lobbyist in the forthcoming General Agreement on Tariffs and Trade (GATT) negotiations. They were drawn from three industries: information technology (IBM, Hewlett-Packard, General Electric, Rockwell International), pharmaceutical products (Bristol-Myers, Johnson & Johnson, Merck, Pfizer), and chemical products (DuPont, Monsanto, FMC). They were joined by movie, video, and recording giant Warner Communications. (Microsoft was not there because it was just a start-up company in those days.) This powerful group was able for the first time to define intellectual property as an integral part of U.S. trade policy.[25] As IP lawyer Myra Tawfik explains, the IPC and the U.S. government developed a three-stage program. First, they identified minimum standards of protection they would accept as adequate. Then they worked (for nearly a decade) to have this protection inserted into international trade agreements such as the North American Free Trade Agreement (NAFTA) and GATT. Third, they vigorously promoted a system of enforcement to ensure that the new rights were protected, using the spectre of "piracy," or unauthorized copying of music, videos, computer software or printed works.

Up to this time, trade issues had been handled by GATT, while intellectual-property rights were the domain of the Paris and Berne conventions. The 1883 Paris Convention for the Protection of Industrial Property (patents and trademarks) and the 1886 Berne Convention for the Protection of Literary and Artistic Works (copyright) established an international bureau in Geneva, Switzerland, that in 1970 became the World Intellectual Property Organization (WIPO). WIPO has a mandate to be "responsible for the promotion of the protection of intellectual property throughout the world through co-operation among [member] states and for the administration of various multilateral treaties dealing with the legal and administrative aspects of intellectual property."[26] But WIPO was unsatisfactory for American purposes. Its conventions were not binding on their signatories, nor did they contain enforcement mechanisms. GATT had both of these, but it had never dealt with intellectual property.

As a first step in reshaping the global trade agenda, the U.S. turned to Canada. U.S. negotiators rehearsed the trade-related approach to intellectual property with Canada in the negotiations for the Free Trade Agreement (FTA) and NAFTA, and were successful in inserting a so-called TRIPs (trade-related aspects of intellectual property rights) code into NAFTA. Then, with the NAFTA success behind them, the negotiators turned their guns on the rest of the world. They also worked in the trade forum to extend IP protection to areas not already covered by Paris and Berne, such as computer software, trade secrets, and biotechnology patents, and to extend the length of term of protection for each type of intellectual property. They were adamant in their demand that compulsory licences for most forms of IP be abolished. This initiative affected Canadians most profoundly in the area of drug prices.

Almost since the beginning of medicare, Canadian government policy had been to control the cost of drugs by encouraging competition between holders of patents and generic drug manufacturers. This was achieved by granting compulsory licences of patents to generic manufacturers at a very low royalty rate. The Eastman Report, commissioned by the federal government, found that in 1983 Canadians had paid several hundred million dollars less than they would have if compulsory licensing did not exist and multinational drug companies held monopoly patent protection. The scheme survived the first onslaught of the 1988 Canada-U.S. free trade negotiations, but it was crushed by NAFTA. Canada was forced to bring in the system of seventeen-year patent protection (the term was later extended to twenty years) demanded by the American drug companies, and Canadian drug prices rose by an estimated $400 million a year.[27]

Canada had been able to fend off most American demands for increased IP protection in the earlier Canada-U.S. Free Trade Agreement, as it did with compulsory licensing. Article 2005, for example, allowed Canada to continue to subsidize, regulate, and control its cultural industries. But it also authorized the Americans to retaliate commercially if they thought their interests had been harmed by such Canadian actions. And the Americans made a few other inroads. Under Article 2006, Canada agreed to amend its Copyright Act to recognize the right of American broadcasters to collect royalties from Canadian cable companies that retransmitted American programs. The Canadian Copyright Board ordered the cable companies to pay $50 million annually for this right. And Article 2007 led to the abolition of Canada's policy of granting indirect subsidies to Canadian newspapers and magazines through favourable tax treatment.[28]

The Americans were more successful in their efforts to entrench IP rights in NAFTA six years later. NAFTA allowed the Canadians to maintain the exemption for cultural industries but inserted a comprehensive IP code. These two provisions were incompatible. How could NAFTA recognize free trade in intellectual property on the one hand and exclude cultural industries on the other? Critics like Myra Tawfik believe that the cultural industries exemption was little more than symbolic. Desperate for continued access to the American market, "Canada agreed to support the U.S. in its view of IP and international trade at the GATT and in NAFTA, even though the adoption of such a position would have a direct and deleterious impact on Canada."[29]

While Canada, the U.S., and Mexico were hammering out the provisions of NAFTA, GATT was wending its way to a conclusion. GATT is an international treaty established after the Second World War to reduce or eliminate "barriers" that hinder the expansion of global business and trade. GATT and its successor, the World Trade Organization, are the pre-eminent codes used to regulate international trade among most major countries in the world. Since GATT's inception, there have been eight rounds of negotiations, with each round amending the agreement to deal with new trade concerns. The Uruguay round was kicked off by ninety-two countries in 1986, but it was not completed until 1993. One reason this round took so long to complete was that its agenda included the proposal to extend GATT jurisdiction to include TRIPs provisions. TRIPs would require the international harmonization (based on American standards) of IP protection, using as a model the code contained in Chapter 17 of NAFTA.

The developing world was highly critical of TRIPs, since they emanated from the technology-producing countries and called for enhanced IP protection. Brazil, India, Thailand, Peru, South Korea, and others asserted that "IP laws by their very nature restricted access to innovations, particularly pharmaceutical medicines and information technologies. Increased protection accorded to IP would seriously undermine their ability to develop economically and would entrench their present dependency on foreign technology. Hence they advocated a flexible, more balanced approach which would take into account the different levels of development within the global trading community."[30] But in the end, the developing world agreed to adopt the TRIPs code.

The U.S. held a big weapon in its arsenal: possible trade retaliation under Section 301 of the U.S. Trade Act and Special 301 of the Omnibus Trade and Competitiveness Act of 1988. Section 301 stipulates that the president can take all "appropriate and feasible action against foreign practices and policies that restrict U.S. commerce."[31] It expressly includes the right to impose trade sanctions on any nation that denies "adequate and effective" protection to American intellectual-property rights. Special 301 goes further, authorizing invasive actions by the U.S. It requires the U.S. trade representative to identify each year countries that do not protect IPR adequately or effectively, or that deny fair market access to American rights holders. Countries on the trade representative's "priority watch list" could be investigated under S. 301, which could in turn lead to trade sanctions. Canada was placed on the watch list because of its policy of allowing compulsory licensing of drug patents – a policy that did not violate any laws or breach any obligations to the U.S. under the terms of any treaty. Such threats had the desired effects on developing countries; they felt pressured to fall into line with U.S.-dictated standards. They were left to pray that the American rhetoric was correct, that liberalized world trade and expanded and harmonized IP protection would mean that all countries would prosper, even if they had to pay more for the IP they imported.

microsoft purges canada of pirates

Enforcement is the final step in the American plan to impose an expanded intellectual-property regime on the world. It is a hard sell, requiring the combined efforts of the propaganda and legal industries. Propagandists are needed to convince users that copying copyrighted software is bad, while lawyers stand by to take copiers to court to enforce corporate owners' rights. To sell its massive assault on the world's cultures and economies, the U.S. elevated copyright piracy and theft to one of the world's great evils. Copyright pirates – countries that did not offer the level of IP protection demanded by U.S. corporate interests – were elevated to the status of "enemies" of U.S. prosperity. Jack Valenti, Reagan's old Hollywood buddy and CEO of the Motion Picture Association of America, told a U.S. Senate hearing that the battle over IP and trade was equivalent to the Cold War, and unauthorized copying to thermonuclear weapons. It was an unusual analogy even for the tough-talking Valenti: he was referring to acts as heinous as copying *Snow White* videocassettes.[32]

Piracy originally meant robbery on the high seas. In fact, there are still pirates plying the South China Sea preying on ships in some of the world's busiest shipping lanes off Hong Kong. These pirates are dangerous – in 1997, fifty-one sailors were killed by pirates, according to the anti-pirate unit of the International Maritime Bureau.[33] Today, however, piracy has a second meaning: "unauthorized use of another's production, invention or conception,"[34] and these pirates – Internet navigators and music fans – are not dangerous at all. When a sea pirate boards a ship, steals goods, and murders crew members, there are losses of physical property and human life. When a land pirate downloads and prints a Web document or copies an audiotape, there is no cost beyond some indeterminable loss of economic potential – creators still have their creations.

Piracy was first used in this sense in England in 1668: "Some dishonest booksellers called land-pirates who make it their practice to steal Impressions of other men's copies."[35] Canadian IP law expert David Vaver dismisses the current meaning of theft and piracy. Theft is "an abusive term used to describe an intellectual property infringement or, sometimes more loosely, any act to which a right-holder objects," he writes. "But intellectual property infringement is not theft in Canada because after the taking, the right-holder is still left with the property. Still, right-holders have never let facts get in the way of a good slogan." And the terms "piracy" and "pirated goods," he explains, are "used by those who know no better or who have vested interests in a strong intellectual property system. They are best reserved for the exploits of Captain Bluebeard."[36]

Although Vaver dismisses the terms, the software industry and the U.S. government make great mileage from their use. During the late 1980s, the Reagan and Bush administrations produced a barrage of highly exaggerated estimates of losses at the hands of so-called intellectual-property thieves and pirates. The U.S. International Trade Commission estimated that in 1986 U.S. industries lost between $43 billion and $61 billion as a direct result of the activities of IP pirates and counterfeiters. Former trade representative Clayton Yeutter (who negotiated the FTA on behalf of the Americans) claimed that the U.S. could reduce its "$170-billion trade deficit appreciably simply by adding proper protection for [its] intellectual property rights around the world."[37] Of course, these were just figures pulled out of various hats.

Studies sponsored by the software industry in 1997 found illegal copying rates ranging from 27 percent in the U.S. to 39 percent in Canada, to 98 percent in Vietnam and 96 percent in China.[38] The percentages are determined by comparing industry data on software sales with estimates of the number of software packages actually being used in a country. These calculations, created by an organization (Business Software Alliance and its affiliates) whose raison d'être is to demonstrate that piracy is a problem of major dimensions, are fraught with inaccuracies. The economic costs of unlicensed use are distorted by the likelihood that software companies price their products higher than necessary to compensate for copying. Another flaw in the studies is that they assume that every unlicensed copy of software will be replaced by a licensed one. If it's free, users will take a look; if they have to pay, they'll be more prudent. Additional revenues accruing to companies will be far less than BSA claims.

Canada was first on the list for strong enforcement measures. In 1988, the year of the FTA with the U.S., the Mulroney government amended Canada's Copyright Act to declare computer programs to be literary works worthy of copyright protection and creating an entirely new category of criminal behaviour. Henceforth, Canadian users of computer programs would have to be licensed by copyright holders. Two years later, Microsoft Canada and other Canadian subsidiaries of American software giants, such as Apple, Claris, Delrina Corp., Lotus Development, Novell, and Symantec, set up the Canadian Alliance Against Software Theft (CAAST) as the Canadian affiliate of the Business Software Alliance. Microsoft Canada provides the association's president, general counsel, and marketing manager and is the power behind this group. Claiming that unlicensed copying of software costs manufacturers more than $300 million in lost business in Canada every year – once again with little basis for this figure – CAAST began collecting evidence of unlicensed software use and turning it over to the RCMP. CAAST's main weapon is an anti-piracy hot-line designed to encourage informers – usually disgruntled former employees, competitors, or angry spouses – to report suspected cases of unlicensed software copying. Early targets were computer dealers who load machines with free software, companies that copy their existing software rather than buying new programs when they purchase new computers, and companies that rent software. The first charges under the new provisions were laid in 1993.

In 1996, CAAST launched "Say Yes to Legal Software," a program targeting thousands of software resellers and users in governments and small businesses, along with individual consumers. The campaign "certifies" retailers as honest dealers and educates consumers about the alleged perils of illegal software. Of course, the industry can never say that the purpose of its anti-piracy crusade is to increase revenues and make Bill Gates even richer. So it couches its activities in terms of benefits to consumers and the economy. Microsoft lawyer Jim Lowe offers that "software piracy is bad news for consumers. Pirated software doesn't come with the assurance of quality, technical support, or warranties of legitimate software. And pirated software can infect your entire computer system with a virus, which can damage your hard disk or destroy all of your data."[39] A 1998 study of unlicensed software copying for CAAST by PricewaterhouseCoopers is titled "The Contribution of the Packaged Software Industry to the Canadian Economy." Reducing the piracy rate, the study argues, will create jobs, increase government revenues, boost productivity in the IT sector, and make Canada's IT industry more competitive on a global scale — all those warm and fuzzy notions that excite policy makers at Industry Canada.[40]

wipo treaties enclose the internet

While Microsoft and CAAST were busy enforcing the laws passed by supportive governments in Canada and elsewhere, their American allies turned to Geneva and WIPO to expand intellectual-property rights even further, this time targeting computer networks and the Internet. The Americans sponsored three new treaties that were considered by WIPO at the end of 1996. The American delegation was led by Bruce Lehman, commissioner of the U.S. Patent and Trademark Office; Lehman is a former copyright lobbyist and a copyright "zealot," according to James Love of Ralph Nader's Consumer Project on Technology. Lehman came with what American copyright scholar Pamela Samuelson calls a maximalist agenda: he wanted to give electronic publishers rights over every temporary reproduction in computer memory (such as copies made when browsing on the Internet), every transmission of copyrighted works in digital form, and every information database, even if the information itself was not copyrightable because it was in the public domain.[41] The U.S. used its economic clout to compel its major trading partners to sign on to two treaties it brought to WIPO, although a controversial article in the Internet copyright treaty was dropped and a second modified at the last minute. An alliance of major corporate and public interests opposed a third treaty on database-extraction rights, and it was not approved.

The eighteen-day December 1996 WIPO conference, formally

titled "Diplomatic Conference on Certain Copyright and Neighboring Rights Questions," was another example of major decisions being made by international bodies far from the reach of citizens and before most national legislatures, including Canada's, had addressed the issues. The large Canadian delegation was headed by Danielle Bouvet, director of Industry Canada's Intellectual Property Policy Directorate. After returning from Geneva, she announced that "Canada [was] very pleased with the outcome,"[42] an interesting comment, given that no more than a handful of Canadians was aware the conference had even taken place, let alone knew what was decided.

Although the U.S. began work on the treaties in 1991, the final draft versions were not made public until August 1996, less than four months before the conference. The Canadian government held one thirty-minute public consultation on November 14, two weeks before Bouvet and her delegation headed off to Geneva for pre-conference meetings. Obviously, this left little time to explore the details and ramifications of the treaties. And news reports were few and misleading. A story by *New York Times* reporter Peter Lewis began, "Copyright laws are under technological siege,"[43] which was hardly the issue. A more accurate opening would have been "Copyright laws are under *corporate* siege," but of course the corporate news media, which stood to benefit from strengthened copyright protection, would never allow anything like that through their filters.

One treaty, which was designed to create for performers who give live performances the right to benefit from recordings of the performance, was not controversial. The second treaty, which was to extend copyright protection to works in digital form, raised a storm of controversy. Although it purported to address the concern that digital works on the Internet could be copied effortlessly and distributed virtually anywhere in the world, it in fact was to end up enclosing another huge chunk of the information commons – one that showed promise of being the most liberating of all. It extended copyright protection to computer programs as if they were literary works (Art. 4) and to databases that could be considered intellectual creations because of the selection or arrangements of their content. Databases with no originality, such as a telephone directory, did not qualify under this treaty, but they were covered by the third treaty on database-protection rights.

As usual, this second treaty on digital formats was couched in the rhetoric of "creators," but the real agenda, as expressed by Bruce Lehman, was to stimulate investment in information infrastructure and to allow businesses to safely offer a whole new array of products and services on-line: "[T]his will provide the security that the people who make information products need to really start to produce dynamite products for distribution through the Internet."[44]

As had been the case with all previous copyright laws, there were two points of view. On one side were those who, like Lehman, say that the protection provided by the treaty would greatly expand the creation of on-line information because it would encourage creators to make their works available, secure in the knowledge that their rights were protected. Lined up on this side were the film and recording industries, some publishing companies, and major computer firms like IBM, Microsoft, and Intel. The other view was that existing copyright protection already applied to the Internet, and that the treaty would erect new barriers to the transmission and sharing of information. Lined up on this side were consumer advocates, libraries, and education groups. According to the International Federation of Library Associations, the proposals were "likely to obstruct rather than assist the flow of information."[45] They were joined by the telecommunications industry and some computing firms, whose opposition revolved around two articles in the treaty.

Article 7 defines the right of creators to receive royalties whenever their copyrighted works are reproduced, directly or indirectly, "whether permanent or temporary, in any manner or form." By expanding the right of reproduction to include indirect reproduction, the article prohibits the creation of temporary copies, unless authorized. The way Web browsers work, a user downloads a fairly substantial chunk of a browsing session into RAM and then onto the hard drive, saving an enormous amount of Internet bandwidth. Article 7 would mean that virtually all Internet users would be violating copyright by reproducing protected works on their hard drives. This article met with much outcry from users and service providers alike. Librarians and academics were also strongly opposed, and issued a statement that read, in part, "If permission and/or payment is required every time a work is even accessed (e.g., viewed on a computer screen), the role of the library to be society's collectors and disseminators of knowledge will be destroyed."[46] Noted Robert Best, government relations director at the Association of Universities and Colleges of Canada, Article 7 would make it impossible for Canada to allow fair dealing – producing royalty-free copies of small portions of a copyrighted work for private study or research purposes. Canadian law allows a person to make a paper copy of a paper work; Article 7 would prohibit a researcher from printing a paper copy of a digital work.[47]

Canada's Information Highway Advisory Council had recommended in 1995 that the Copyright Act be amended to provide a definition of "browsing," which it defined as "a temporary materialization of a work on a video screen, television monitor or similar device," but went on to say that it "should be left to the copyright owner to determine whether and when browsing should be permitted on the Information Highway."[48] Such an approach was fashioned as a compromise between the user and industry representatives on the council. But IHAC's copyright subcommittee went further, reflecting the approach of Lehman and the "copyright maximalists" and recommending that "the act of browsing a work in a digital environment should be considered an act of reproduction," and thus be subject to copyright. This is not surprising, given the make-up of the subcommittee – four copyright lawyers (including Michael Eisen, lawyer for Microsoft's Canadian Alliance Against Software Theft) and two representatives of major database vendors.[49]

In Geneva, however, the opposition of librarians and academics may not have been as decisive as a letter sent to President Bill Clinton from the chief executive officers of eleven major U.S. Internet and telecommunications firms, including BellSouth Corp., NYNEX, Bell Atlantic Corp., MCI Communications Corp., America Online, CompuServe, UUNet Technologies, and PSINet. They sent representatives to the WIPO conference to argue against Article 7 and delivered their letter to the president midway through the discussions. The letter said that unless Articles 7 and 10 were revised to address the group's concerns, "we will have no choice but to work to prevent its ratification by Congress." Article 7 was dropped on the last evening of the conference.[50]

Article 10, meanwhile, deals with the right of communication, and in fact creates a new and additional copyright for any work that is simply made available to the public over the Internet. The article goes so far as to state that "any communication to the public" has to be authorized. Even if someone puts a picture, article, or other work on their Web site, in other words, they have to do more than get the permission of the person who created the work. They have to pay royalties for making the work available to the public – even if no one picks it up. Many nations' copyright acts, including Canada's, cover the right of a copyright holder to communicate a work to the public by telecommunications (transmission by cable, radio, satellite, or telephone wires, where such transmission is made to the public). IHAC's copyright subcommittee extended this right, arguing that placing a work on a computer bulletin board (that was March 1995; today it would include Web sites) constitutes a communication of the work to the public, even if Web surfers access the site at different times. If the work was communicated to the public without permission, copyright would be infringed.

The article doesn't address the question of who pays. If work on a Web site is authorized and someone accesses and downloads it, who is liable for copyright? Is it the owner/operator of the Web site, the Internet service provider, the customer who accesses the site, or a collective group of customers? Pressure from the eleven CEOs and several consumer groups led to the reworking of this article at the last minute so that ISPs and public carriers would not be liable for illegal reproduction activity that might occur on their networks, but the article was still adopted by the WIPO conference.

ken thomson's quest for a property right in databases

The Draft Treaty on Intellectual Property in Respect to Databases, the third on Bruce Lehman's agenda, provoked the greatest opposition. Some scholars called it the end of the public domain. It gave protection to compilers of data rather than to the original owners of the data, so that even a telephone directory could be copyrighted. As James Love explains, the database treaty would have established "a new property right that has the potential to create private monopolies on data and documents that have traditionally been in the public domain."[51] In fact, it would have destroyed the public domain in information altogether by declaring that even facts could be copyrighted.

The treaty was promoted by large electronic-publishing companies such as West Publishing, the world's largest producer of legal databases, and the Anglo-Dutch publishing giant Reed Elsevier as a response to the 1991 U.S. Supreme Court decision in *Feist Publications* v. *Rural Telephone Service.* This landmark ruling rejected a claim of copyright for a telephone directory's white pages, arguing that facts cannot be copyrighted. The court further ruled that obvious items such as listing names, addresses, and telephone numbers in alphabetical order contain no "original expression" and therefore are not sufficiently creative to qualify for copyright protection. In reaching its decision, the Supreme Court went back to the copyright provision of the U.S. Constitution: "to promote the progress of science and useful arts." Compilations of data can receive copyright protection, the court said, only if the creator of the compilation can show some originality in the selection and arrangement of the data. The counterargument, proposed by the phone company, was that large databases can be expensive to create and require a great deal of effort, although they are rarely original in their selection of materials. The court rejected this "industrious effort" or "sweat of the brow" theory.

The *Feist* decision alarmed West and Reed Elsevier. Although they were already protecting their databases through contracts with their customers, contracts that placed restrictive conditions on the reuse or dissemination of the information compiled, they wanted stronger protection and lobbied for a new *sui generis* property right to protect the contents of databases. A bill proposing the creation of a new form of intellectual-property protection for compilations of information was introduced in the U.S. Congress in the spring of 1996. It did not pass, but then reappeared, with Lehman's backing, in almost identical form as the proposed WIPO database treaty several months later. This new right could not be called copyright, since the *Feist* decision expressly forbid that. But if granted, the treaty would have vastly expanded the ability of database owners to regulate and restrict the public's right to use data, without the types of safeguards that exist in copyright law today. The doctrine of fair use (or fair dealing in Canada), under which individuals can make single copies of works for their own personal use or study, would not have applied to data protected under this new right.

The database treaty was opposed by a wide array of interests, from library, education, and public-interest communities to major corporate players that would have been penalized by it. Database vendors like Dun & Bradstreet and Bloomberg feared that the treaty would give stock exchanges permanent ownership of the share-price statistics in their databases.[52] Broadcasters and STATS, a disseminator of sports statistics, worried that they would have to pay sports leagues heavily for statistics, since the leagues would own facts like official box scores.[53] The omission of a fair-use provision, meanwhile, automatically made librarians and educators dedicated foes of the treaty. And scientists were outraged at a threat to the free flow of research results. (The treaty defines the practice of creating abstracts of scientific articles, many of which are published in Reed Elsevier scientific journals, on Web pages as an infringement of database extraction rights.[54]) The presidents of the National Academy of Sciences, the National Academy of Engineering, and the Institute of Medicine wrote a joint letter to the secretary of commerce expressing their grave reservations. They said the treaty "would seriously undermine the ability of researchers and educators to access and use scientific data, and would have a deleterious long-term impact on our nation's research capabilities."[55] Even John Young, co-chair of Clinton's Committee of Advisers for Science and Technology, joined the groups opposed to the treaty. In the end, Lehman was asked to take it off the table.

West Publishing, meanwhile, stood to gain most from the database treaty. West is the only comprehensive publisher of U.S. federal circuit and district court opinions, and also prints state court opinions from all fifty states. The page and paragraph numbers in West court reports are the basis for citations used by scholars, lawyers, and judges. West also makes corrections to the text of court opinions, typically after working with the judge who wrote the opinion.[56] If the database-protection proposals had been enacted, West would have had a firm monopoly on decades of judicial citations and corrections to judicial opinions, says James Love (who, along with many legal scholars, believes the corrected text of court opinions, and the citations to those opinions, should be in the public domain). Love argues further that even the current West monopoly has delayed the development of new information products and services for legal researchers.

Although West lost the battle in Geneva, it has launched a series of lawsuits in an attempt to maintain its monopoly and prevent others from using its page numbers or the corrected text of court opinions without securing a licence. Clearly, West was not out of the game yet. It had a long and enviable record in getting what it wanted – legal recognition of its ownership of the system for citing federal court opinions – and often resorted to hardball tactics to achieve this.

- During the 1980s and 1990s, West paid for dozens of high court judges, including seven U.S. Supreme Court justices, to travel first class and stay at luxury resorts while they were on a West-sponsored selection committee. Many of these judges had opposed a proposal to create an organized database of court decisions with guaranteed low-cost access, a serious threat to the company's business.
- West, and donors associated with the company, contributed nearly a million dollars between 1989 and 1994 to members of the U.S. Congress, which, in 1992, considered a bill that would have prohibited copyright of citation and numbering systems for federal and state laws and court opinions. The bill died in subcommittee without a vote.
- West-financed congressional representatives and federal judges opposed a 1994 proposal by U.S. Attorney General Janet Reno to improve public access to federal court opinions.

West continued to battle against public-interest advocacy groups wanting more open access, as well as smaller companies wanting a chance to sell competing systems. The controlling Opperman family of Minnesota, perhaps tiring of the fray, decided to sell. Who might be interested? "Obviously Thomson [Corp.], as a big content provider, I think, would certainly be someone that would look at us or, as we determine which direction to go, that they would certainly be in the playing field," said West spokesperson Ruth Stanoch (a former chair of the Minnesota Democratic Party).[57] Six months later, Thomson announced it would pay $3.4 billion (U.S.) to become the biggest legal publisher in the world. It was a "transformational event" in the company's trek from owner of valuable newspaper franchises to owner of even more valuable proprietary databases. *Globe and Mail* reporters Casey Mahood and John Saunders cheerfully reported that West was the "800-pound gorilla of the business, armed with a copyrighted citation system used by almost everybody in the U.S. legal system to identify cases."[58] But it was a stretch to claim that West had a "copyrighted" system. That's exactly what West had been working so hard and paying so much to achieve.

After the defeat of the Draft Treaty on Intellectual Property in Respect to Databases in Geneva in December 1996, West, now owned by Thomson, went back into action. In October 1997 Rep. Howard Coble, chair of the House of Representatives subcommittee on the courts and intellectual property, introduced Bill HR 2652, the Collections of Information Antipiracy Act, which bore an eerie resemblance to the database treaty. Once again, West and Reed Elsevier – joined this time by Microsoft, which had graduated to the big leagues of database compilers – worked behind the scenes with Lehman to push the bill through Congress. And once again the bill ran into extensive opposition. After ten months of fruitless efforts to get the bill passed before Congress was dissolved for the 1998 election, its proponents withdrew, vowing to return in 1999. And they did. Less than a month after the start of the new Congress, Rep. Coble reintroduced a revised version of the bill – it was HR 354 this time – and the battle was underway again.

database protection in canada

Canada was also affected by the *Feist* decision. Until 1997, legal protection for databases or compilations had been more favourable to compilers, who simply had to show "industrious collection" or "sweat of the brow," and not the element of originality mandated in *Feist*. However, a decision by the Federal Court of Appeal in *Tele-Direct (Publications)* v. *American Business Information* moved the goalposts. As a result of NAFTA, the federal court ruled, the definition of "compilation" had to be changed to accommodate the *Feist* decision, which said that selections and arrangements must have an element of originality to qualify for copyright protection. The Canadian court followed *Feist* and denied protection to the compilation of information found in the Yellow Pages telephone directories.

As a result of this decision, Industry Canada and the Canadian heritage ministry quietly began work on a Canadian database policy. They commissioned University of Victoria law professor Robert Howell to survey existing protections for databases and identify legal and policy issues that needed to be addressed by government. The direction of his October 1998 report was not encouraging. Of twelve issues identified by Howell, the words "public" or "user" appear in just three. One says vaguely that "the balancing of database protection and users' rights of access to data may need ongoing attention." Another wonders if "some data, such as non-confidential information held by governments or public authorities [should] be declared public domain data or information." A third asks, "What extent or nature of legal protection of data or contents of databases is necessary to encourage the creation and maintenance of high-quality databases and to ensure a level of accessibility that is reasonable in the public interest?"[59] As to what government might do with this information, Industry Canada notes in its 1998 discussion paper on electronic commerce that "databases are more and more important in a knowledge-based economy," and wonders "whether a special form of IP protection should be developed for databases."[60] Ominous words from the people who represent the information industry in government. Ken Thomson can sleep easier.

reasserting the public interest

At the millennium, little remains of the public interest in works of the mind, and if Bruce Lehman and John Manley have their way there will soon be even less. In the hard-driving campaign to extend and enforce intellectual-property protection, the delicate balance between the rights of authors and the rights of society, as established in the eighteenth century, has been crushed. Citizens no longer seem to have any rights at all. Why did this happen? Why did society willingly turn over such awesome monopoly powers to the likes of Thomson, Disney, and Microsoft?

James Boyle, in his intriguingly titled book *Shamans, Software and Spleens*, suggests a simple reason – we continue to be persuaded that authors are creative geniuses and that their works are worthy of strong protection. The entire IP regime, he argues, is built on this flimsy foundation. In fact, this idea has its roots in an eighteenth-century belief that the only way we can protect creators so they will continue to produce works of genius and near-genius is to grant them monopoly rights. As publishers and distributors gain more control over those monopoly rights, their need for the author-as-creator myth is stronger than ever. Says Boyle: "A striking feature of the language of romantic authorship is the way it is used to support sweeping intellectual property rights for large corporate entities. Sony, Pfizer and Microsoft tend to lack the appeal of Byron and Alexander Fleming."[61] Take away the myth of romantic authorship, and the infrastructure of copyright laws loses its moral suasion and can be seen for what it is: naked economic monopoly power. Copyright was centuries in the future when Sir Thomas More wrote *Utopia*, Chaucer gave us his *Canterbury Tales*, and Shakespeare composed his great plays. The works of these great geniuses and many more are evidence that creativity occurs without copyright.

How unique are most books, films, computer programs, and musical works? They consist mainly of words, sounds, images, facts, and ideas that derive from the common culture and are picked up free from the common store of such information. We go to the taxpayer-supported library and use reference books. We learn about subjects in taxpayer-supported educational institutions. We take taxpayer-supported creative-writing and music-composition courses. We talk to people who freely convey information and opinions to us. We read newspapers and magazines and watch television, picking up ideas from them. We listen to music and hear sounds around us.

The answer, of course, is that often a work does present new information, or a new way of looking at old information. We do receive fresh insights about our world from music, films, videos, books. A creator puts his or her unique stamp on them, and perhaps does add to the common pool of ideas and information. And we need to ensure that such a supply of ideas continues to be provided. Authors and creators must be compensated for their work − the very future of society may depend on their producing new ideas and new ways of understanding our world. But the current legal regime rewards corporate interests, not creators.

In fact, IP laws may impede creativity, preventing new ideas from being widely disseminated or slowing the pace with which ideas are spread. One of the most interesting developments in software is the rapid spread and high quality of Linux, a computer-operating system that is freely available on the Internet. According to Lehman's maximalist view, strong copyright protection is necessary to spark the development of new software products and services. Because they are freely available, products like Linux should rapidly collapse, or at least fall far behind rival software produced by Microsoft, with its iron-clad copyright-protected source code.

There is another view about the effectiveness of strong copyright protection. Computer consultant Keith Porterfield claims that in fact most networking developments are based on free or open-source software. His evidence is convincing: one-half the Web sites on the Internet are powered by freeware such as the Apache server; most active content (such as filling out forms and animation) is generated by freeware programming languages such as Perl; the freeware Majordomo package is the most popular e-mail list manager; most e-mail is managed by the freeware Sendmail program; the Internet's Domain Name System, which does the mapping between numeric and human-readable addresses, is almost totally dependent on a free software package called BIND (Berkeley Internet Name Daemon).[62] The view that information wants to be free was recognized in the early 1980s by computer programmer Richard Stallman, who created the non-profit Free Software Foundation to promote non-proprietary programming.

Linux began life in 1990 as a few lines of computer source code written by a twenty-one-year-old Finnish computer engineering student, Linus Torvalds, who wanted to see if he could run the Unix operating system on a desktop PC. Torvalds decided to distribute Linux through Stallman's foundation using a general public licence dubbed copyleft, which allows users to duplicate, alter, redistribute, and even sell the software as long as the same freedom to copy and modify is passed along to subsequent users.[63] He posted the code on a bulletin board, where it was picked up by programmers around the world. They made their modifications and improvements, and then reposted their code on bulletin boards and the Internet. Eric Raymond is a software developer who published a paper on the Internet in 1997; in it, he expresses his astonishment at the rapid rise and high quality of Linux, which follows a model he calls the bazaar. In the bazaar mode, "hundreds of top-level programmers on the Internet . . . flexibly group and regroup around particular projects, releasing code often and gang-blitzing the bugs." No commercial developer can match the pool of talent the Linux community can bring to bear on a problem, Raymond argues. "Perhaps in the end the free-software culture will triumph . . . simply because the commercial world cannot win an evolutionary arms race with free-software communities that can put orders of magnitude more skilled time into a problem."[64]

Raymond's paper was one of the factors that persuaded Netscape to release its browser source code to the public domain and license Netscape Communicator 5.0 for free to all users, foregoing about 13 percent of sales revenues. Netscape hoped to spark an outpouring of applications that would strengthen its position in the market. Let the programming community freely exploit these codes, in other words, and the Internet will be flooded with a plethora of high-quality software products, giving the beleaguered Netscape a chance to compete with Microsoft (a company that Raymond characterizes as fitting into the "cathedral-building" model of creating software). "In the cathedral mode, source code is kept in the hands of a few select individuals who develop and maintain it. Bug fixing is very difficult, painstaking work entrusted to the best programmers on staff."[65] And of course, the cathedral model depends critically on protecting source code with strong copyright laws. The bazaar model requires no such protection.

By 1998, Linux was good enough to attract the attention of several major corporations that were trying to break Microsoft's dominance with its Windows operating system. Ottawa-based Corel Corp., for instance, released a no-charge Linux-based version of its WordPerfect software in its David-and-Goliath struggle against the Microsoft behemoth. Major PC makers such as Compaq, Dell, Hewlett-Packard, IBM, and Silicon Graphics all discussed shipping computers with Linux pre-installed, as they do with Windows. Major software companies like Oracle Corp., Netscape, Informix Corp., and Computer Associates announced plans to revamp their products so they can run on Linux. It's still an unequal contest, however. At the end of 1998, Windows had 300 million users to 7 million for Linux. But more and more software developers are beginning to look to Linux as a low-cost, open-standard alternative to Windows NT, the dominant operating system for computer networks.

The biggest coup for the freeware movement came in 1998, when the Mexican government decided to install the Linux system in 140,000 elementary- and middle-school computer labs. Installing Windows 98, MS Office, and a server running Windows NT at each school site would have cost the Mexican government about $125 million (U.S.). The total cost for Linux for the entire system is fifty dollars. And because Linux is faster, more reliable, more adaptable, and more efficient than Windows – it doesn't crash as often – the government can use older computers and less expensive equipment that does not need to go through costly upgrades.[66]

Linux demonstrates that creativity can occur, and the public can benefit, without copyright protection. Nonetheless, the creator-author fiction continues to mislead people. In 1998, WIPO commenced a campaign to extend copyright protection for an additional twenty years after an author's death. The argument used is that post-death protection was established to provide for at least the first generation of an author's heirs, and that since people are living longer, a longer period of protection is needed. What wasn't emphasized is that the bill would extend protection for corporate owners of copyright from seventy-five to ninety-five years. Since in most cases copyright is assigned or transferred to a corporation that exploits it for the entire duration of its protection, the protection is mainly for the benefit of corporate holders (although the myth of the author-creator is required to mask this fact).

The U.S. Congress beat WIPO to the punch by pushing through a bill in 1998, just before Congress dissolved for the elections. The bill was titled the Sonny Bono Copyright Term Extension Act, and while Bono's grandchildren might benefit years down the road from royalties on his songs the true beneficiaries are Disney and Time Warner. (The Disney Corporate Handout Act might be a more appropriate title.) Mickey Mouse was copyrighted in 1929, and was to enter the public domain in 2004. A similar fate faced Bugs Bunny and the song library of George Gershwin. To forestall these calamities, the entertainment industry pumped millions of dollars into the Republican Party's campaign war chest, hoping to get the bill pushed through before the election. As a result, Walt Disney is guaranteed at least another twenty years of cash flow from the Mickey Mouse marketing machine, while the company's assets increased in value by as much as $1 billion, which it can borrow against to buy other companies or expand into other businesses.

In all the IP grabs, in the relentless enclosure of our common information resources, one fact is ignored. All national copyright, patent, and trademark laws, and all international agreements and treaties that codify intellectual-property rights, were *granted by society* through its elected and appointed representatives. IP rights are not found in nature; they are granted by society. We should recall the words of Thomas Jefferson, whose view was that the grant of an exclusive right to a creative work "was a creation of society – at odds with the inherent free nature of disclosed ideas – and was not to be freely given."

academics build their
intellectual property portfolios

....

Because the universities and research organizations have
traditionally been early adopters of next-generation networking
technologies . . . [t]hey are in the best position to test the
network and help develop it to the point where it will be
robust enough for commercial use.

                      — Taken from CANARIE's Web site, June 25, 1997

Faculty should also be alert at all times to the potential
monetary value of their research.

                      — Canadian Institute for Advanced Research

The commercialization of science has resulted in a new regime
of secrecy which is very concerning to the scientific community.

                      — Irving A. Lerch, American Association for
                      the Advancement of Science

Bill St. Arnaud is CANARIE's director of network projects. During
1996 and 1997, as part of CANARIE's outreach program, he presented
audiences across Canada with a map that displayed all of CANARIE's
networks — thirteen regional Internet service providers serving more
than a million Canadian Internet users, twelve regional test networks
connecting most researchers in Canada, plus four connections to the
United States and one to Europe via Teleglobe Canada. It looked com-
plicated, and from an engineering and systems perspective it was. As

St. Arnaud explained, "The total composite of all these networks is probably one of the most complex research and education networks in the world, with all sorts of connectivity. . . . [It is] one of the world's longest networks, [at] over 6,000 kilometres, a hierarchical network supporting ATM and IP services and protocols."[1] Yet behind this apparent complexity was a startlingly simple concept: the network operationalized a flow of knowledge from publicly funded government and university research labs to the product-development and marketing divisions of private-sector corporations.

The corporate-dominated CANARIE board was well aware that most advances in knowledge that might have commercial value were made by academic and government researchers working in publicly supported labs. So CANARIE adopted a strategy of providing Cadillac facilities – the highest bandwidths and fastest networks possible – to taxpayer-supported researchers. Let them make the discoveries, the strategy went, give them state-of-the-art equipment for testing, and, two to three years after the discoveries are made, turn them into commercial products and services. St. Arnaud had laid out a blueprint for an electronic assembly line for knowledge. "The research and education community is the first to try [to] test these applications, stub their toes, and then the commercial community will take over," he explained to his audiences.[2] To get the assembly line operating smoothly, CANARIE cobbled together a high-speed national test network from fledgling regional operations, like OCRInet in Ottawa and Rnet in B.C. Then, after experimenting with names like Internet 2000 and Internet Next Generation, CANARIE created CA*net II, the first "next generation" network, which would be operated by Bell Canada. Less than a year later, in 1998, CA*net II was replaced by CA*net 3, an even faster electronic assembly line for researchers, also operated by Bell. It is one defining image of Canadian scientific research at the millennium.

Running parallel to CANARIE is another set of networks, not of computers, switches, and fibre-optic lines, but of university researchers and corporate sponsors. These individuals and organizations are brought together in fourteen networks of centres of excellence to pool their research results and divide the benefits flowing from any discoveries. "The Networks of Centres of Excellence [NCE] program facilitates the transfer of knowledge and technology from universities to industry," says the Chrétien government's 1996 science paper.[3] How it does this is illustrated in the TeleLearning Research Network's 1995 application for funding, which includes a diagram of its business model showing science and technology research entering one side and revenue exiting the other. The TeleLearning NCE provides a second image of science research in Canada. CANARIE and TeleLearning work together. CANARIE needs the applications being developed by the NCEs to justify its efforts to build high-speed networks. TeleLearning needs CANARIE's networks to allow its far-flung researchers to communicate their results to each other, as well as to transmit its education products to consumers across Canada and around the world.

Of course, CANARIE and the NCEs are far from being the entire science and technology picture. Of a total of $6 billion a year in federal government support for science and technology, CANARIE will spend only $161 million over nine years and NCE about $47 million a year. But these two overlapping programs, which were among the few research programs to be spared Paul Martin's budget-cutting axe, epitomize the direction of science-research policy in Canada as the country reaches the millennium. They're essential ingredients in John Manley's Connecting Canadians program. In his first priority, Manley promises that CANARIE will deliver the fastest network in the world by 2000. CANARIE's CA*net 3 will do that. His third priority is to increase Canadian content on-line. TeleLearning will help make Canada "a leading-edge supplier of online content to the world."[4] For that to happen, though, on-line content needs to be protected as intellectual property owned by corporate backers and academic researchers.

The CANARIE-NCE approach, which emphasizes applied, commercially oriented research at the expense of more basic science, has sparked criticism from experts like Canadian Nobel Prize–winner John Polanyi, who said in a 1993 presentation to the Professional Institute of the Public Service of Canada, "If we increasingly restrict our basic science to the areas which will benefit existing Canadian industries, we run the risk, little by little, of converting our university laboratories into state-subsidized industrial laboratories."[5] Nearly four years later, he warned that "to go much further along the path to commercialization of university research would destroy our universities."[6] One shudders to think what he will say in another four years.

Polanyi is a passionate defender of basic research — "experimental or theoretical work undertaken primarily to acquire new knowledge of the underlying foundations of phenomena and observable facts, without any particular application or use in view."[7] Leslie Millin, another advocate of basic research and a former secretary of the Science Council of Canada, which was axed by the Mulroney government, argues that succeeding federal governments have squandered Canada's world-renowned scientific legacy. Like Polanyi, Millin is incensed by the shift to applied research. "Nor have they understood that wealth flows not so much from applied research as from basic research, because it is basic research that produces the major breakthroughs that in turn produce the huge profits."[8] Although pure research may bring national wealth in the longer term, it is applied research that helps companies in the short term, and that seems to be the overarching imperative for recent governments. As John Hardy, one of Canada's pre-eminent nuclear physicists, bitterly commented after the 1997 federal budget killed his seventeen-scientist sub-atomic research group at Chalk River, Ontario, "When the applied guys finish applying the ideas we've generated . . . they're not going to have any more ideas to apply because there's no one around in this country discovering them." Hardy subsequently took a job at Texas A&M University, where he would oversee a cyclotron project that promised to be of the same high quality as the one he left in Chalk River.[9]

Even the idea of basic research is being eroded by pressures to be more "relevant" and "productive." There is now a sub-category called oriented basic research, or pre-competitive research, which is expected to "form the background to the solution of problems or possibilities."[10] Some government funding programs expect applicants for basic research grants to have at least expressions of corporate interest and financial contributions (if not outright corporate sponsorship) lined up before they receive government support. This is where the

NCEs fit. "The novelty of the NCE approach was its emphasis on the pre-competitive nature of much of the research, providing industry with opportunities to take advantage at the leading edge of science."[11] Whether the research is pre-competitive or applied, the emphasis placed on the commercialization of that research distorts the national research agenda. Worthy questions are being ignored because there is little money to support them and the graduate students working in those fields. In the realm of applied research, many issues of great concern to Canadians go unstudied because there are no corporate sponsors. One troubling consequence is that the next generation of researchers, scientists, and technicians, having come to maturity in an era of corporate-oriented research, may perceive that to be the norm. Non-commercial, public-interest research, which could support a public information network and democratic media, for instance, is becoming an endangered species.

intellectual property or public resource?

In an environment where taxpayer-supported scientists are expected not only to disclose the results of their research to the public through journal publication and conference presentation, but also to sign non-disclosure agreements with corporate sponsors, there is a danger that the public interest will lose out. What are scientists' obligations to the public that pays their salaries and provides them with the secretaries, graduate students, buildings, lecture halls, offices, and research labs in which they teach and do research? Can their own private interests create conflicts? Will the free discussion of ideas and active collaboration on research projects be stifled by concerns for corporate confidentiality?

The American Association for the Advancement of Science was so concerned about these issues that it held a conference called "Secrecy in Science" at MIT in early 1999. One official estimated that private capital was paying for 25 percent of research at MIT, up from 5 percent in the mid-1980s. The free exchange of ideas and results is the hallmark of scientific enterprise, yet conference participants heard story after horror story of secrecy. They explored three cases involving biomedical researchers, one of whom was Dr. Nancy Olivieri of the University of Toronto, who met corporate and university resistance when they tried to publish some of their results.[12]

The public should benefit from publicly funded research, but most industrial agreements to fund academic research include delays on disclosure so that company officials have time to establish the financial potential of the findings and get a head start on commercial development. Proprietary interests in research results can even cause important findings to become corporate secrets, hidden from the rest of the scientific community until safely patented or copyrighted. According to one historian, all products and useful information resulting from the labour of university scientists is becoming private intellectual property owned by professors, funders, or the university, a development that has transformed the university's role from a producer for the general society to something more akin to a leased research team.[13]

Subtle changes in research direction help industry more than the public; graduate students are pressured to become involved in research that could benefit the private sector, and free and open lab practices are eroded through competition for profitable research results. There are few voices left defending the public interest in university science research when pressures from all directions – federal and provincial governments, funding councils, universities themselves, and of course, industry – are pushing towards greater commercialization.

The Natural Sciences and Engineering Research Council (NSERC) directs hundreds of millions of dollars towards university researchers each year. In the background material on its Research Partnerships Program grants, the NSERC cautions university researchers not to reveal project results "inadvertently or prematurely," so that intellectual property can be protected and the corporate sponsors can take advantage of the findings. "The industrial partner may wish to negotiate prior screening rights with the university or to ask for reasonable delays in presenting or publishing results." Delays are usually of the order of 30 to 90 days and rarely over 6 months. "The university or the researchers employed by the university usually own the rights to the intellectual property arising from NSERC grants." NSERC warns that to avoid conflicts, university, researcher, and company should "negotiate a research agreement before starting the research project."[14]

In 1993, the NSERC launched a program called Intellectual Property Assessment to help universities manage their intellectual property by protecting their discoveries, demonstrating their commercial relevance, and easing the transfer of the technology to the private sector. The NSERC warned:

> Urgent action is needed on this front. Not only has the volume of intellectual property managed by universities exploded over the last 5-10 years, but the difficulty and expense in protecting intellectual property have emerged as major impediments to knowledge transfer. Moving an idea from university lab to market depends on convincing a company that the idea is commercially viable and protectable.[15]

In the TeleLearning Network, corporate sponsors that provide significant resources have rights defined by the research contract they sign when they enter the network. Intellectual property is handled by a technology-transfer committee, which is to identify promising technologies and interested partners. The network is even funding one project to develop methods for commercializing TeleLearning services and products. This would enable them to scan the market to provide potential partners and researchers with the information needed to assess the commercial potential of their technologies.

A key to TeleLearning's strategy for positioning its products favourably in the global marketplace is to make extensive use of field trials. Its salespeople can then claim that the products are superior to others because they have benefited from real-life testing and refinement. Of course, other telelearning-product developers also use field trials, so the battle is on for claims to the best testing procedures. Because TeleLearning's strategic advantage lies in the way it conducts its field trials, it must keep its testing procedures secret. But because the tests involve human subjects, TeleLearning needs to receive ethical approval from funding agencies and university ethics committees. York University historian David Noble sees this human experimentation as TeleLearning's "Achilles heel." In the field trials, he says, students are experimental subjects. What the students are not being told is that while they're studying the courses, the courses are studying them. They are required to participate on-line to provide data for the field trial, which is information to improve the product and develop the market. Rather than paying for the courses, they should be paid for being experimental subjects. They're not told that all their communications with each other and with the professor are monitored and permanently stored by use by the vendor. . . .[16]

Standing in contrast to the intellectual-property approach to research is public-interest science, which investigates questions relevant to the lives and concerns of people in the community. Public-interest research must occur with the active participation of those concerned, not just the self-interested corporate sector. Its subjects can include community health, worker health and safety, environmental integrity, and applications for a public information network, and it must take place in a context that involves citizens in determining research priorities. Dick Sclove of the Loka Institute in Amherst, Massachusetts, has been creating an alternative national research system and has produced some promising results that are attracting the attention of Canadian social sciences and humanities researchers.[17] Such a research network could be an alternative to the corporate-dominated networks of CANARIE and the NCEs.

Sclove speculates that a democratized science agenda would lead to different and more sensible research priorities. There'd be less research directed towards military weaponry, chemical- and machine-intensive medical interventions, and job-displacing factory and office systems, and more towards alternative and preventative medicine, women's health concerns, organic agriculture, public transit, job-preserving innovations, and local economic self-reliance. There'd be more attention paid to enhancing community life and less to the relentless corporate drive to expand personal consumption.[18]

In Canada, a citizen-determined science policy could finally reverse the trend to CANARIE-sponsored information highway applications and direct research towards sorely needed public information networks. There'd be less directed at developing commercial learning products and more directed at literacy and community action. Network participants would be universities; research-oriented, non-profit organizations; and sympathetic researchers working in federal laboratories. University involvement is critical because community research gives students practical experience working on socially engaged projects. Students can be remunerated with college credit rather than money, so additional costs are small. The participation of community-based, research-oriented, non-profit organizations is also critical, since they help ensure that universities remain well grounded in actual community concerns and perspectives.

TeleLearning, by contrast, treats student learners as subjects whose responses provide data to help researchers refine telelearning products and ready them for commercial exploitation. The public-interest approach would have student learners participate as equals in determining priorities. Since the mid-1980s, unfortunately, neither governments nor universities have demonstrated much enthusiasm for public-interest research, preferring the pay-offs from CANARIE and the NCEs. Many researchers do keep public-interest science alive, but they face dwindling resources and a lack of networks attuned to the needs of public-interest, community, environmental, women's, anti-poverty, and citizen groups.

university researchers network with corporate executives

The unique contribution of the Mulroney government's 1989 Networks of Centres of Excellence program is that government funds are provided only when corporations have been signed up. Another novelty is that top researchers from across the country working in a similar field are brought together to share approaches and findings with each other and with corporate sponsors. The degree of participation of private firms in the research program of a proposed centre is an important factor in determining which applicants will be successful.

Soon after the program was announced, a committee of international and Canadian scientists chose to fund fifteen of the 158 proposals submitted to the government; the projects selected covered a range of subjects, such as genetic diseases, telecommunications, microelectronics, and high-performance concrete. The fifteen projects received a total of $240 million for five years of operation. In 1994, after a peer-reviewed competition, ten of the fifteen original networks were selected to continue in a second phase of the program for another four years, with an additional $197 million in support. One network did not reapply and the other four failed, presumably because they did not meet new requirements imposed at that time. Says an outside evaluation of NCE in 1997, "The changes to the selection criteria . . . were intended to increase private sector involvement in all network activities, including the establishment of research priorities."[19] The study observed that:

> one premise of the program is that strengthening the linkages
> between university, government, and private sectors will facilitate
> the exchange of information and technology, stimulating the private
> sector's ability to capitalize on frontier research and accelerating
> the commercialization of research results from the network.[20]

In 1995, four new networks were added to the ten approved in phase 2 in areas that had been targeted as "priority areas of strategic importance to Canada in terms of economic, social and environmental benefits."[21] These new networks were in the areas of advanced technologies, the environment, health research, and technology-based learning – telelearning – areas that the government believed could be levered to economic advantage.

The outside evaluation of the program was undertaken by ARA Consulting Group, a Canada-wide management and economics consulting firm, towards the end of the second phase. ARA produced a glowing report, and the government subsequently made the NCE permanent, with its own budget line in the annual estimates to Parliament. The evaluation found that high-quality research was being carried out by high-quality researchers; some projects were leading to "big winners," with significant social and health benefits; high-quality training was being provided to large numbers of graduate students and post-doctoral fellows, most of whom stay in

Canada; the networks were multidisciplinary and multi-sectoral, and were being run reasonably well; university researchers had greatly increased the exchange of knowledge; and the networks were producing a high and increasing output of peer-reviewed articles.

These are all worthy outcomes, but they occurred within the relentlessly commercial context of the program. The inescapable fact is that the NCE formalized the connection between academic research and industrial development, particularly after it became a permanent program in 1998. Within an NCE, the boundaries between university and corporation blur; previously separate institutions begin to merge. Organizations participating in a network must sign an internal agreement that covers such matters as the responsibilities, obligations, commitments, and privileges of each organization; how the network will be managed; how funds will be distributed; what level of internal reporting is required; how corporate and academic partners will interact with each other; who will own the intellectual property produced by the network, and how will it be disseminated; how and by whom will research results be published; who will own the equipment; who will pay for insurance; and how conflicts of interest will be dealt with.[22] Thanks to the NCEs, such internal agreements will become a standard feature of university research in Canada.

Academic participants may end up with greater commitments to their corporate partners than to their university colleagues. And the network may end up doing the research that industry won't do but still expects to benefit from, creating another institutionalized subsidy for business. ARA's evaluation makes this interesting observation: "There are a substantial number of projects that are expected to lead to significant economic and/or social benefits to Canada through application by the private sector. . . . The companies often would not have done the work at all, or in some cases would not [have] done it as early, without the Networks of Centres of Excellence."[23] Most networks have specific committees and/or staff positions that are responsible for the exploitation of their research. The networks protect their intellectual property through non-disclosure agreements, patents, and licences in fields where these are relevant.[24] By 1996, ARA reports, 157 patents had been applied for and 32 granted; in addition,

50 licence agreements and 158 non-disclosure agreements had been concluded. (These are conservative estimates, since some networks would not provide information for ARA's evaluation.) In addition, networks created spin-off companies, developed R&D investment funds, and incorporated "arm's length" commercialization entities. Clearly, the Networks of Centres of Excellence are permanently shifting the balance away from public interest to intellectual property.

telelearning and ibm–"a marriage made in heaven"

The TeleLearning Research Network is controversial because some academics harbour suspicions that the purpose of the project is to replace teachers and classrooms with copyrighted software and computer networks operated by university-corporate partnerships. It's not that on-line teaching systems threaten the established education system. Education technology cannot by itself improve teaching or discard teachers. It's how it's used, by whom, and for what purposes, as well as how the technology is integrated into existing social and political structures, that will determine technology-based learning's impacts. That's where the corporate bias becomes a problem.

The concept of telelearning has existed for many years as the distance-education departments of universities and colleges across Canada. And in those forms, which were intended to serve underprivileged rural populations, distance education has enjoyed widespread support. The difference with TeleLearning's approach is the commercial bias of the enterprise. Courses are being designed to be sold everywhere, so that the social concerns of local residents, say, in Labrador or northern Alberta, cannot be taken into account. Only courses with profit-making potential will be developed, and others, those of social and community value but not purely profitable, will not be.

TeleLearning, led by SFU's Linda Harasim and Tom Calvert, was approved as a second-phase network and received $13.1 million in funding in 1995. It brought together everyone in Canada working on large-scale government- and industry-funded electronic distance-education projects. Key to the network were four major research projects, called beacon technologies (perhaps echoing the Stentor

Alliance's Beacon Initiative of several years earlier). TeleLearning's mission was to develop, field test, and commercialize the beacon technologies.

Joanne Curry, director of SFU's University/Industry Liaison Office (UILO), was hired as TeleLearning's executive director, a move that signalled the project's direction. Her job at UILO had been to help SFU researchers commercialize their discoveries, and her greatest satisfaction, she told an SFU in-house publication, had been "helping to launch spin-off companies."[25] Industry partners were recruited from five market segments: employee training (Bank of Montreal, CUPE, IBM Canada, Human Resources Development Canada), content providers and publishers (McGraw-Hill Ryerson, Prentice-Hall), software developers (NovaSys, MPR Teltech, Communications Research Centre, EduPlus Management Group), network service providers (Rogers Cablesystems, Stentor Resources Centre, AT&T Canada), and equipment manufacturers (Bell-Northern Research, Northern Telecom, and Kodak Canada). Many of these corporate partners were also participants in the "beacon technology" projects.

David Noble of York University is an implacable critic of TeleLearning, and even expressed outright hostility in a lecture he gave at Simon Fraser University, the network's home base, in March 1997. Noble electrified his audience by charging that the network was "a front organization for a consortium of primarily U.S. corporations."[26] The initiative, he said, came from MPR Teltech, a wholly owned subsidiary of BC Telecom, which in turn was a subsidiary of U.S.-based GTE Corp. "All decisions of the TeleLearning Research Network are made by a board, and the board is headed by Ian Dowdeswell, vice-president of business development at MPR Teltech," Noble declared. When TeleLearning co-leader Tom Calvert, who was in the audience, took the microphone, he did not deny that the network was a front organization for U.S. corporations, *or* that all decisions were made by a board, *or* that the board was headed by Ian Dowdeswell. He denied Noble's claim that Dowdeswell was a vice-president at MPR. Dowdeswell had left three years earlier, Calvert said.

Noble was wrong on this detail but correct on the larger issue. MPR Teltech *was* the research arm of BC Telecom, British Columbia's incumbent telephone carrier, which was 50.1 percent owned by GTE Corp. With 750 employees, MPR was one of the oldest and biggest high-tech companies in British Columbia. Dowdeswell was no longer at MPR only because the company no longer existed. On GTE's orders, the research company's twelve technologies had been put on the auction block in late 1994 and sold off over the next two years, after which the company dissolved. In fact, MPR's video-conferencing product, called Wave, was responsible for bringing MPR and the tele-learning researchers together in the first place.

Wave allows video signals to be compressed, transmitted on high-speed networks, edited, and decompressed, all without losing quality. It was just the ticket for distance education. In the early 1990s, MPR started working with Harasim and Calvert in the awkwardly named Canadian Online Exploration and Collaborative Environment for Education (COECEE), which received a $1-million grant from CANARIE. The project's goal was to use MPR's Wave technology and Harasim's education software to create a package for on-line courses called Virtual Interactive Environment for Workgroups. COECEE also included Stentor Resources Centre, the telco alliance arm which pro-vided telephone network connectivity; the Open Learning Agency, which developed open-learning programs and courses in the province and would provide a market for the product; the B.C. government's Education Technology Centre, which promotes increased use of tech-nology in education; and Science World, a non-profit science centre in Vancouver (which was also developing an electronic science maga-zine it later licensed to Concord Pacific developer Terry Hui).

When GTE ordered MPR to be dismantled and sold off, BC Tel turned to IBM Canada as a potential buyer. The two companies were already partners in ISM-BC, one of the largest computer outsourcing firms in the province, so it seemed a natural choice. IBM bought the Wave division and its forty employees and moved into MPR's space in Discovery Park, SFU's research facility at its Burnaby Mountain campus, alongside SFU's Faculty of Applied Science, home of Harasim and Calvert. The TeleLearning Network also has its office there. At about the time IBM acquired Wave, it signed a memorandum of understanding with the B.C. government to explore the possibilities of taking over parts of B.C. Systems Corp., the Crown corporation that ran the province's computers and information networks. These difficult and lengthy negotiations would eventually lead IBM to establish the Pacific Development Centre (PDC) at Discovery Park.

In December 1996, IBM global headquarters bestowed on PDC a worldwide mission to develop distance-learning courseware for the Internet. Dave Hunter, manager of the distance-learning operation, says TeleLearning was a key reason why IBM decided to locate the mission in Canada. "Access to the research in innovative learning models . . . is a critical input to developing a product that will compete world-wide. . . . We also see the TL-NCE as playing a key role in developing highly skilled graduates, several of whom we have recently hired," Hunter said.[27] Next, IBM formed a partnership with SFU that would see the computer company provide support services for on-line education courses while the university supplied the content. At a 1996 TeleLearning-sponsored seminar, where academic and corporate partners shared the stage for joint presentations on their projects, Calvert appeared with IBM's Hunter and exclaimed that theirs was a "marriage made in heaven."

With the TeleLearning connections, IBM quickly expanded its distance-education activities in B.C., working with the B.C. Ministry of Education (which already had 40,000 distance learners in the province) and the Open Learning Agency (which had 27,000 distance learners). PDC is partnering with local and international universities, colleges, institutes, and schools to develop applications that will provide the timely services students expect and demand from universities, all accessible with a Web browser.[28]

IBM's focus on global markets mirrors that of Harasim and TeleLearning, whose 1995 funding application to the NCE raised the spectre of "American telelearning services" being delivered to Canadian markets, which "would have profound effects on our social independence, cultural vitality and intellectual sovereignty if our institutions and service companies were non-competitive."[29] This was an odd angle to promote, given that most corporate partners were Canadian subsidiaries of American multinationals, like IBM Canada, Kodak Canada, Microsoft Canada, and even MPR Teltech itself. But the preoccupation of the application was the market for telelearning equipment, systems, and services, which in Canada was worth about $5 billion and in the U.S. could exceed $50 billion. "Suppliers with effective 'leading edge' technology from the TL-NCE, and who identify and supply the 'early adopters' market, which the TL-NCE will reach through conference presentations, will gain a competitive advantage in this marketplace."[30] The partners will "become exporters of leading-edge telelearning technologies, equipment, services and expertise in the global market."[31]

The business market will develop first, the application notes, but the real opportunities lie in the K-12 and post-secondary markets because of their sheer size (they're worth about $500 billion in the U.S. and $55 billion in Canada). Commercially marketable hardware and software products will flow from TeleLearning's research program, and will include "courseware and other learning products, interactive information sources, testing and marketing systems, products for training the workforce, products for lifelong learning."[32] And all of this can be delivered anywhere, anytime, over CANARIE's high-speed networks.

In 1996, as SFU and IBM were hammering out their partnership agreement, Harasim and Calvert established a company called Virtual Learning Environments Inc. (VLEI) to market their Virtual-U software. The company and the university signed a licensing agreement that gave VLEI the exclusive right to produce and distribute Virtual-U programs. In return, the company agreed to pay the university $500,000, plus additional royalties if the venture is successful, provide equity in the company, and assign to the university the rights to any improvements in the technology. VLEI had already chalked up some international sales to institutions such as Aalborg University in Denmark and the University of the West Indies in Jamaica.[33]

canarie's electronic assembly line

Technologies like MPR-IBM's Wave and software like Virtual-U need high-speed guaranteed network service to be usable in the video-conferencing applications demanded by telelearning projects, and that's where CANARIE fits into the picture. Distance education is a CANARIE priority "simply because it is regarded throughout the Internet community as one of the most important applications of this new broadband technology," said CANARIE president Andrew Bjerring.[34] CANARIE's missions were to set up a high-speed test network and to develop applications to run on that network. Both were critical for telelearning. High speed and guaranteed bandwidth are vital for university courseware and other education applications that need to exchange multimedia content in real time, and CANARIE's program to back the development of applications provided early and sizeable funding for telelearning-related projects. The goal was to install networks and software so that, for example, a professor at one university could deliver a lecture with slides, videos, and other multimedia content, and students at another university on the other side of the country could view the lecture and then participate in a real-time discussion via videoconferencing.

To get to that point, the network went through three iterations. The first was called National Test Network (NTN), and it allowed IT companies to test new products and network applications inexpensively, using facilities funded mainly by the information industry and telephone companies, but with significant CANARIE contributions. NTN was merely a beginning, however. CANARIE needed a "next generation" network that could meet several crucial requirements: provide support for a larger base of network and application developers; handle high-bandwidth applications providing simultaneous voice, video, and data transmission; be able to prioritize traffic depending on type; and move from a "best efforts" to a "quality of service" network. This new research network was called CA*net II, and it was announced at CANARIE's Showcase in Ottawa in June 1997. It was billed as the first "next generation" network in the world and, in the spirit of the electronic assembly line, would be made available only to universities and government research labs. Anyone else who wanted to use the network would have to obtain approval from CANARIE.[35]

CA*net II consisted of three elements: regional advanced networks in each province; a mesh, or "cloud," of high-speed networks linking the regional networks; and connecting points, or GigaPOPs ("giga" meaning billions of bits per second, and "pop" meaning point of presence), performing the complex routing between the local networks and the backbone. The GigaPOPs had the task of segregating traffic (i.e., sending "commodity" traffic over the commercial Internet and traffic destined for another institution – say, from one TeleLearning researcher to another – over the high-speed network).

CA*net II was fifteen times faster than the existing Internet, and it provided better audio- and video-transmission capabilities (because data signals were not routed until they reached a GigaPOP). Most important, CA*net II provided guaranteed quality of service for specific applications and allowed for multimedia content delivery. The commercial Internet was a "best efforts" network, so there was no guarantee that an advanced application, like TeleLearning, would have access to adequate bandwidth to perform properly. In the case of a video feed, for instance, Internet Protocol packets must arrive at the destination in the correct order and on time or a video won't play properly. With congestion, frames can get lost, resulting in jerky motion or no motion at all, and the video can stop altogether while the receiving computer waits for packets to arrive.[36]

The greatest beneficiaries of CA*net II seemed to be the telephone carriers. Bell Canada, AT&T Long Distance Canada, and Teleglobe Canada provided the underlying asynchronous transfer mode (ATM) infrastructure for the network and paid $45 million of the two-year, $60-million cost of CA*net II, since they would be able to develop advanced commercial Internet services from their participation. "Since [CA*net II] is constructed around Bell's ATM network, everything we learned designing and building CA*net II can be transferred to Bell's commercial customers right away," said John McLennan, president and CEO of Bell Canada, at the official launch of the network.[37] In fact, the telcos had a major impact on the design of CA*net II, proposing the configuration as a virtual network within an ATM "cloud" that would also support the business-class Internet service they would soon role out.

CA*net II was just the ticket for TeleLearning too. "People would really like to make a lot of use of multimedia in their courses," Tom

Calvert remarked in a newspaper interview when it was announced. "But with the current networks, you have to limit that just because of the bandwidth. If you put in a lot of rich multimedia it takes so long to transmit, it doesn't work very well." York University, for example, has been using Virtual-U's software to create "very rich multimedia courses," Calvert said. "But we can't really take advantage of that because the link across Canada currently is so slow."[38]

CA*net II was barely operational before it was deemed obsolete. The wave of the future, CANARIE opined, was an all-optical Internet based solely on the Internet Protocol (IP), which is orders of magnitude faster than the mixed system of asynchronous transfer mode (ATM) and IP that constitutes CA*net II. Because it was so much faster, CA*net 3 was even better for applications like telelearning. Manley contributed $55 million to the enterprise, and the rest of the $120-million cost came from the companies that would benefit from it. CA*net 3 uses a technology that multiplies the bandwidth of a fibre by driving it simultaneously with thirty-two different colours of laser light. This allows much more data to be transmitted than via conventional fibre technology. The fibres are then directly connected to high-performance network routers.

Bell Canada led the consortium that won the contract to build the new network; the other members were Northern Telecom, Cisco Systems Canada, Newbridge Networks, and JDS Fitel, which together provided the mix of technologies to do the job. But while the technologies were new, the model was the same electronic assembly line, only faster. The network was made available only to researchers at universities and government labs who were working on optical Internet technologies or developing the applications essential to make the system fly. The network is framed as a research venture, but corporate interests are always just around the corner.

While the consortium was installing the network for CANARIE, its member companies were wheeling and dealing on a grand scale. JDS Fitel, which makes the wavelength division multiplexing systems (WDM), merged with its chief rival in a deal worth $6.1 billion (U.S.). Nortel, which buys WDM systems from JDS Fitel and incorporates them in its fibre-optic networking equipment, merged with a leading computer-network firm in a $9.1-billion deal, and Bell Canada, which incorporates Nortel equipment in its high-speed fibre-optic network, sold a 20 percent share to U.S. giant Ameritech Corp. for $5.1 billion.

CANARIE had education research (along with health and electronic commerce) firmly in mind for its high-performance bandwidth. In 1995, it set up three ad hoc committees focusing on these areas to help the board define what CANARIE's role should be. The focal point was its Technology Applications and Development (TAD) program, which was set up to find applications that could run on the high-speed network CANARIE had cobbled together. The education committee was asked how the 1996 TAD competition could better emphasize education applications.

The committee selected seven education projects, including Linda Harasim's Virtual-U, the newly incorporated offspring of her earlier VIEW, which had been part of COECEE's $1-million CANARIE grant in 1994. Other projects included Blackstone Multimedia Corp.'s Education Operating Network, designed to accelerate the use of multimedia courseware in the classroom; DeltaWare System's PEI Collaborative Learning Alive! Pages, which were to deliver curriculum over the Internet; and the Learner Workbench by Vancouver's Knowledge Architecture, meant to provide an Internet-based program for school and non-school projects. These and other projects selected for funding in 1997 and 1998 all seem designed to make public education more dependent on corporate computer programs and Internet services.

mulroney charts the course, chrétien follows

CANARIE and NCE are the culmination of fifteen years of federal government efforts to bring academic research and industry closer together. As early as 1984, the Mulroney government was urging universities to transfer technology to the private sector for commercial development whenever possible. Canadian governments have long been obsessed with the poor research performance of the Canadian corporate sector, whose R&D efforts are proportionally lower than those of other G-8 countries and Canada's other major trading partners. Not that industry doesn't fund research in Canada. Private-sector R&D

spending rose significantly (in inflation-adjusted terms) over the past two decades to become the largest component of Canadian R&D. Yet the fact remains that Canadian industry does not invest nearly as much as the private sector in other developed nations, not in absolute terms or as a percentage of GDP.

Two explanations are commonly offered for industry's lacklustre performance. First, the Canadian economy is still resource-based, and resource-extraction industries spend less on R&D than manufacturing industries. What's to research? Just dig it up or cut it down and haul it out. Second, there is a high level of foreign ownership in Canadian manufacturing. Most research, aside from product development for local markets, is done in head-office, not branch-plant, countries.[39] Rather than deal with the ownership issue, Mulroney opened the door wider and tried to solve the problem by encouraging and enticing industry to do more research in Canada. If that didn't work, his plan was to encourage and entice academic researchers to do it for industry.

An early Mulroney government initiative to encourage industry to do more was the 1985 Scientific Research and Experimental Development Program, which provided companies of all sizes with tax breaks for approved research. Revenue Canada estimates that tax credits in excess of $1 billion are being granted annually on more than $5 billion of industrial R&D funded by the private sector. Since these tax credits are themselves taxable as income, the revenue the government foregoes is somewhat less than $1 billion. A 1994 Conference Board of Canada study estimated that our nation's tax treatment of R&D was the most favourable of eleven countries (including all G-8 members), although some have questioned whether the program does actually lead to increased research activity. In any case, industry has deemed the taxpayer-subsidized program to be an essential ingredient of corporate research in Canada. Business leaders especially like this approach because government doesn't tell them what kind of research their companies should undertake. In a 1998 brief criticizing the national revenue department's audit procedures, industry made a thinly veiled threat: "This program is considered to be critically important if companies developing leading-edge tech-nologies are going to be able to justify keeping their Research and

Development in Canada."[40] In other words, government could tinker with, but should not dare cut, the program.

The next step was to focus federal government thinking about how public research could help private profit. The formerly independent Ministry of State for Science and Technology was folded into "a department concerned primarily with industrial development. This move . . . resulted in the entrenchment of a business approach to academic research . . . inside the federal government."[41]

The Liberals continued down the same road, putting their own stamp on the policy by creating even closer ties with industry. To differentiate the Liberals from the Tories, Industry Minister John Manley undertook his own science policy review. He started out with a considerable bargaining chip in his back pocket – the recommendations of the Information Highway Advisory Council. IHAC had a lot to say about what government should be doing in science and technology. It supported a proposal to enlarge the fiefdom of its political master, Manley. "The Council considers S&T spending as economic policy," IHAC declared, and therefore Industry Canada (and John Manley) should be in charge.[42] IHAC went on to argue that "Canada must establish business-related conditions to encourage aggressive, commercially driven R&D and applications."[43] This was the old "privatize, commercialize" refrain. IHAC also urged that "federal R&D tax credits be expanded significantly, irrespective of the size of the firm, for R&D that is directed at Information Highway products, technologies and applications,"[44] a self-serving idea, since most IHAC industry members represented large firms that would benefit directly from such tax credits.

Manley's policy was formulated in an environment of severe budget cuts during the mid-1990s. Every aspect of federal S&T activity – except CANARIE and the Networks of Centres of Excellence – came under Paul Martin's knife. Government spending on S&T shrank by about $500 million while Manley was conducting his review, and didn't recover to the level it had been at the beginning of the Liberal reign until the 1998–99 budget. With his budgets cut and his labs working more closely with industry, Manley released his long-awaited report, *Science and Technology for the New Century*, in

March 1996, predictably calling for increased partnerships with the corporate sector.[45] "The federal government must respond to the challenges of the knowledge-based economy by becoming a more effective partner in the innovation system," the report declared.[46] The commercial application of technology expands investment, jobs, and growth, Manley said, and he promised to work with business. Indeed, the policy says "some activities once carried out exclusively by the federal government are now being conducted as public-private collaborations or are being transferred fully to the private sector."[47]

research councils deliver the message

The federal government controls what happens in its own labs by directing them to do certain kinds of work and not others. Its control over university research is less direct and operates through funding councils. The government sets up the councils, appoints the members, and provides the funding. It doesn't direct funding to particular projects or even to particular types of projects. But the government does create a climate of expectations through its policies and statements. Not surprisingly, the Liberals' obsessive drive to tie government spending on research more closely to the needs of industry became the mandate of the granting agencies.

Academics must do research – that is part of the system. They publish their results in scholarly journals and present their findings at conferences, efforts that are necessary to secure tenure and promotion and to enhance their status in their particular spheres of academic enterprise. Many academics depend on financial support from the federal government for their research. Before 1960, funding for academic research was delivered through the National Research Council, but there were ongoing conflicts between NRC scientists and university researchers. To counter this, the Medical Research Council was established in 1960 and the Natural Sciences and Engineering Research Council and the Social Sciences and Humanities Research Council in 1978. The granting programs of these three arm's-length funding agencies are the mainstay of Canadian university research. They provide funding on a competitive basis through peer review, which involves reviewers from relevant fields sitting on agency selection and advisory committees. The NSERC has the largest budget, comprising about 55 percent of the federal dollars that go to university research; it funds science, engineering, applied science, computing, and communications. The MRC provides about 30 percent for health and medical research, the SSHRC just over 10 percent for the social sciences and humanities, and the NRC provides about 5 percent. Total funding in fiscal 1994–95 was $882.8 million. Martin slashed away at this for the next three years before restoring it to $862 million in 1998–99, with plans to raise it to $903 million in 2000–2001, but in inflation-adjusted dollars this will still be lower than 1994–95 spending.

Most NSERC funds still go into research grants that do not require commercial partners. But this type of funding has been declining for nearly twenty years. As we've seen, the new direction in government S&T policy ties funds to corporate priorities. In 1994, the NSERC released a new strategy called Partnerships in Knowledge, which endorsed even closer ties between universities and business, anticipating the direction the Liberals would take. "The development of closer links between universities and other sectors offers many exciting opportunities for those with the interest and drive to participate in these activities," it claimed. The document denied that "support of basic long-term research will be abandoned in favour of solving immediate industrial problems, [and] that university laboratories will become industrial research centres."[48] Nonetheless, partnerships became the NSERC's watchword.

Tom Brzustowski, from the office of Ontario's deputy minister of education, was brought in to lead the NSERC in its new direction. His view was that education should produce "a greater capability of the people of Ontario to create wealth, . . . [to] export products in which our knowledge and skills provide the value added, . . . [and] to develop new services which we can offer in trade in the world market."[49] Just before Brzustowski's appointment, his predecessor said that academics who resist working with business to develop new technology may find themselves obsolete. "They make the silliest arguments I've ever heard," Peter Morand said. "We can't afford to have these characters who beat their breasts and say, 'Respect what I'm doing.'"[50]

After a meeting in Saskatoon in October 1995, perhaps one of the first chaired by Brzustowski, the council made major modifications to its programs to "better represent the extent of partnerships and collaboration already present in NSERC activities and to promote stronger links between researchers and research users." It created a Research Partnerships umbrella for "all activities that involve partnerships beyond the academic sector, and that are characterized by significant partner involvement and clear evidence of ability to use the results."[51] The NSERC would fund a greater variety of activities that included partners, from basic to the most applied research. In all programs under this umbrella, corporate partners must actively participate in and/or make financial contributions to the research. Even basic or pre-competitive research would be included. "The investigation may be for exploratory studies or discovery of new knowledge, but the research must be of relevance to a company's line of business and the company must contribute an amount equal to the NSERC grant."[52] One new program, Technology Partnerships, went even further in its goal of commercializing technologies developed in university labs. The program funds university research activities that can demonstrate to companies, before they risk full-scale development, that an idea originated in a university laboratory is technically feasible. In return, partnering companies must be able to show that they can take the technology to the next stage of commercialization. The NSERC even helped establish an investment fund that would invest in companies attempting to commercialize technologies developed in university labs.

partners or handmaidens?

The pressure is on the universities to produce for industry. For companies, the pay-off is obvious. Partnerships can shave years off the time needed to develop new or improved products. Bell-Northern Research is a participant in the Canadian Institute for Telecommunications Research, an NCE that is developing wireless-communications technologies. Bell-Northern assistant vice-president Dave Robertson expects ideas being researched to be in use within three or four years. "It is an excellent opportunity to push the limits of our technology," Robertson says. "Although some are unachievable, a small percentage of the time they come up with ideas we have not thought of . . . that could yield incredible results."[53]

For governments of all political stripes operating in an era of triumphalist neo-conservative ideology, the motivation is also obvious. They see support for industry as the only option available for national or provincial development, a sharp contrast from the past, when governments played an activist role in countless large and small ventures and set up their own labs to undertake basic and applied science research. As in so many initiatives to commercialize information, Industry Canada leads the way, not only through its own programs, but also through the labs, which report to the minister, and the granting agencies, which fund academic research.

In 1995, Industry Canada commissioned the Canadian Institute for Advanced Research (CIAR) to survey university officials and produce a report on how Industry Canada could help the institutions commercialize their research.[54] In the jargon of academia, it's called technology transfer (although technology can mean just about anything and can be transferred to government agencies and non-profit organizations as well as to industry).

To be able to transfer technology, universities must first establish who owns it, and most have internal policies that govern the ownership and rewards for intellectual property. Usually, ownership resides with the researchers, not the institution. If they so desire, the professors can leave with their inventions or innovations and start their own companies, which some do. The majority, however, assign their rights to the university in return for a share of future benefits.

Even where the universities own intellectual property, such as is the case at the University of British Columbia, most are handing a bigger share of the pie to faculty and other researchers. In 1990, the University of Toronto, the third-largest research organization in the country, began giving faculty members the option of taking personal ownership of their inventions, with U of T retaining a 25 percent share of revenues. Ten years later, about 90 percent of discoveries at U of T were retained by their inventors.[55]

By 1990, an infrastructure to facilitate commercialization was put in place in most universities, where technology-transfer offices identify promising research discoveries, fund the development of prototypes that demonstrate their feasibility, patent them, find interested and able corporate partners, negotiate licences, draft agreements, and create spin-off companies. At SFU, Daphne Gelbart is an "innovation detective," a University/Industry Liaison Office technology-transfer officer; she scouts SFU's laboratories, meeting rooms, and offices on "reconnaissance missions" and scans papers published by faculty members, searching for new processes, technologies, and inventions that can be commercialized. Al Fowler, manager of intellectual property at UBC's Industry Liaison Office (which tries to attract investors to technology developed at UBC), notes that the office has grown substantially: it was collecting $20,000 annually in royalties in 1985; by 1995 it was reeling in about $1 million a year in cash and equity positions. The University of Waterloo leads Canadian universities, with royalties and other revenues of about $2 million a year.[56]

Of course, even with returns in the range of $1 million to $2 million per university, per year, these offices don't pay for themselves; they depend on various taxpayer-supported programs to keep them afloat. The NSERC provides money through its Intellectual Property Management Program, provincial governments contribute in various ways, and various administrative units and faculties within the university also contribute. Key support comes from the NRC's Industrial Research Assistance Program, and from Industry Canada in the form of an Internet service called Trans-Forum, which links UILOs across the country and provides information to assist officials in their marketing efforts.[57]

When a new technology is invented, industry-liaison offices either license it to an established company, or they create a spin-off company to develop it for commercial application themselves. Licensing a technology to an existing company provides a quicker return to the university. The company obtains an exclusive or non-exclusive right to exploit the technology, while the university and the inventor receive royalty payments when the company starts earning revenues. The university and the inventor may also take up shares in the company. In 1997, 195 licences were granted by universities to existing companies, boosting the total number of outstanding licences by 41 percent to 672.[58]

Spin-off or start-up companies are more problematic for universities because new companies might not produce revenue for five to ten years, if ever. But they might also create jobs and add to the ability of industry to make greater use of university research in the future, and so are considered important by federal government and university policymakers. Since 1984, UBC's University-Industry Liaison Office has participated in the creation of seventy-two spin-off companies. Normally, UBC would receive royalty payments for its share of the enterprise, but in 1988 the university began negotiating equity options instead. This provided additional support to start-ups, because it reduced the cash burden imposed by royalty payments and, at the same time, enabled the university to capture growing capital values in companies that do not begin to earn revenues for up to a decade after inception. In 1997, the university held equity in twenty-eight companies, all but one of which had been created from UBC research. That same year, the University of Toronto started eleven companies. In 1996, the University of Alberta also started eleven companies, while UBC, SFU, and the University of Calgary each started seven. The grand-daddy of spin-off companies is aerial- and satellite-mapping firm MacDonald Dettwiler Associates, incorporated in 1969 as a spin-off from UBC. The now American-owned company has revenues of over $100 million and a Canadian workforce of 850.

The new system seems to be working, at least from the perspective of researchers and administrators. "We don't lose a lot of people," says Peter Munsche, U of T's assistant vice-president of technology transfers. Most professors associated with discoveries stay on at the university to teach and do further research, and find somebody else (like a graduate student) to run their spin-off company for them.[59] Perhaps they read *Business Week*'s 1998 report on the 120 millionaire academics at British universities, including Cambridge University communications and engineering professor Andy Hopper (worth an estimated $10 million (U.S.) and computer lab researcher Stewart Lang ($8 million). At Oxford, engineering professor Brian Bellhouse is worth $20.5 million, while David Potter, a former lecturer in physics at London's Imperial College, tops the list with a family stake in a hand-held-computer firm worth $184 million.[60]

too close a partnership?

To achieve their new-found wealth, universities may be getting too close to their partners. In 1997, Northern Telecom donated $8 million ($1 million a year for eight years) for the Nortel Institute for Telecommunications at the University of Toronto. The funds went towards two research chairs; three associated faculty positions; equipment for two new labs; a fourteen-month, $25,000 master's program in telecommunications; and student scholarships. The institute's strategic direction is overseen by a joint university-industry advisory council, which is co-chaired by Gedas Sakus, president of Nortel Technology, and Adel Sedra, U of T provost and vice-president of academic affairs. Nortel also set up a "permanent on-site position at the U of T to co-ordinate and manage continuing relations between Nortel and the university."[61]

The agreement was cheered by Jon Gerrard, then-federal secretary of state for science, research, and development, who called it a knowledge-sharing partnership. The NorTel–U of T team won a 1998 Synergy Award for university-industry R&D partnerships from the NSERC and its own partner, the Conference Board of Canada. But a different interpretation was placed on the deal after details were leaked to a student newspaper. David Vaver, a York University law professor and expert on IP law, said the agreement "seems to set up an institute within the university, [which] uses the resources of the university, but which looks very much like the lab of a NorTel subsidiary. NorTel is in a position to control the way in which significant information developed under a NorTel program is exploited." He went on to say, "The faculty and students who work on the project are never the owners of what they produce on a NorTel-funded program." (U of T inventions policy says that if faculty or staff members are working under the direction of the university, rather than on their own projects, then the university gets exclusive rights to the end product. In this case, U of T has assumed rights to inventions stemming from NorTel-funded research, selling to the company the option to buy the rights from the university.[62])

NorTel president Sakus was correct when he said he would ensure that the company "gets the best bang for our buck."[63] The partnership helps NorTel "maintain its position as a world leader in communications technology and product innovation," said Claudine Simpson, NorTel's vice-president of global external research and intellectual property, at the gala dinner in Halifax where NorTel–U of T received their Synergy Award. And NorTel knew what it was supporting: U of T researchers had already helped pave the way for the components of high-speed fibre-data transmission systems for NorTel, systems similar to those NorTel was developing for CA*net 3. As for the university, it gets some money, new equipment, training for graduate students, and a chance to continue to help solve NorTel's problems.

reconnecting research to the public interest

As this chapter has indicated, citizens, taxpayers who fund science research, people affected by the consequences of research projects, and those who might have alternative perspectives on research priorities are noticeably absent from the table when science policy and funding priorities are decided. There is an alternative called community-based research, which is rooted in the community, serves a community's interests, and frequently encourages citizen participation at all levels. Academic researchers can form partnerships, not with IBM or NorTel, but with groups that traditionally have been left out of the research agenda, including public interest, trade union, community, anti-poverty, women's, and Aboriginal groups. Citizens can collaborate with university experts, as well as with organizations dedicated to helping them undertake research. Community-based research aims not merely to advance understanding, but also to ensure that knowledge contributes to making a concrete and constructive difference in the world.[64] In some European countries, students can earn university credit for conducting research on behalf of communities, workers, public-interest groups, and local government agencies. The Netherlands has a national network of thirty-eight community research centres, or "science shops," at thirteen universities; the centres respond each year to 2,500 requests on issues surrounding the needs of disadvantaged groups, workplace safety, industrial pollutants, and all types of public policy. Most Dutch community and non-profit organizations know how to contact the network when they need research assistance. There is thus in the Netherlands a nation-wide system to direct effective research capabilities towards concerns defined by the community.[65]

In the United States, the Loka Institute works to make science and technology more responsive to social and environmental concerns. Loka is a non-profit organization that was founded in 1987 by Richard Sclove and is situated on the campus of Hampshire College in Amherst, Massachusetts. One of its major projects is to set up science shops in the U.S. through the agency of a National Community Research Network. Each shop could provide communities, workers, public-interest groups, and local governments with the resources to investigate their concerns and to act on them. Many other projects have been suggested by Loka, including encouraging local participation in technology assessments; urging citizens and public-interest groups to participate in telecommunications policy issues; and facilitating worker participation in studies of workplace health and safety, as in the design of workplace technologies, and in labour policy decisions.

In March 1995, Sclove wrote an influential article about the Dutch science shops in the *Chronicle of Higher Education*.[66] The article sparked interest in the U.S. in working towards a community-based research network. Establishing such a network was particularly critical and timely in 1996, because severe budget cuts in federal programs addressing social and environmental problems were forcing community groups and local governments to take up the slack. The article also impressed members of the Humanities and Social Sciences Federation of Canada, who felt the model could apply here too because of the federal cuts to transfer payments for social programs and vicious attacks on disadvantaged groups by governments in

Ontario and Alberta. Although many organizations and universities were already doing community-based and participatory research in Canada, they were often invisible to those who could most benefit from their assistance, and they were frequently unaware of each other's work. They lacked awareness of themselves as part of something larger, a nation-wide system or even a social movement.

The University of Quebec–affiliated Groupe de recherche-action en biologie du travail, which was later renamed Le Centre pour l'études des interactions biologiques entre la santé et l'environnement (CINBIOSE), undertakes research projects for unions to improve workers' employment conditions, health, and well-being. A committee of union and university representatives receives project requests from the unions, and then chooses which projects to pursue. Workers are encouraged to "participate actively in all stages of the research – selection and identification of the problem, choice of hypotheses and methods, analysis and interpretation of data – contributing to their knowledge of the situation and assuring that the research corresponds to their needs."[67]

In one case, researchers were contacted by slaughterhouse workers who complained of many health problems – including backaches, articular pain, menstrual pain, and warts. After discovering that little work had been done on occupational hazards in the poultry industry, the researchers initiated a new study. Workers participated in designing, distributing, and collecting questionnaires; taking measurements of the workplace environment; analyzing and interpreting data; and reporting the results. Because of the study, the employer agreed to raise the slaughterhouse temperature, install benches for employees to sit on while working, sharpen instruments, allow more toilet breaks, and provide workers with gloves that fit. The participatory research methodology had an additional benefit: slaughterhouses with high worker involvement in the research saw conditions improve more than in slaughterhouses with less worker involvement.

The Humanities and Social Sciences Federation worked with Montreal consultant Patricia Roman, who participated in Loka's July 1996 Community Research Network Planning Conference in Amherst, to produce a proposal for what they called Community Research and

Information Crossroads (CRICs). CRICs would bring together faculty members and students in the humanities and social sciences at twenty-five universities across Canada. They would address issues of concern to specific communities, such as child poverty, violence, literacy, the changing workplace, and an ageing population. In July 1997, the federation released its proposal, a well-conceived concept with wide academic and community support.[68] CRICs were quickly adopted by social-science and humanities-research communities as a way to boost their sagging fortunes in the face of government's love affair with science, engineering, and medical research, activities with more relevance and benefits for the corporate sector. But because the federation proposed that CRICs should be financed primarily by the federal government, that meant the concept would be subject to the priorities of Industry Canada.

The Social Sciences and Humanities Research Council (SSHRC) set aside $3 million from its 1998–99 budget for sixteen CRICs, but made some significant changes to the concept. CRICs became innovation centres; their purpose became to promote knowledge transfer between universities and the community; they would be open to proposals from private-sector organizations; they were renamed Community University Research Alliances (CURAs); each centre would have to focus on one research theme; and community groups, as well as universities, could become centres. Specific CURAs have yet to be approved by SSHRC, let alone begin operating, so it is too early to tell whether the science-shop approach, as modified by the federal government and the funding agency, can take root and flourish in Canada.

A successful Canadian science-shop initiative such as CURA could begin to shift the balance of research priorities away from the corporate and towards the public and non-profit. This same kind of strategy is needed in another area of vital public information targeted by the information industry for commercialization: public education. Often it is the same companies, such as IBM, that are engaged in both types of commercialization.

colonizing new markets:
ibm goes to school

Learning and training will be an integral part of the knowledge economy, and the learning and training industry will be one of the major growth sectors.

— Final Report, Information Highway Advisory Council, 1995

. . . an addressable market opportunity at the dawn of a new paradigm.

—Morgan Stanley Dean Witter, Wall Street brokers

The information industry's plans for education may have been revealed on October 9, 1997, when Canadian Press sent out a wire story reporting the contents of confidential government notes from a March meeting billed as the Minister's Round Table on Technology in Learning and chaired by John Snobelen, at the time Ontario minister of education. The notes suggest that schools and classrooms will vanish by 2005, and textbooks will be available only on the Internet. "Technology will be the vehicle towards guided self-reliant learning at the post-primary level. . . . Learners will learn at their own pace, anytime, anywhere, anyplace," the document says, eerily echoing a trademarked Microsoft phrase. Within seven years, all Ontario students — even those in kindergarten — will have a "personal electronic

notebook" on which they can call up their curriculum, something traditionally delivered by teachers. The education ministry will be combined
with the ministry of economic development under the direct supervision of the premier.[1]

The story was released just before Ontario's teachers went out
on an "illegal strike," as the *Globe and Mail* took every opportunity
to report. *Globe* editor-in-chief William Thorsell insisted that the
teachers' action failed the test of civil disobedience,[2] but Ontario
General Division Court Justice James McPherson disagreed. He said
the walkout was more likely a political protest, and threw out the
government's application for an injunction to force the teachers back
to work.

Not surprisingly, the *Globe and Mail* did not run the story about
the leaked notes. The subtext of the *Globe*'s reporting and editorials
was consistent: the issue was not about education but about curbing
the unbridled power of those nasty unions. The Snobelen notes would
have lent credence to the teachers' claim that the real purpose of Bill
160 (the Education Quality Improvement Act), which had sparked the
teachers' protests, was to centralize control of education at Queen's
Park. Once it had control, the government could implement its (largely
secret, corporate) agenda, which involved cutting billions of dollars
from the education budget, firing teachers and replacing them with
computers and lower-paid teaching assistants, opening classrooms to
business, and ultimately incorporating education into the information
industry's global networks, where content companies like TeleLearning
spin-offs could create their own curriculum and profit from its distribution over the Internet. The *Globe* refused to allow that there was
any centralization agenda, even though the legislation clearly spelled
it out.[3]

Ironically, the day before the Canadian Press story hit the wire, the
Globe distributed a ten-page advertising supplement from IBM Canada
called "Focus on Business Solutions – The Canadian Education
Industry." The "lead story" – actually IBM advertising copy – was
headlined "High-Tech Tools Open New Vistas in London: Ontario
City's School Board Integrating Technology and Education." The copy
featured IBM's SchoolVista, "a complete teaching software package."

School board computer consultant Linda Brown said the software was the school's "main education operating system." The word "teacher" appeared in the 700-word copy only twice. In the IBM vision of the education "market," teachers are adjuncts to the software (or "facilitators," as the Snobelen notes had it). The software ran the school, and it was the patented property of IBM, which licensed it to school boards.[4] Other "stories" in the IBM insert told readers that "for educators, the best is yet to come: Canadian learning institutions are gearing up for the second phase of their technological revolution," and that one Alberta school "dismisses idea of boundaries."

Words like "technological revolutions" and "blurred boundaries" are code for the corporate education agenda. Translated, they mean replacing the teacher-oriented system with one ruled by corporate-owned technology and transferring school curriculum to the Internet, where it can be delivered anywhere in the world.

IBM has been fomenting education's "technological revolution" and attempting to blur boundaries for decades, ever since computers in education first became fashionable in the 1960s. The company revved up its activities in 1995, when, to staunch the flow of red ink from its books, head office in Armonk, New York, restructured into fourteen industry-specific global organizations (there were operations dealing with retailing, government, health care, and education, among others). The company still retains geographically based organizations such as IBM Canada for legal and political reasons, but these national branch plants are not operating entities. IBM Canada is merely the sum total of all the industry-specific units that operate north of the forty-ninth parallel. For example, IBM's Pacific Development Centre, based near Vancouver, has a mandate to go after distance-education business anywhere in the world. Manager Chuck Hamilton boasts of the 2,700 tools the centre has available for anything remotely dealing with education. Its job is to drum up business with Canadian schools, colleges, and universities.

In a slow-growth economy such as Canada's has been for the last twenty years, new revenue for businesses such as IBM lies in cultivating areas of social and cultural life that have not previously been subjected to business transactions. Social activist and technology critic Heather Menzies calls this activity "colonizing" new areas of society:

> The corporate priorities are to find new markets for their information systems, to hook more customers into their infrastructures, and generally to fill the constantly expanding carrying and switching capacity of the capital-intensive information systems. In short, their priorities are in an important sense to colonize new sectors of the economy (especially health care and education in the public sector).[5]

Education is one of Canada's largest economic sectors, with annual expenditures (excluding public and employer-based training expenditures) of $56.4 billion annually. Much of this goes to wages and salaries for education workers (about 66 percent of operating costs). Replacing teachers with IT hardware and software services and less expensive teaching assistants is one way for industry to divert some of this revenue stream into its own coffers. The largest "market" is kindergarten to Grade 12, which has 6.5 million potential customers. The post-secondary sector includes fewer students but requires more sophisticated programs, so there is an opportunity to provide value-added, and therefore more profitable, services such as entire courses or programs. Helping IBM and other firms colonize education using IT has been an essential task of the Chrétien government, with Finance Minister Paul Martin cutting spending and Industry Minister John Manley spreading IT and corporate partnerships. The result will be a gradual disappearance of shared public information and community values, hallmarks of Canadian public education for a hundred years. Once corporations have successfully "partnered" with educational institutions and built their own libraries of curriculum, there's little to stop them from establishing their own electronic-education centres and competing with the public system, which meanwhile is faced with dwindling resources and an incessant corporate propaganda campaign to discredit its legitimacy.

ontario's new deputy minister of education

Six months before the Minister's Round Table on Technology in Learning, the Mike Harris government hired Veronica Lacey as Ontario's deputy minister of education and training. During the political fallout surrounding Bill 160, it was revealed that Harris's office had negotiated a confidential performance contract with Lacey – the leaked copy was unsigned – setting out a $667-million cut she would need to make in the province's education budget to be eligible for annual personal bonuses of up to $32,000.[6] This was one of one hundred tasks on Lacey's list of things to do, as set for her by the Harris government; another was to produce a long-term vision for technology in the classroom, such as was outlined in the Snobelen notes, that would serve as a guide for individual technology decisions.

Cutting education budgets and expanding the use of technology in the classroom are the kind of challenges Lacey had faced in the past. Before becoming a key functionary in the Harris government–IBM agenda, Lacey was director of the North York Board of Education and a keen advocate of partnerships between schools and the information industry, which she believed were vital for the success of the education system. Her board cut $45 million from its budget between 1992 and 1995. "Given the cutbacks that education is facing, partnerships with business, government and the community are needed now more than ever," she explained at the time. The key to successful partnerships, she maintained, was ensuring that the benefits to students were clearly stated. "We do not promote the commercialization of our classrooms. We are not passive players in our partnership arrangements," Lacey emphasized. "In fact, we are usually the initiators, and we can control the agenda at all times."[7]

And what might that agenda be? We might get an indication from CyberArts, a computer-based arts program in two North York high schools, Northview Secondary and Don Mills Collegiate. CyberArts is a partnership between the school board and five companies: Silicon Graphics and its subsidiary, Alias-Wavefront; Apple Canada; Kodak Canada; and cable carrier Rogers Cablesystems. Using expensive, state-of-the-art equipment that the companies helped buy, students spend half their school time learning skills in creative and digital imaging, 3-D animation, photography, design, and special effects. The program cost about $800,000 and the companies provided about $300,000 of that in equipment, software, and training support for teachers and students. "That program could not be offered if it weren't for the business community," said Ross Parry, public-affairs officer at the board. "What makes this partnership unique is that *we have individuals from the partner companies right in the class teaching. A lot of the teachers don't know how to use the equipment. So rather than us spending money to train teachers, we bring [business people] right into the class*"[8] (italics added). And once the teachers are eliminated by the Harris government, partner companies can get on with the business of running the program and turning out the skilled people required in an industry dominated by Silicon Graphics–Alias Wavefront equipment and Walt Disney content.

Lacey was an early public-sector appointee to the CANARIE board – David Black of Silicon Graphics was another early director – and later to John Manley's Information Highway Advisory Council, where Rogers Cablesystems had a seat. She chaired IHAC's Learning and Training Working Group, which produced the quote at the beginning of this chapter. After CANARIE completed its job of upgrading and privatizing the Internet in Canada, the organization turned its attention to developing content for the networks. Lacey was picked to chair the education steering committee, which advises the CANARIE board about education-technology projects deserving of financial support.

In 1996, Lacey won a National Iway award, which was conceived by CANARIE and the Canadian Advanced Technology Association and sponsored by the Royal Bank of Canada. The awards recognize "demonstrated leadership in the development of Canada's emerging information society." Lacey was cited for using the information highway to educate North York students (through programs like CyberArts) and for promoting the highway across the country. She shared the spotlight with New Brunswick premier Frank McKenna, who won his award for paving his province in fibre and inviting dozens of call-centre sweatshops to set up business there. Lacey and

McKenna had already co-launched, in 1993, the National Network for Learning, an "electronic highway for Canadian schools" that promotes the development of "exemplary curriculum materials by teachers and by commercial enterprises."[9] If the Harris government's goal is to replace teachers with computer-based education systems, there are few in Canada better suited to lead the way than Veronica Lacey.

the agenda to colonize education

To achieve a private-sector-controlled electronic highway for Canadian schools, the first step was to cut public funds to education. Hysteria about government deficits and debt was created through a major corporate propaganda campaign, which kicked off in earnest in the 1980s under Mulroney and reached a peak under Chrétien. Corporate-funded think-tanks like the C.D. Howe and Fraser institutes (and later, AIMS) were front and centre, churning out a steady stream of studies claiming that deficits would destroy the country, so we'd better cut spending on social programs and education. The Chrétien government led the assault, backed by a phalanx of provincial governments, like those in Ontario, Alberta, and New Brunswick. The Ontario Alternative Budget Working Group estimated in October 1998 that Ontario had cut $1.4 billion — or more than 10 percent — from its education budget since the Conservatives came into power in 1995. According to working group co-chair Hugh Mackenzie, research director for the United Steelworkers of America, the cut between 1997 and 1998 was close to the $667 million stipulated in Veronica Lacey's performance contract (and she may have received her bonus for the year).[10] One result of the cuts was that hundreds of schools were shutting down.

Spending cuts left school boards and post-secondary institutions in a state of crisis, desperate for alternative sources of funding and curriculum to maintain their level of services. Even if cuts didn't lead to the immediate layoff of teachers, they forced schools to hold bingo tournaments and sell chocolate bars to pay for field trips, extracurricular sports, and drama productions. And they spooked Canadians into favouring closer ties between education and business, as a July 1997 poll by Environics Research Group indicated. When those polled were asked if provincial governments, school administrators, and school boards should forge more links with business, 90 percent said they approved of such ties at the post-secondary level, while 75 percent supported them for primary and secondary schools. Canadian School Boards Association president Betty Green, a Manitoba trustee, wasn't surprised at these results, believing that education cuts made the public open to the idea of links with the business community.[11] Carol Green Levenstein has run Children's Creative Marketing since 1989. Companies like broadcaster A&E and BASF Canada came to her when they wanted to provide business-sponsored curriculum to schools. Until 1994, it was always a tough sell to get into the schools, she notes. Then the federal Liberals cut transfer payments to education, a move that was followed soon after by tight-fisted Ontario government policies. By 1996, she says, classroom doors that were once shut tight had opened.[12]

After budgets were cut and the education community thrown into a state of crisis, the next step was to promote information technology in schools as a way to take up the slack. Brian Mulroney's Steering Group on Prosperity – Lacey was a member – started this campaign in 1992 with a call for an increase of 30 percent a year in the number of computers in schools. Offering an IT lifeline to education was Manley's special assignment. His department was the point agency prescribing technology (and private-sector partnerships) as the remedy for the deficit "disease." Industry Canada's 1994 discussion paper *The Canadian Information Highway* set the stage: "Soaring costs in health care, education and training coupled with large federal and provincial deficits are stimulating interest in the electronic delivery of public services."[13] Have no fear, educators, there are solutions to spending cuts! In fact, we should be thankful for the cuts, because we have been inspired to come up with something even better: "An advanced information and communications infrastructure [that will] act as a driver for experimentation and testing of new ways for service delivery."[14] The results of these experiments will be better educational services, improved availability, and quality of education. We can do better with less if we embrace information technology.

Industry Canada successfully tied the information highway to the deficit. In fact, this would become a dominant theme in selling the highway and Connecting Canadians to Canadians. We need it so we don't fall behind our competitors in the race to profit from the global economy, the argument went, and we need it to temper the pain of budget cutting. The discussion paper served notice that education, health, and government services would be decimated by budget cuts over the next three years, and that to save themselves they should get on the IT bandwagon immediately.[15]

Many provincial education ministries, school boards and schools, and even some individual teachers echoed this refrain. And remarkably although education budgets (and every other kind of budget) were being cut, money was available for technology. Even as his government cut $1.4 billion from education, Minister Dave Johnson told the Ontario branch of the Information Technology Association of Canada, the industry lobby group, that it was committed to technology and was spending $135 million to connect classrooms to the Internet.[16] In the meantime, Ottawa-based Corel Corp. signed a deal with Ontario, Newfoundland, and British Columbia to provide up-to-date software at bargain-basement prices. Says market development manager William Pope, "Teachers are being retired and they're not being replaced. . . . This [video-conferencing] technology allows" schools to share teacher resources.[17]

In Alberta, the Ralph Klein government cut its education budget by $224 million between 1993 and 1996, but was able to find $45 million in 1996 for classroom technology. The Alberta Department of Education also revised its teacher-certification requirements to include competency in information technology. School boards and schools quickly began employing "more hardware and software for computer technology," observed Ray Lurette, an education manager at Edmonton's Westworld Computer, a software reseller that previews and recommends educational software and computers. His company had its best year ever after Klein slashed education funding.[18]

The mainstream news media helped focus parents' and educators' attention on the technology issue. One *Vancouver Sun* article in a back-to-school issue was headlined "Why Your Child Needs to Be Computer Savvy." "Some kids are now sending CD-ROMs to colleges as part of their applications," the paper warned. "With that kind of competition, it is critical for children to acquire as much computer knowledge as possible, as early as they can."[19] Every education special in the *Globe and Mail* seems to be about technology, as if that's the only issue. In fact, this media over-reporting on educational technology (and charter schools) at the expense of other issues is an example of agenda-setting: the media cannot tell us what to think, but they do an excellent job of telling us what to think about, what's important. The *Globe*, the *Sun*, and other papers move technology to the top of the education agenda.

With the notion that information technology can be an excellent response to budget cuts firmly planted in the public mind, the next stage of colonization becomes evident: disseminate the idea that education is just another area of business activity. The Economic Council of Canada's hatchet job on public education fallaciously called the school system a large bureaucratic monopoly that required freedom of choice for students and partnerships between employers and schools.[20] This theme is echoed persistently by neo-conservative columnists and editorial writers across Canada. In a move to privatize economic policy, Mulroney eliminated the council in 1992, and its work was enthusiastically taken over by the network of right-wing think-tanks being set up across the country, including the C.D. Howe Institute, the Donner Foundation, the Atlantic Institute for Market Studies, the Conference Board of Canada (Veronica Lacey was a director), and the Fraser Institute. The constant repetition of this message by pro-business commentators and reactionary think-tanks, as well as the wide publicity given it by the corporate media, put it on the agenda and made it relevant.

Manley's Information Highway Advisory Council blurred the distinction between education and business. In IHAC's view, the knowledge society and the knowledge economy were one and the same. The relevant chapter in IHAC's final report, *Connection Community Content*, is titled "Learning and Training: The Knowledge Society," and it's the creation of Veronica Lacey's Learning and Training Working Group. Despite its title, it begins by saying, "The Information Highway is part of the larger landscape of the *knowledge economy*"[21] (italics added). Later, the council reveals its "vision statement" for education:

> Learning and training comprise an integral part of the knowledge
> economy. Canada will provide an environment for lifelong learning
> in which all Canadians will have access to the widest possible variety
> of learning opportunities and tools in order to succeed in such an
> economy.[22]

If IHAC has its way – and it did, since Manley thought so much of
its work that he reassembled the group in June 1996 for a second
round of ruminations – the notion of public education will disappear
from public discourse. Instead, we will talk about the "learning and
training industry." Indeed, what is hindering us from building the
information economy, the council says, is the "formal connotation"
(meaning public) of education – shades of the Snobelen secret notes.
Think differently, and you will be amazed to realize that "the learning
industry is already one of the nation's largest economic sectors."[23]

Is that how we should think about public education? IHAC says
yes. Its focus is on creating markets for education software, and it
calls on the federal government to develop a "technology-based
learning and training industry in Canada, particularly for the benefit
of small- and medium-sized enterprises,"[24] while the provinces and
territories should "be encouraged, in partnership with the private
sector, to develop Canada-wide full-credit courses, which should be
made available to all Canadians."[25] If education was merely part of
the economy, the learning and training business, IHAC concluded,
then industry had a legitimate role to play in schools. Public acceptance of such a view would allow for less controversial infiltration of
education by the private sector.

Next on the program is the implementation of a wide-ranging
array of partnerships between business and education. When colonizing a new territory, after all, you need guides who know the terrain,
a Pocahontas for your John Smith. Corporations need to "partner"
with educational institutions to learn the "business" so that they can
target markets they might not otherwise access. BC Tel's installation

of a sophisticated two-way video-conferencing network called Ubiquity is one example of a "successful" partnership. Part of the Burnaby 2000 initiative by the Burnaby school board in suburban Vancouver, this installation allows BC Tel staff to rub shoulders with educators and education administrators, an important market group for the company. "This is an extremely competitive business," explains Donna Serviss, BC Tel's manager for community investment. "If we're not plugged into the education system and interacting with teachers, with principals and with students, we're out of the ballpark."[26]

Of course, the corporate sector is not the only one searching out partnerships. Other levels of government, research institutes, and non-profit associations are also active. But the overwhelming majority are with business. Council of Canadians chair Maude Barlow wants "partnerships with schools [to] be established with sectors of our society besides business – environmental groups, labour, community-action people. Sure, business should be one player," she says, "but it shouldn't be the dominant player."[27] One problem, however, is that many of these, information-based or not, are not true partnerships; they are merely business transactions touted as partnerships. Companies trying to sell their products to kids like to call the arrangement a partnership when it's actually a blatant marketing effort. And schools looking for corporate handouts refer to their efforts as a search for partnerships when they might better describe what they are doing as positioning the school as a charity.

Getting into the schools is a tremendous opportunity for companies whose products are used by kids, notes John A. Torella, a senior consultant and principal for the J.C. Williams Group, a retail consultancy in Toronto.[28] According to him, the Toronto school board's controversial $1.14-million contract with Pepsi-Cola Canada for exclusive rights to supply the city's schools was simply a business deal between the school board and one of its suppliers. Although it was nothing more than naked marketing, it was sold as a partnership. Similarly, Ottawa-based Corel Corp.'s bitter struggle with Microsoft was played out in the classrooms of Canada. Corel's software deal with three provinces was criticized for being nothing more than a plot to cultivate brand loyalty among the customers of tomorrow. In fact, this was part of Corel's highly successful "seeding" mandate, a program that includes Corel managers whose job is to drive the company's sales into the education "marketplace." In one case, Corel signed a $500,000 contract with the Ontario government to provide business software to all primary and secondary schools in the province. The Ontario government slashed its budget, then welcomed Corel with open arms.[29]

Many IT companies will be satisfied with partner relationships, and that will be the extent of their involvement with schools. But for some there may be a fifth and final stage, which will come when corporations have achieved an understanding of the education business and no longer need to partner. They'll be able to fly solo, setting up their own businesses and providing education products and services to consumers who can afford them, thus capturing a greater share of the revenue flow. William Kennedy, who has taught history, English, and math for eight years at College Street Secondary School in downtown Toronto, says, only half jokingly, that the most profitable course for computer companies would be to have technology replace teachers entirely. "They would want distance education everywhere, even if your school was a block down the road from where you live."[30] Greatly diminished provincial educational authorities could establish curriculum requirements and these could be met by private companies or public agencies. Once corporations have been invited inside the classroom, it may be difficult to escort them out again.

business's second goal for education

Colonizing the education market is one goal of business. A second is to ensure that students receive the training business deems appropriate for the workforce of the future. Both come together in computer-animation programs at Sheridan College and Centennial College. Sheridan's Oakville, Ontario, facility has a reputation for turning out animators who are snapped up by film and animation studios; it has a better than 90 percent placement rate. About 20 percent of Disney's California animators are Sheridan alumni. And this is what education should be about, says the *Globe and Mail*'s *Report on Business*. A 1996 ROB profile of Sheridan and two other high-placement programs admonished readers that "too many schools are out of touch with the demands of the job market. They should take a lesson from these . . . post-secondary masters at turning out job-ready graduates."[31]

And how are these "masters" planning to turn out job-ready graduates in the new millennium? In 1997, the Harris government provided $12 million for a new animation centre at Sheridan, a grant whose ultimate goal is to cut public support for the program, perhaps to zero, and to increase student fees 300 percent or more. The government grant was conditional on the private sector ponying up an equal amount, a condition that was met handily by the line-up of companies anxious to profit from the new centre. The private sector contributed far more than its required share ($30 million spread over five to eight years), although the contributions were in hardware and software, not cash, which is still provided by taxpayers. IBM provided the infrastructure for the centre. (IBM and Sheridan also did a side deal to work together at IBM's Pacific Development Centre on the West Coast.)

California-based Silicon Graphics (SGI), which makes high-performance computer workstations and stood to benefit the most, provided the lion's share of contributions, $22 million in equipment, software, and animation tools.[32] SGI had positioned itself in the burgeoning animation and animation-training markets in February 1995 with a $500-million takeover of Alias Research of Toronto, which creates software for special effects in Hollywood films, and Wavefront Technologies of Santa Barbara, California. SGI then set up a new subsidiary, Alias/Wavefront, to develop business in the education sector. In Ontario that meant Sheridan and the Bell Centre at Centennial College in Toronto. Overseeing the partnership is Sheridan's new chair, Glenna Carr, a former powerful Ontario civil servant whose previous posts include stints as deputy minister of skills development, commercial relations, and on the management board of Cabinet. After leaving government, she began specializing in promoting private-public partnerships, and in 1998 became president of the Canadian Council for Public-Private Partnerships, whose primary objective is to promote various forms of creative partnering as a supplement to traditional tax-based public-service financing and delivery.

This is the new model of education in Ontario, according to Robin

King, director of the animation school: "As an educational institution we have to . . . move ourselves away from being dependent on public funding. I think this is a leading-edge example of the government's initiative to go forward with that."[33] King believes that the government-corporate partnership will result in more funding for Sheridan than it received previously from the provincial ministry of education. In fact, Sheridan plans to repay the $12 million to the provincial government, once fees can be deregulated and rise to an estimated $8,600 a year (fees were $1,300 in 1996). Sheridan has no problem introducing such huge increases in fees, since, it argues, its grads are in high demand and the pay is good. When the day comes when grads are no longer in demand and the pay is no longer as good, perhaps the public sector will have to rescue the program.

Meanwhile, Sheridan's instructors maintain close relationships with industry, and many consult on industry productions. Their exposure to ongoing changes in the industry provides Sheridan with its competitive edge over other schools. Such intimate connections can be beneficial both to students, who are exposed to the most up-to-date techniques and trends, and to industry, which gets well-trained entry-level workers.

A Sheridan rival, the Bell Centre for Creative Communications at Centennial College, is also "in the business of training people who are going out there in the world and seeking work," said Walter Stewart, former dean of communications and general studies. Industry involvement in the learning environment can be of great practical advantage to his students. "The more effective and relevant our program will be, the better equipped our graduates will be."[34] There would be no one-time corporate donations. Instead, Centennial structured ongoing relationships with its technology partners to keep the facility on a par with new developments. Heading Centennial's list of partners are Bell Canada, which paid enough to have the facility named after itself, Silicon Graphics and Alias/Wavefront, and Sony of Canada. (Silicon Graphics cemented its relationship with the centre by recruiting Stewart, Centennial's former dean, who had left to take over the presidency of Smart Toronto. At SGI, Stewart became the company's market development manager for education and research.)[35]

These companies contributed more than $13 million through hardware, software, training, and services, for a total investment in the Bell Centre of $33 million. So even though Ontario's taxpayers invest 50 percent more than private corporations, they receive no acknowledgement.

The Bell Centre opened in January 1995 and at the time featured one of the highest-bandwidth networks in the country, one able to transfer 10 megabytes of data per second anywhere within the building. Each of the one hundred workstations consists of a Silicon Graphics high-performance computer and a digital camera. Information in any form – a page of text, a video, or a song – is converted to digital streams that can be shared by a variety of electronic devices, such as laser printers, computers, fax machines, and CD players.

It's a neat arrangement for the company whose equipment and software have been used in *Jurassic Park, Toy Story, The Lion King*, and *Titanic*. SGI supplies computers and software to train the next generation of animators who will work on its machines; the company can then use the facilities for training, testing, and development. SGI no longer has to fly film to Los Angeles for post-production work. Instead, Centennial will help the company retrain technicians in Toronto to do the job. Interacting with people who might one day be working for their company is also of interest to SGI.[36] And with the research capability of the college installations at its disposal, it can work on the next generation of special-effects tools. Early in the new millennium, SGI predicts that these special-effects artists will be able to create simulated human actors real enough to fool viewers. Several years later, the technology will be economical enough to put those actors in starring roles. With the soaring salaries demanded by leading actors, Hollywood studios are pushing impatiently for this development. It won't be long before virtual stars and virtual Academy Awards appear on the scene, and the global media corporations can pocket an even greater share of audience revenues. And it also won't be long before the college centres become an arm of industry, with benefits accruing to shareholders of global computer and information corporations while costs are underwritten largely by Canadian taxpayers.

a lifelong learning treadmill?

In some ways, tying education to business is not new. Business always wants education to prepare young people for their places on the shop floors and in the offices of industry and commerce. And the education system has always complied. "The encouragement of mass literacy, the development of compulsory education, mechanics' institutes, the founding of civic universities and the growth of technical colleges and universities have in their different ways been oriented around the needs of business and industry," wrote Kevin Robins and Frank Webster in an analysis of British education that applies equally to Canada. But there was "a liberal and critical dimension to education that resists subordination to the market and aspires to other — intellectual, imaginative and aesthetic — truths and values," they observe.[37] Business tolerated the traditional ideals of the civilizing, socializing, and inspiring nature of education as long as it didn't have to pay for these. What is new is that with today's budget cuts and the prospects of lower levels of public funding in the future, there will be no one left to pay for critical, liberal education. Universities and colleges like Sheridan and Centennial will provide the training and education that business wants because there will be money for this, but they will neglect the liberal and critical aspects of education because there will be little money for this.

Such a strategy is ironic. A 1998 study by UBC labour economist Robert Allen found that graduates in humanities and social sciences have a better chance of finding jobs, moving up the corporate ladder, and ending up in professional or managerial positions with higher pay; those who graduate with specific skills from technical and vocational programs start their careers with higher pay and better positions but stagnate in their thirties and forties. The difference lies in what an arts degree gives students: analytical abilities and good reading, writing, and basic computer skills, Allen notes.[38] Yet industry seems uninterested in people with these skills. It wants graduates of technical programs like those at Sheridan and Centennial, people able to quickly fill what are usually lower-level programming, animation, and systems-analysis jobs. The lack of workers for these jobs consti-

tutes the so-called skills shortage, which industry takes every opportunity to complain about.

The earlier system of mass education, as Robins and Webster
explain, was a response to the needs of a mass-production and -con-
sumption society. The purpose of education was to produce good
workers and citizens for a system whose goal was to create identical
products as quickly and as cheaply as possible. Students completed
their education, went out into the work world, and probably never
returned to school.

The new system of education is based on the notion of lifelong
learning, "the idea that seeking knowledge and understanding should
be a lifelong pursuit," writes SFU communication professor Linda
Harasim, who leads the TeleLearning Network of Centres of Excellence,
which is developing education products for global markets. There is
nothing new about this idea, she notes. "Socrates spoke forcefully on
this point. . . . What is new is the *economic importance of lifelong
learning*," she suggests, echoing the words of the Information Highway
Advisory Council. "Because of the rate at which jobs change in their
knowledge requirements, the human-resource needs of society now
demand . . . lifelong readiness to learn on the part of individuals"[39]
(italics added). As Rory McGreal of TeleEducation New Brunswick
puts it, workers in all industries will need almost constant education
to stay abreast of new technology and upgrade their skills.[40]

For Tony Bates of the University of British Columbia's distance
education centre, lifelong learning is a national duty. "The wealth of
nations will depend increasingly on knowledge-based, high-tech
industries. . . . These are highly competitive, global industries," Bates
writes. "Keeping even a few months ahead of the competition, in
terms of innovation and knowledge, is critical to survival, as is the
quality of product and service. This means that education and
training, not just in the pre-work years, but throughout a lifetime, are
essential elements of a successful workforce."[41]

In the past twenty years, industry has shifted from mass to customized production in services and goods, a system called flexible
specialization. In this economy, the goal is to produce small, customized batches, tailored to the customer's needs and incorporating

the latest technological developments. This system involves shorter, ever-changing production runs and projects, and uses workers' knowledge to reduce costs and improve quality. Decision-making is decentralized to the front lines. Production often occurs in mobile and temporary locations.

In this economy, workers are hired for specific production runs and laid off when projects are completed. As a result, education for such an economy must be continuous, or "lifelong." Having been laid off when a production run is completed, workers must upgrade their knowledge and skills, most likely at their own expense if the Sheridan College model becomes standard practice, to be competitive for the next production run. Flexible specialization means that global corporations can move products and services rapidly around the world, searching for the lowest costs and the right mix of qualified workers.[42]

Here's where telelearning comes in. If skills-upgrading courses can be delivered to unemployed workers anywhere in the world, then employers will have a larger pool of talent from which to choose, competition for jobs will be global and fierce, and wages can be ratcheted down even further. Telelearning ensures that competition for jobs cannot be contained within borders. Let's consider one example: Sheridan College works with IBM's Pacific Development Centre to mount courses on the Internet. It then signs a deal with Kimkokwing Institute of Creative Technology in Kuala Lumpur, Malaysia, which sees the Malaysian school donate $4 million to give its students access to Sheridan's courses and a chance to study in the Sheridan International program option. Students are awarded Sheridan's postgraduate diploma in digital animation upon completion of the program. As a result, Sheridan graduates will have to compete with lower-paid Malaysian grads for plum Hollywood jobs. In fact, much animation work already occurs in lower-wage areas like the Philippines and other Asian countries.

The lifelong learning, knowledge-based society presumes the changes that are occurring are inevitable – the myth of technological determinism once again – and all we can do is adapt to them by dismantling our successful hundred-year-old education system and creating something new and untested. But we need to be aware of the consequences of privatized, commercialized learning and training. (The word "education" is dropped, probably because it is associated with the word "public.") With lifelong learning go lower wages, fewer benefits, and minimal security for most workers, and higher wages, greater benefits, and increased security for the lucky few who become part of a company's small permanent workforce, which is needed to maintain the company's ongoing viability.[43]

Self-paced learning is sold as one of the great advantages of using IT in schools, but an inherent feature of IT is its monitoring and sur-veillance capabilities – a computer can keep records of every keystroke a user makes. True, students can work at their own pace, but if they're slow completing a curriculum module, that information will surely become part of their record, available for inspection by a prospective employer, especially if the employer establishes cur-riculum, as Silicon Graphics does at Sheridan College. Students will learn to solve problems on terms amenable to the controller of the system, and the system will sort out those who are most willing and able to do so. "Less able" students will be funnelled to less cogni-tively complex computer work to prepare them for lower-skilled jobs or for permanent unemployment. Each lifelong learner will be on his or her unique track, searching worldwide for that particular combina-tion of courses that will provide a competitive edge.

casting schoolnet wide

Education technology is not the problem. It's the purpose for which it is introduced that causes the concerns and creates the threats to democracy. One of the greatest challenges to public information is Industry Canada's SchoolNet program, Canada's "champion of life-long learning," as its mission statement tells us, and a showcase for the Chrétien government's Connecting Canadians strategy. SchoolNet was launched in May 1993 and touted as a means to "plug kids into the world," as government spin doctors put it. Led by Doug Hull, director-general of science promotion and academic affairs at Industry Canada and a member of CANARIE's education steering committee, SchoolNet is ostensibly meant to provide teachers and students across Canada with an easy-to-use single platform to access the Internet. Ottawa budgeted $52 million over four years to hook up 15,290 schools to the Internet.

SchoolNet went through two phases. The first raised suspicions that the program, under the guise of providing access, was really about developing markets for the so-called learning and training industry; the second phase confirmed these suspicions. This is not surprising, given SchoolNet's sponsorship by Industry Canada, which has neither the mandate nor the jurisdiction to support education. Industrial development is the name of this game, although in the first phase this agenda was tempered by traditional education concerns. SchoolNet was guided by a large (and unwieldy) advisory board of fifty-five, and the board members represented many interests, from industry groups such as Stentor and the Information Technology Association of Canada (ITAC) to school administrators, teachers, school boards, home and school associations, principals, other public institutions such as the Canadian Library Association and Science World, and the educational networking operations of all the provincial education ministries. Industry Canada and Human Resources Development Canada were the federal representatives. Freenets, CA*net, and CANARIE were also represented.

Many members of this board supported commercialization, but there were alternative and critical voices too. Heather-jane Robertson reported one attempt, led by Marita Moll of the Canadian Teachers' Federation, to undermine a 1995–96 communications plan that contained strategies to attract sponsors and partners to the program and to get the message out to the media about the importance of the information highway to education. This initiative came from SchoolNet's Communication and Partnership Committee, which was chaired by Douglas Knox of ITAC. As a result of this mini-insurrection, Robertson reports, Industry Canada convened the board only once during the next two years, while government technocrats and industry executives could get on with the job at hand.[44]

With the four-year funding period coming to an end and a second phase beginning, the advisory board was disbanded and its members presented with letters and certificates recognizing their contributions (repeating the pattern of the CA*net board, which a few months earlier had turned the Canadian Internet over to CANARIE and Bell Advanced Communications and voted itself out of existence). The new board of twenty-one, appointed by Industry Canada shortly after, was more amenable to the commercialization agenda.

In the new phase, which extends broadband connectivity to 250,000 classrooms, SchoolNet acts like a broker, which allows information and technology companies – the learnware sector, Doug Hull calls it – to market their products and services at cut-rate prices directly on-line to budget-conscious schools. The new SchoolNet Web site intermingles offerings from educational institutions and commercial vendors without identifying their origins. You can select sites like teenSIZZLE, an on-line magazine that contains edifying articles such as the one about a thirteen-year-old "businessman" who's a Grade 8 student in a West Vancouver school and has an Internet business creating Web pages for local companies.[45] Or you can click on "the Brainium" on SchoolNet's homepage and be told that the Brainium is an award-winning on-line science resource for Grades 4 through 8. Click again and you are whisked, in the blink of an eye, from the .ca domain to .com and the Brainium homepage.[46] Click on "Information" and, in the fine print at the bottom of the page, learn that Brainium is produced by MultiActive Education. Click on the "MultiActive Education" button and you are taken to another corporate site, where you find out that MultiActive Education is an industry leader in the production of on-line education resources for the global marketplace and a subsidiary of MultiActive Group, which you later learn is owned by Vancouver billionaire Terry Hui, head of Concord Pacific Developments Corp., which is developing the former Expo 86 site on Vancouver's False Creek (and which paid $500,000 to get its name on the Vancouver Public Library memorial cards when the new building opened).[47]

The brains behind the Brainium is David Vogt, a SchoolNet advisory board member and the former executive director of Science World, the golfball-shaped centre nestled snugly beside Hui's Concord Pacific land at the east end of False Creek. In 1994, Vogt was part of a research team developing a common technology format for all levels of education — K-12, post-secondary, and informal — in COECEE, which included BC's Open Learning Agency, Simon Fraser University, MPR Teltech, the research arm of BC Telecom, and the Stentor Alliance, as well as Science World. Science World's target was the K-12 market with its electronic science magazine called *Science Eh*? Vogt recognized that he had a "hot product" on his hands, but he did not have the capability to take it forward.[48] Enter neighbour Terry Hui, who was starting his second fortune in communications and IT, wiring all his buildings with fibre-optic cable, forming a partnership with BC Telecom to offer cable services to Concord Pacific–developed buildings (getting up Ted Rogers's nose in the process), and acquiring a popular software package called Maximizer, which allows companies to fire sales staff and automate their activities.

Vogt soon left the science centre to work on the electronic magazine — renamed Brainium — for Hui, who plans to spend $11 million over six years to commercialize the product around the world. (To compensate Science World, MultiActive donates some of the proceeds from licensing Brainium to the Science World Foundation to promote science literacy.)

Hui and Vogt got off to a fast start. The B.C. ministry of education licensed Brainium for three years, paying $500 a school, which allows any of the 1,100 schools in the province to register with MultiActive and receive the product and customer support.[49] SchoolNet did a similar deal with MultiActive, and that's how Brainium ended up on the SchoolNet Web site. SchoolNet claims Brainium's teacher materials are professionally written, and they certainly are, but the balance in some of Science World's earlier work under Vogt has been questioned. For instance, the Minegames Gallery, a partnership between Science World and the mining industry of Canada, was a major project for Science World in 1994. The "mining industry is facing the problem that nobody wants mines any more," Vogt told an audience in 1996, "because the environmental lobby was so strong about every mine . . . polluting and [being] destructive. We don't want the message put out that mines are good, but we want people to understand how complex the issues are and get away from the emotional side. . . . We aren't predisposed to any kind of message," Vogt assured his listeners, "but here is a huge industry that needed to get a message across and wasn't able to do so with TV and brochures and other media that people are largely immune to."[50] Science World came to the rescue.

SchoolNet's GrassRoots Projects Program gives $300, $600, or $900 to teachers to create projects that can be mounted on the Internet. Industry Canada's objective is to create content of interest and relevance to teachers and students, and thus increase the number of students using the Internet. GrassRoots builds, very cheaply, a database of content for CANARIE's high-speed networks and promotes the message that children need computer-technology skills if they are to compete in the knowledge-based economy. In phase 1 of GrassRoots, funding came from Industry Canada and the taxpayers; in phase 2, Bill Gates and other corporate interests provide the funds. At a news conference in Toronto in October 1998, Gates and Manley announced the launch of the GrassRoots National Campaign, and Gates contributed $1 million over three years to provide teachers with software (Microsoft software, of course), funds, and access to training. The first phase produced only 600 projects. The new phase was expected to produce 20,000 projects, involving 5 million students. With Gates's money in hand, Manley would have to shop around for another $14 million to reach his target. Gates's largesse was nothing more than a donation to a government department by a private company. The most disturbing aspect of the event is that Manley seemed not even aware that there could be a problem with conflict of interest. His spin doctors (Earnscliffe Strategy Group, which also acts for the Microsoft-dominated Canadian Alliance Against Software Theft) framed it as a constructive and innovative form of partnership.[51]

SchoolNet also displayed questionable judgement when it helped resurrect the discredited Youth News Network (YNN). YNN is a Canadian knock-off of Chris Whittle's infamous Channel One in the States. In exchange for a free satellite dish and TV monitors, students are required to watch nine minutes of news and three minutes of youth-targeted advertising daily. Nearly half of all schools tune in every morning to Channel One. In 1992, promoter Rod MacDonald began pitching YNN to Canadian education ministries and school boards, largely unsuccessfully. Even though school administrators salivated at the prospect of getting their hands on the free equipment, most parents bridled at the thought of their children becoming members of a captive audience for such blatant commercialism. After all, twelve minutes a day adds up to seven full school days a year. MacDonald's spin was that YNN was about "media education," and that it was good for students because it was a "tool to understand how media work." But that was before the Internet and SchoolNet.[52]

In 1998, MacDonald was back again, with the same basic hustle but in a new wrapping. YNN would deliver news and current-affairs programming and, as before, the ads that pay for the service, and would also provide "leading-edge multimedia computer labs." Each school that signs up will be equipped with a satellite-receiving dish, internal cabling system linking classrooms, one 27-inch TV monitor per classroom, and a computer lab equipped with multimedia computers. A daily 12.5-minute program – with 2.5 minutes of ads – will be downloaded to the school satellite. To get these goodies, schools must sign a five-year contract that obliges the school to show 90 percent of all programs to 90 percent of the population of their school. YNN is a service for high schools only, and it targets the 2.5 million high-school students in Canada, the demographic segment with most money to spend.[53] In the U.S., advertisers pay up to $200,000 (Cdn.) for a thirty-second spot. A 1997 study by the Consumers' Union found that 80 percent of Channel One's news content was slanted towards the sponsor's product. The educational benefits are minimal, but students' retention of the ads is very high.[54]

YNN's new approach was all about hardware, software, education content, and backbone infrastructure. MacDonald could rest assured that he had all the buzzwords correct: he retained the services of Hill & Knowlton Canada, one of Ottawa's most powerful PR and lobbying operations. Hill & Knowlton consultant Jeff Smith, who came to the firm from the office of Liberal Cabinet minister Sheila Copps, was the registered lobbyist for Microsoft Canada in all its information highway activities. MacDonald had chosen wisely: Hill & Knowlton know exactly what moves Industry Canada. He launched his marketing campaign for the new YNN on February 8, 1999. The news release was on the SchoolNet Web site the next day, with a link to the

YNN site.[55] MacDonald hopes to have a million pairs of eyes watching his daily ads by June 2002. With SchoolNet's help, he might just do it.

frank mckenna meets mighty microsoft

SchoolNet's role in aiding the colonization of public education can be seen everywhere. Perhaps the best example is New Brunswick, where the information industry is an equal partner in education, thanks to Premier Frank McKenna's determination – and New Brunswick Telephone's business strategy – to transform the province from lobsters and maple syrup to call centres and education technology. McKenna was the first premier with an e-mail address and NB Tel the first telco to fully digitize all services and install fibre-optic wiring in urban areas.

Fundy Communications, the province's leading cable operator, even built its own fibre-optic network. To make their investment worthwhile in a small, slow-growth province, NB Tel and Fundy rely on business and support from the McKenna government. McKenna and NB Tel teamed up to market New Brunswick as a good location for call centres, for example. (McKenna retained his connection to the telephone company after retiring as premier – he was quickly appointed to the board of Bruncor, NB Tel's parent company.) By 1998, more than fifty companies had heeded the call, attracted by New Brunswick's telecommunications infrastructure, a bilingual workforce that was rarely late for work (according to one call-centre company, which decided to expand operations in New Brunswick), lower wages, and McKenna's personal touch – often his would be the voice on the phone when a company contacted the provincial government with questions about call centres. There was also the controversial policy of providing a $10,000-a-job subsidy for employee training. Jobs were created, but most were not new and had merely relocated to New Brunswick because of its compelling package of benefits and inducements.

To encourage New Brunswickers to embrace the information age, become trained for call-centre jobs, and purchase telecom and cable services, McKenna's government made basic computer literacy a requirement for high-school and community-college graduation. It's significant that this new directive was announced at the same time as

NB Tel and Northern Telecom made public their plan to wire 60 percent of New Brunswick with fibre-optic cable. Thanks to SchoolNet, every school in the province was connected to the Internet by 1995; in 1996, McKenna gave a $250 sales-tax rebate to residents who bought home computers that could access the Internet. NB Tel's high-speed Video Active Network (VAN) provides video-on-demand services, and its 1997 trials delivered educational materials to homes and schools.

Toronto-based Digital Renaissance, which develops software for interactive services, is NB Tel's partner in its video-on-demand service.[56] It has some powerful owners: BCE with 20 percent and Atlantis Communications, Canada's largest producer of movies and TV programs, with 10 percent. Thus the ducks are lined up to pour commercial offerings into New Brunswick schoolrooms. Around the same time as NB Tel's trials, the province spent $6 million to lease 3,400 new computers and connect them to the Internet over NB Tel's VAN, providing new business for the phone company and its partners, and bringing to 13,000 the number of Web-enabled computers in the public-school system. The deal would also help Rory McGreal's TeleEducation operation.

TeleEducation was distance education in New Brunswick in the pre-Web era. It linked the province's universities, colleges, and secondary schools to more than fifty scattered distance-learning sites, where students could take courses electronically. TeleEducation didn't offer its own courses but delivered to individual learners courses put on by public and private institutions, the result of a 1992 federal-provincial co-operation agreement worth $10.5 million. It was decidedly low-tech – 486 PCs, 14.4 Kbs modems, Windows 3.1 operating systems, and a conferencing system called Smart, which allows students to communicate with each other in real time – but it worked. TeleEducation provided access to educational programs to all New Brunswick residents, reducing the historical inequities between New Brunswick's urban, rural, and isolated regions.[57]

Educating residents of rural New Brunswick was certainly necessary for McKenna to be able to continue selling the advantages of his well-educated, computer-literate workforce to prospective call-centre operators. But he had a second goal: he wanted to use education as a lever of economic development, designing courses and programs that could be delivered anywhere in the world over the Internet. Such a strategy might create new jobs by encouraging a home-grown information-technology industry. TeleCampus, a TeleEducation off-shoot, is exactly this kind of economic development masquerading as education, the result of a second Canada–New Brunswick Regional Economic Development Agreement. "We in New Brunswick see education as an industry," said TeleEducation director Rory McGreal,[58] echoing the words of the IHAC (McGreal was a member of its Learning and Training Working Group) and of CANARIE (he was a member of the education steering committee).

The provincial ministry of advanced education and labour and TeleEducation together put up $14.5 million over four years to bring together public and private educational offerings on the Internet. Their goal is to have 10,000 students taking on-line courses by the year 2000. McGreal feels a sense of urgency to develop TeleCampus into a fully functioning "virtual" campus. "The key is that whoever gets content out there and on-line fast enough will be successful," he said.[59]

So the race is on, but the question is, Whose content? The answer: It doesn't matter. TeleCampus went on-line in September 1997, providing some English- and French-language courses from New Brunswick Community College and the universities and some from private vendors. Significantly, the TeleCampus Web page – headlined "New Brunswick Institutions Offering Online Courses" – does not differentiate between public and private offerings.[60] One of these New Brunswick "institutions" is Scholars.com, which is based in Fredericton, the provincial capital, and received most of its start-up financing from the New Brunswick government, but it is not a New Brunswick institution, nor is it about education, despite the catchy name. Scholars.com is a subsidiary of CBT Systems, the world's largest developer of self-paced training in information technology. CBT is based in Menlo Park, California, and the parent company's head office is in Dublin, Ireland. Scholars.com specializes in software training, and offers Microsoft (and a few Novell) training courses to prepare students to write certification exams.[61] It is nothing more than a private training institute, of which there are thousands in

Canada. Such institutes fulfil a valuable function for a narrowly defined purpose. The difference here is that because Scholars.com is on-line, it is sanctioned and promoted by TeleCampus and the ministry of advanced education. And it provides one more link between the McKenna government and Microsoft.

Microsoft first appeared on the provincial scene in 1995. The software giant began building an education and training network in more than forty countries and a dozen languages as one spin-off of its Windows 95 and Microsoft Network products. Microsoft chose New Brunswick as a Canadian test site because of the McKenna–NB Tel team. Microsoft's managers liked NB Tel's burgeoning fibre-optic network, and they saw McKenna as one of them, a highly entrepreneurial man committed to the new technologies.[62] (Although, as John Ralston Saul points out in *Voltaire's Bastards*, political leaders and corporate managers, by definition, can be neither capitalistic – they use other people's, not their own, capital – nor entrepreneurial – they're members of bureaucracies and don't take personal financial risks – but they both can and do spout the rhetoric of capitalism, and perhaps that's what attracted Microsoft.)

All public schools in the province were tied into the Microsoft Network when it was launched. Under the Microsoft plan, courses from kindergarten to Grade 12 are offered via computer link-up through a school's computer centre, a library, or at home. After signing on, users become registered students, free to roam the campus and use its resources, and are charged a fee for courses they take. Microsoft provides the network and some computer training, while the education department approves courses. The network can be expanded to encompass training schools accredited by the New Brunswick government, such as Scholars.com. All participants, of course, have to use Windows 95.

The project cannot help students without access to a computer. But Microsoft Canada general manager Frank Clegg argued, "We have always believed that if you offer a service, people will find a way to find access to the hardware"[63] – yet another "build it and they will come" visionary! In 1995, the Microsoft spin doctors designated this as the Microsoft Institute. But perhaps that sounded too clinical, because several years later the name was changed to Anytime, Anywhere Learning and was tied to a requirement that students have access to laptop computers, reducing further the need for schools, and perhaps teachers too (although in 1995 Frank McKenna tried to reassure teachers by saying that the Microsoft Institute was "an aid to teachers, not a replacement to teachers"). Not only does Microsoft Network connect New Brunswick with education resources around the world, it connects worldwide users with New Brunswick's education offerings. "Wherever you happen to live in the world, you could sign up and get a New Brunswick education," commented Ken Nickerson, director of technical services for Microsoft Canada. "You could live in Malaysia, get your New Brunswick high school credits, and then apply for admission to any university in the world."[64]

Microsoft has been signing the same deals with national, state, and provincial governments, as well as universities and colleges around the world, so it will have the right to distribute Microsoft software packages at deeply subsidized prices. As a result, few students are likely to pay the full price to buy a package from any competitor, such as Corel, which mimicked Microsoft's strategy in some provinces with deeply discounted WordPerfect and other software packages, but is a flea beside the 800-pound Microsoft gorilla. As Nathan Newman, project director for NetAction, an on-line activist organization, explains the U.S. situation, "Microsoft is using strategic monopolistic pricing in the education market, with the government's assistance, to turn our state university systems into private workforce training programs for Microsoft."[65] Deep discounts of 90 to 95 percent cost the software giant nothing, since the cost of reproducing software is nearly zero. Under the guise of charitable donations to education, Newman claims, Microsoft is effectively locking in its software monopoly. The process is economic dumping disguised as generosity, he says. Once a monopoly is locked in, Microsoft can raise prices, as it has done with its Office and BackOffice products. And once Microsoft dominates the education market and knocks out the competition, the sweet deals to universities and provincial governments will likely disappear and students will see prices jacked up, Newman predicts.

For Microsoft, accessing the education market is not just about gaining a monopoly over software. The company targets the training market too, spending hundreds of millions of dollars a year to ensure workers are trained in its technology so that business executives will feel pressured to adopt Microsoft products.[66] With the exception of Novell, Microsoft is the only software vendor to have its own professional certification credential.

Scholars.com is a small piece of Microsoft's worldwide training and certification program, Skills 2000, which trained more than 1.2-million technicians in 1997. Anyone in New Brunswick taking Scholars.com courses is eligible for a Microsoft Skills 2000 loan, which provides "a flexible low-cost way to begin a new career in the IT field or to enhance your current IT skills."[67] It reaches these prospective customers through a combination of partnerships with computer vendors, commercial training centres, a free television-based training program, training sessions linked to conferences around the country, and provincial education officials. But New Brunswick education officials should be asking if private training institutes like Scholars.com provide unbiased technical education or merely act as a marketing arm of Microsoft.

Microsoft also goes after the academic market, hooking up more than 300 academic institutions and 40,000 students a year through its Authorized Academic Training Program. It provides free technical training to teachers and educators and has shaped those academic programs to create Microsoft-certified professionals. It then adds an academic stamp of approval to its own programs with its Twenty-First Century Campus in the Connected Learning Community, piling up all the buzzwords into one unsavoury heap. Instead of working in classrooms, buildings, labs, and libraries, learners will have twenty-four-hour, seven-day-a-week access to Microsoft Exchange servers, Windows NT operating systems, and Microsoft Office word-processing, spreadsheet, and database programs from anywhere in the world. With training and software standardized around Microsoft, campuses will likely find it too expensive in the future to switch back to a more diversified computing environment.

The extent of Microsoft's ambition to dominate the education market is epitomized in the ill-fated California Education Technology

Initiative (CETI). This consortium, which included hardware allies GTE Corp., Hughes Aircraft, and Fujitsu, signed an unprecedented deal with California State University in 1997 to give it a monopoly – Microsoft's favourite situation – over the telecommunications infrastructure and marketing and delivery of on-line courses to 500,000 students and faculty in the system for a ten-year period. The consortium would invest $365 million in infrastructure and receive an estimated $3.12 billion in revenues over the ten years of the deal. Campus administrators went for it because state legislators were unprepared to spend $365 million themselves. Given Microsoft's traditional profit margins of 50 to 80 percent of revenues, it was a sweet deal indeed. As Nathan Newman of NetAction explains,

> For Microsoft, control of the central servers and software
> standards for the largest university system in the country will give
> it an unprecedented opportunity to expand its control of computing
> standards. . . . By supporting only Microsoft's spreadsheets, databases
> and word processors, Microsoft will make sure that the only
> integrated approach to computing on campus with technical
> support will be through Microsoft products.[68]

The ill-conceived project was finally killed as a result of intense opposition from students – who objected to being turned into a captive market for company products – and faculty members – who were not consulted and feared that CETI would dictate content for their courses based on what would sell. California-based competitors like Apple, Netscape, and Sun Microsystems also opposed the deal because they were excluded (not one company in the consortium was California-based).

Nathan Newman and NetAction distributed carefully researched materials questioning the legitimacy of the deal through its Web site and e-mail lists. Eventually, the commercial media picked up the story. The ensuing negative publicity convinced Microsoft to withdraw. Open computing standards that can lead to creativity and innovation are what public and post-secondary graduates need, not competency in one company's (perhaps inferior) products.

public resource or private market?

Unfortunately, few people in Canada are raising questions about the education-technology fiefdoms being created by Microsoft, the telephone companies, Silicon Graphics, and IBM. Little controversy was sparked by Bill Gates's donation of $1 million to SchoolNet, when questions should have been asked about the ethical propriety and pedagogical value of the gift. There may be real benefits from on-line education technology, but these need to be carefully and realistically evaluated in light of corporate strategies. Courses offered by private training organizations that enhance IT skills are an example of how the on-line format makes good sense, as long as there is an arm's-length relationship between public and private education authorities. Expensive executive MBA programs are another example. Students are often mature, busy, high-level, highly paid business people, and they sometimes live and work in locations that are remote from the university program they wish to take. They, or more often their companies, can afford to pay for the expensive multipoint video-conferencing systems that allow a lecturer in one location to maintain real-time contact with students in many locations.

On-line education technology also gives people who live in remote parts of Canada equal access to courses and programs. This was key in the initial development of distance education and remains a worthy and desirable goal, one that needs to be pursued. But since most Canadians live in urban areas, the question remains: How can such a marginal use, while beneficial, justify large investments in information infrastructure? Clearly the corporate target is people living in urban areas. Here too, though, education technology can be a benefit. It can be used, for instance, by people who live near educational institutions but cannot attend on-campus or day courses because of parental responsibilities, full-time employment, disabilities, or any other obstacle that makes them physically unable to reach educational establishments. Distance education can also help people who live in one province and want to attend a university in another province without incurring heavy travel and living expenses.

But the benefits need to be placed beside the costs of turning education into a market. With hundreds of partnerships being consummated in dozens of locations in each province, all creating content to be used internally or to be marketed elsewhere, there is a great danger that authorities will lose control of the public education agenda and the setting of common curriculum. There will be mini-curricula everywhere, with an inevitable diminution of public information – information that we all need to be members of a community. And once corporations have successfully partnered with educational institutions and built up their own libraries of courses, what's to stop them from establishing new education centres tied to large corporations and their need for core and contingent workers?

Many teachers worry that the emphasis on computers is coming at the expense of programs in art, physical education, and music, all hit by government cutbacks to education. Then there's the concern, expressed by labour leaders and others, that corporate partners will influence the curriculum, if even unconsciously. Will a curriculum unit on technology, with IBM as a partner, provide the views of technophobes like Neil Postman and Clifford Stolle? Will all points of view continue to be presented impartially to students? Will the concept of technological determinism (as discussed in Chapter 3) be subjected to critical study in a Microsoft-sponsored curriculum unit, or will it be presented as fact? Will Microsoft rewrite history?

And should computers be a priority, especially in poorer inner-city areas? Toronto's Leslieville Public School has only nineteen computers for 500 students and half were acquired through the efforts of parents and teachers. Says principal Charles Carr: "We are an inner-city school, so we don't necessarily have all the resources of other schools. But our kids have to be provided with an equal opportunity to succeed as affluent kids with home computers in Rosedale."[69] Eighty percent of students at Leslieville are East Asian, and their first language is either Cantonese or Vietnamese. Very few have home computers. Asks Simona Chiose in *This Magazine*, "Can a computer and a modem in every classroom really improve the high-school drop-out rate, or make computer scientists out of kids who fall asleep in class because they didn't have breakfast? Unfortunately we may be counting on a techno-fix for political and social problems we are simply unwilling to address."[70]

Some teachers aren't listening. As if in a mass trance, educators from coast to coast have seen the light and its name is information technology. Without computer skills, they attest in workshops that verge on religious revivals, their wards, once out of school, will be thrown on the dunghill of eternal joblessness. Salvation lies in learning those skills. Students, trade in your textbooks for IBM laptop computers and Microsoft software at deeply discounted prices. At a news conference held in Toronto in October 1998 to announce Bill Gates's $1-million contribution to Industry Canada's GrassRoots Program, a Grade 11 student proclaims via satellite feed from Iberville, Quebec, "Two years ago, I had never touched a computer keyboard. I now have a multimedia company I started with my friend . . . to serve local businesses."

Hallelujah, brothers and sisters! Steel yourself against the devil himself, who, disguised as Neil Postman, doubts there is any need for schools to set themselves up as teachers of computer skills, since students seem to pick these up on their own. Even more sacrilegiously, he doubts that schools should focus on training for employment, especially in computer-related jobs. The skills taught today in school will be obsolete in a few years, and no one can know what future employment trends will be. Better to teach students thinking and problem-solving skills they can use in any kind of future, he suggests, heretical thoughts for edutech fundamentalists.[71] There's accumulating evidence that music training improves education performance. The U.S. College Board, which administers the Scholastic Aptitude Test (SAT) for university admissions, found that music and drama students outperformed others by 42 points in math scores. Another study showed that piano instruction beat computer instruction in enhancing children's abstract reasoning skills, those needed for learning math and science.[72]

But the devil won't go away. He returns with a question that should have been obvious all along. In the discussions about lifelong learning and the knowledge economy, hardly any thought has been directed to the purposes of education beyond providing skills industry wants. Is there no nobler aim than this? Why are we educating our children?

One possibility, Postman suggests, is that we should want them to learn how to live on a finite planet, an option he calls Spaceship Earth. It is the story of human beings as stewards of the earth, caretakers of a vulnerable space capsule. In this scenario, the purpose of education would be to inculcate in children a value of lifelong caring for the environment, not necessarily lifelong learning for industry. And if we are to care for our planet, we need first to learn to care for our schools, our neighbourhoods, and our cities.[73] Information technology might have a role in this vision of education, but not a major one. Face-to-face communication and group interaction are the dominant information networks. How distorted, then, that IBM's worldwide advertising slogan is "Solutions for a Small Planet," without acknowledging the problems its products and services are meant to solve – certainly not those of Spaceship Earth. But "Solutions for a Small Planet" works because it is classic propaganda, conflating society's need to survive with business's need for profit.

what does industry want?

*The 20th century has been characterized by three developments
of great political importance: the growth of democracy; the growth
of corporate power; and the growth of corporate propaganda as
a means of protecting corporate power against democracy.*

— Alex Carey, *Taking the Risk Out of Democracy*

*Democracy and capitalism have very different values. Democracy
believes in radical equality. . . . Capitalism believes in radical
inequality.*

— Lester Thurow, *Boston Globe*, 9 September 1997

The colonization of education is a radical agenda, and one that few
citizens will support if they are given an adequate explanation of
what business is doing. But if it follows the same route as the FTA,
NAFTA, tax and pension "reform," and other important issues, citizens likely won't receive that adequate explanation. Canadians were
kept confused or misinformed, and these schemes went ahead even
though they were not in the interests of most citizens. This is cause
for concern. Business seems eminently successful at achieving what it
wants with relatively little public opposition, even if what business
wants goes against the interests of most citizens.

Alex Carey, Australia's critic of corporate power, would not be surprised by any of this. He has identified three major political developments in the twentieth century: the growth of democracy, the growth of corporate power, and the growth of corporate propaganda to protect corporate power against democracy. Carey defines propaganda as "communications where the form and content is selected with the single-minded purpose of bringing some target audience to adopt attitudes and beliefs chosen in advance by the sponsors of the communications." Successfully selling NAFTA, with its charter of rights for corporations, Carey would say, is one major victory by corporate propaganda over democracy. He contrasts propaganda with education, where, "at least ideally, the purpose is to encourage critical enquiry and to open minds to arguments for and against any particular conclusion, rather than close them to the possibility of any conclusion but one."[1]

The word "propaganda" is a harsh one for North Americans. An activity we have been "propagandized" into believing can be applied only to the "bad guys," the Hitlers and Stalins of the world, never to us and our political and corporate leaders. "The success of business propaganda in persuading us, for so long, that we are free from propaganda is one of the most significant propaganda achievements of the twentieth century."[2] We condemn the management of public opinion in totalitarian states such as Nazi Germany, the Soviet Union, and China because it implies the loss of personal freedom and democracy. But we applaud, or at least tolerate as good business and public-policy practice, the management of public opinion in a democracy like Canada. Why is there such a double standard? asks Carey. His answer is that business interests are never promoted as special interests (i.e., we never acknowledge that business interests are all about wanting to preserve wealth and privilege). Rather, corporate propaganda has been successful in merging the national interest with business interests.[3] We are told — and we accept without blinking an eye — for instance, that we need to promote our IT *industry* by giving it subsidies and tax breaks so that *Canada* can survive in the global age. In this way, Canada and industry have been cleverly joined together as one: what's good for business is good for the country.

Another great triumph was industry's success at tying individual freedom, a value we all deeply cherish, to free enterprise and the free market, concepts we instinctively suspect (as if the freedom to exploit people and damage the environment was an inherent right of humankind). A small but powerful sector of society has convinced us that "the free-enterprise system which sponsors [propaganda] is some kind of bulwark and guarantor of a democratic society."[4] Most people will recognize that Carey's characterization of propaganda applies to advertising and public relations, the instruments by which public opinion is managed in a democracy. Indeed, he argues that through advertising and PR, propaganda is more highly developed and sophisticated in Western industrial democracies than it ever was in Nazi Germany or the Stalinist Soviet Union.

Modern propaganda and public relations are distinctly American creations that resulted largely from that nation's entry into the Great War in 1917. Within a week of declaring war, President Woodrow Wilson set up the Committee on Public Information (CPI) to sell his Crusade for the American Way to a sceptical and largely pacifist public. By the end of the war, committee chairman George Creel and his phalanx of journalists, publicists, advertising executives, novelists, historians, and muckrakers, using every available medium of communication, turned CPI into an effective organ for shaping public opinion. The war that was reported to the American people was the war CPI wanted them to see.

After the war was over, many Creel operatives turned their efforts to another crusade: making the world safe for business. They applied the lessons they had learned in wartime to the marketplace and the domestic political arena. One Creel alumnus was Ivy Lee, the first great PR man, who taught business how to use the press. He established his reputation by helping John D. Rockefeller clean up his image, no mean feat given Rockefeller's brutal treatment of workers in the Ludlow, Colorado, massacre and during a coal-miners' strike in West Virginia, as well as his ruthless crushing of competitors.

Another Creel graduate, Edward Bernays, a member of the committee's foreign press bureau, developed and dominated the new public-relations and domestic propaganda field for the next thirty years. He had no difficulty in associating the PR industry with the word "propaganda" – he even titled his 1928 book on the industry *Propaganda*. Bernays earned his place in PR annals for his ability to create news – he would place self-serving stories favourable to his clients' interests in the news media without indicating the origins of the stories. It's a tribute to Bernays' genius at manipulation that even today studies estimate that 60 percent of news stories originate with corporate and PR sources. He also offered a rationale for the use of propaganda in a democracy. An article Bernays wrote on this subject in 1947 raised Carey's ire. He claimed that Bernays "firmly and deceitfully asserted" that engineering consent is "the very essence of the democratic process, the freedom to persuade and suggest."[5] This article became the bible for corporate interests. The same year, *Fortune* magazine started pushing the line that it is as hard to imagine a genuine democracy without the science of persuasion (i.e., propaganda) as it is to think of a totalitarian state without coercion. By the 1950s, the belief that democracy was not possible without public relations (i.e., propaganda) was commonly held.

Joseph Goebbels and Adolf Hitler had been much impressed by the Americans' propaganda success in the First World War, and they sought to ensure that the Nazi regime followed the principles that Lee, Bernays, and their fellow collaborators had established. Hitler's *Mein Kampf*, published in German in 1926, described how effective Allied propaganda had been in contrast to Germany's, which, Hitler believed, contributed to the demoralization of German soldiers and the country's eventual defeat. *Mein Kampf* also outlined the Nazis' basic propaganda principles: appeal to emotion, not reason; repeat a few ideas constantly; use stereotyped phrases; put forward only one side of the story – an accurate description of modern advertising. In 1933, through German industrialist I.G. Farben, the Nazis invited Ivy Lee to meet with Hitler and Goebbels and provide advice on PR matters. Farben had retained Lee to help improve Germany's image in the U.S., a task that provoked an enormous American backlash when it became known.

The Second World War was a draw between the Allies and the Germans on the propaganda front, as both sides furiously applied the principles developed by the Committee on Public Information and refined by Bernays. After the war, the word "propaganda" disappeared from the academic literature because of its negative connotations, only to be replaced by "persuasion" and even "communications." Generations of academics in sociology and communication departments received corporate funding to study how to persuade people and shape public opinion.

Advertising and public relations burrowed deeply into North American thinking, becoming an accepted part of the modern landscape, while propaganda was erased from the public mind. A 1998 biography of Bernays, written by a *Boston Globe* reporter, was titled *The Father of Spin*,[6] and the review in *Business Week,* written by a former bureau chief who had worked in PR, was headlined "The High Priest of Hype." Hype and spin are a long way from propaganda.

The word "propaganda" reappeared in the late 1970s in the work of Noam Chomsky, Edward Herman, and Carey, who studied with Chomsky.[7] At the same time, business changed the way it managed democracy as a result of the successes of the early environmental movement. Within a very short period – five years – business's reputation had suffered a precipitous decline as a result of environmental activism. Something new had to be tried to combat its growing negative image. This time business combined its traditional grassroots propaganda campaigns with a greatly expanded treetops approach. As we learned in Chapter 4, grassroots propaganda is intended to reach as large a number of people as possible, and to change public opinion through a combination of advertising, public-relations, and opinion-polling activities. Treetops propaganda, by contrast, is aimed at influencing the leaders of society – politicians, bureaucrats, news editors, reporters, economics commentators – and its ultimate goal is to set the terms of debate and determine the kinds of questions that will come to dominate public discussion.[8]

In the early 1970s, American conservatives from various backgrounds created a movement that would come to be known as the New Right. It brought together "idea people" like Paul Weyrich and Ed Feulner and "money people" like the heads of the Olin, Coors, and Richard Mellon Scaife foundations.[9] They took two existing right-wing institutions, the Hoover Institution on War, Peace and Revolution (established in 1919 to develop anti-Bolshevik propaganda) and the American Enterprise Institute, and created a network of think-tanks that operates on both grassroots and treetops levels. Carey saw this as an "elite version of the factory system," where think-tanks recruit intellectuals who convert millions of corporate dollars into up-market propaganda for corporate interests. Within a few years, corporate money had set up treetops-oriented think-tanks in the United Kingdom, the United States, and Canada (including the Canada West Foundation in 1972, the C.D. Howe Institute in 1973, the Fraser Institute in 1974, the Business Council on National Issues in 1976, and the Conference Board of Canada, which had existed as an arm of the American National Institute Conference Board since 1954, but was established as a separate legal entity in 1981). They proceeded at an increasingly frenzied pace to attempt to reverse the gains in political, social, and economic rights that had been achieved by citizens in the first seventy years of the century. In the U.S., their work in the late 1970s to early 1980s led to the defeat of labour-law reform and consumer protection laws, the downfall of some prominent liberal senators, a rise in the proportion of Americans who thought there was too much government regulation, and the election of Ronald Reagan. The victories of Margaret Thatcher and Brian Mulroney followed soon after.

By the 1990s, the industrialized world was saturated with right-wing propaganda institutes. In the U.S., a powerful handful dominates the national political scene, including the well-funded Washington, D.C.–based American Enterprise Institute (1996 revenues, $16.5 million [U.S.]) and the Heritage Foundation (1996 revenues, $28.7 million [U.S.]). Business interests have deemed it necessary to develop a parallel set of propaganda institutes at the local level, since they also need to change public opinion about issues of state/provincial and municipal governments. In the U.S., most states have one propaganda institute, some have several. Canadian corporate interests followed this regionalization pattern, establishing AIMS in Atlantic Canada, the Frontier Centre for Public Policy in Winnipeg, and the Canadian Property Rights Research Institute in Calgary during the 1990s. They "publish reports advocating deregulation, privatization, property rights, school choice and a few other topics. And each produces reports that sound the same as the others."[10]

As the combined grassroots-treetops strategy succeeds, Carey observed in the late 1970s,

> public discussion no longer assumes, for example, that affluent societies have a first responsibility to provide jobs for all who want them, and the debate is instead about whether 6 or 10 percent is a "natural" (and, by implication, acceptable) level of unemployment. It no longer takes for granted that we have a right to clean air; rather debate centres on how far the cost to industry for polluting the community is economically acceptable. The debate ceases to be about how far and in what areas it is necessary for government to be involved in the economy and centres instead on arguments for reduced government involvement and timetables for achieving this. . . . And finally, with successful treetops propaganda, the debate will never be about the curtailment of the manipulative power of contemporary corporations.[11]

propaganda in canada

"Propaganda" is such an emotionally and politically loaded term that critics of the corporate agenda use more neutral words like "myth" or "hype." Murray Dobbin's exposé of corporate power is titled *The Myth of the Good Corporate Citizen*, while Linda McQuaig's *Shooting the Hippo* is subtitled *Death by Deficit and Other Canadian Myths*[12] and McQuaig talks about the popular mythology of the deficit. In fact, Dobbin and McQuaig both document carefully crafted corporate propaganda campaigns of major proportions. But although McQuaig's book is about propaganda, she never uses the word. Granted, "myth" is a useful expression — it does convey the idea of a mismatch between what is claimed and what is real — but it fails to recognize a key question: Who is doing the myth-making, and why? "Hype" is another often-used word — Heather Menzies uses it in her article "Hyping the Highway,"[13] for example — but it suggests good-natured exaggeration, not out-and-out deceit and manipulation, which is what the corporate propaganda machine intends.

McQuaig begins her book by detailing a February 1993 story on CTV's "W5" about New Zealand's deficit situation. Host Eric Malling alleged that a baby hippo had to be shot in a New Zealand zoo because the government was so far in debt it couldn't afford to expand the hippo pen. The piece was watched by 1.7 million Canadians and had an enormous impact on public opinion about government deficits. Yet it was largely fabrication. What actually happened was that in 1984, New Zealand experienced a currency crisis caused by an over-valued dollar. After the election that year, the dollar was devalued by 20 percent, and the crisis ended. The hippo probably lived to a ripe old age.

McQuaig acknowledges that Malling was a "master in the art of persuasion." But in truth, this is not persuasion, which requires debate and interaction. The currency crisis wasn't even mentioned in Malling's account, this relevant fact being suppressed perhaps because it might get in the way of the message. If we follow Carey's definition, we can see that Malling's hippo story was a masterful piece of propaganda, with the form and content of the program intended to manipulate viewers into adopting attitudes and beliefs that have been chosen in advance by the sponsors of the communication. In this case, the sponsors of the communication, the C.D. Howe Institute and its corporate backers, were nowhere to be seen, and the story used significant symbols and values, such as murdering a defenceless baby hippo, to affect people on an emotional level. Several pages later, McQuaig writes: "[The story] about living beyond our means and hurting our children . . . [is] a distortion of the real story, a mythologized account designed to persuade us to accept what we don't want."[14] McQuaig also remarks on the use of constant repetition by corporate propagandists, until the message becomes "clatter in people's heads," as Jim Winter asserts – or as Noam Chomsky and Edward Herman put it, until it is "internalized largely without awareness" and becomes "common sense,"[15] a principle that Adolf Hitler understood well.

But Eric Malling and the C.D. Howe Institute are just small cogs in a wheel in a very big machine, which, as Carey notes, has been constructed since the 1970s to protect and advance corporate interests in Canada and elsewhere. Today, corporate propaganda is a force of awesome magnitude. Millions of dollars flow from the deep pockets of Canadian and foreign right-wing foundations and corporations into the hands of tax-deductible charitable foundations like AIMS, the Fraser Institute, and the C.D. Howe Institute. These corporate-funded think-tanks produce their own in-house studies or contract with sympathetic academics to produce studies that support corporate goals. The results of the research are disseminated widely and repeatedly through the corporate-controlled print and electronic media to influence the public mind. As Adolf Hitler learned from the American propaganda successes of the First World War, the secret of success is constant repetition, which is the formula adopted by the corporate propaganda machine.

Three propaganda messages are relevant to the successful selling of the corporate agenda for the commercialization of public information. The first is that, given the deficits and the debt, we can no longer afford to provide adequate funding for social programs and public information. The second is that information technology will eventually benefit everyone in society. The third is that the private sector must provide these services, since the public sector is incompetent to do so. Sometimes these messages are combined. For example, the Information Highway Advisory Council tells us that "facing growing fiscal pressure, governments have no choice but to use information and communication technologies to improve productivity and service and save money." This neatly combines about three separate propaganda messages into one enormously misleading statement.

first myth: deficits require spending cuts

Deficits were caused by out-of-control government spending on social programs we can no longer afford. Governments had to cut spending on social programs to get rid of the deficit (and that means cutting spending on institutions that provide public information).

This is the first attack on public information in Canada. It claims that Canada's ballooning deficits and accumulated debt resulted from unrestrained, irresponsible federal and provincial government spending on social programs we can no longer afford. It is one of corporate Canada's greatest propaganda triumphs. Without its success, social-spending cuts would have had a rougher ride, and public information would not be threatened.

Even as late as 1994, Canadians did not consider the deficit to be a significant issue as most opposed cuts in spending and considered unemployment as the biggest issue. Five years later, after severe slashing away at social programs and a constant stream of supportive messaging, the situation had changed dramatically. A *Globe and Mail*/Angus Reid poll in late January 1999 asked Canadians what the federal government should do with surplus money. The leading responses were to reduce the accumulated debt (39 percent) and cut taxes (33 percent). Spending more on government programs was third, at 24 percent.[16] Two additional options — restoring spending to its former level and increasing taxes on the wealthy — were not even mentioned in the survey, but no one seemed to notice. Five years of constant repetition, of media scare stories, of Liberal manipulation of budget information, and of Reform Party frenzy during the 1997 federal election campaign had achieved the desired result: a likely permanent reduction in the services and programs provided by the government, including those that supply public information. As Angus Reid executive vice-president Darrell Bricken noted, "[Canadians'] sense is that governments have been a bit out of control in the past ... and ... they are not necessarily prepared, except in very specific circumstances, to see government get that active on the spending side." And once public information is diminished, propaganda will have an easier time of it.

But none of this was true. As Linda McQuaig so carefully documents in *Shooting the Hippo*, the deficit was not out of control, nor was it caused by social spending. She introduces us to Vincent Truglia, a senior analyst specializing in Canada for Moody's Investors Services in New York, and one of the handful of people who ranks Canada's credit worthiness for foreign investors. In June 1993, he issued a Moody's "special commentary," which described Canada's debt as "grossly exaggerated" and pointed out that Ottawa's fiscal position was "not out of control." It was good news the corporate elite did not want Canadians to hear, and so was reported briefly without comment by the business press and then largely ignored.[17]

But if the deficit was not out of control, it could still have been caused by social spending. In June 1991, Statistics Canada published a study in its *Canadian Economic Observer* that made the basic point that social spending had not been the cause of explosive debt growth. An earlier version of this study, reports McQuaig, tallied the contribution social programs made to debt growth: only one percent was due to unemployment insurance costs, 4.5 percent to welfare programs, 6 percent to old age pensions, 3.4 percent to housing programs, and 8 percent to programs intended to protect persons and properties (military, police, and prison systems). Other programs had already been slashed, so family benefits programs had actually reduced debt growth by 11 percent, and cuts to public transit and communication services (largely Via Rail and postal services) had reduced debt growth by 8.2 percent. These figures did not appear in the *Canadian Economic Observer* article, but the figures that did appear could have contributed enormously to discussions about the causes of the deficit.[18] Not surprisingly, the report was largely ignored by the mainstream news media. It reappeared briefly in 1995 at the height of the Paul Martin budget-cutting frenzy and was ignored once again by the commercial press, leading Vancouver-based Project Censored Canada to select it as one of the top under-reported stories that year.

And Canadians also did not hear much about the real causes of the deficit, one of which was Bank of Canada governor John Crow's single-minded obsession with inflation (with the unflagging support of Finance Minister Michael Wilson). He kicked off his anti-inflation campaign in 1988, and it continued under his successor, Gordon Thiessen, with the assistance of Finance Minister Paul Martin. Crow's tight-money policy – restricting the amount of money circulating in the economy – ratcheted up real interest rates (interest rates minus inflation) to the highest level of any G-8 country and choked the Canadian economy into a severe recession in the late 1980s and early 1990s. High interest rates led to high levels of bankruptcies, foreclosures, and, most important, exceedingly high unemployment levels (they soared from 7.5 percent in 1990 to almost 12 percent three years later), which reduced tax revenues. Fewer people were working and paying taxes, adding to social-assistance costs. High interest rates also increased the government's borrowing costs on the existing debt, adding directly to the deficit and increasing the debt even further. Interest costs rose from $29.6 billion in 1987–88 to $42.5 billion in 1990–91.

Why did Crow and Wilson embark on such a seemingly reckless adventure? Price stability, reports McQuaig, was Crow's concern.[19] Bonds held by investors should not lose their value to inflation over time. If inflation is higher than the interest rate paid on bonds, the investor loses. If inflation is less, the investor wins. And if inflation is a lot less, the investor's profits are even larger. McQuaig notes that Wilson had been a Bay Street bond trader before going into politics, and he was intimately aware of investors' concerns.[20] After he left politics, Wilson headed back to Bay Street to work for investors, who were no doubt pleased with what he accomplished for them, as a consultant for RBC Dominion Securities. Crow left the Bank in 1994 – after a series of lavish farewell parties paid for by taxpayers but attended only by the financial elite – to become a fellow-in-residence at the C.D. Howe Institute.

McQuaig quotes studies that estimate the increase in the deficit – ranging from $15 billion to $30 billion of a total deficit of $49 billion – resulting from Crow's obsession. The numbers may vary, but the conclusion is clear: a significant proportion of the deficits racked up between 1989 and the first years of the Chrétien-Martin administration were the result of high interest rates and a tight monetary policy, not social spending. Another portion of the deficit had been put in place nearly twenty years earlier, when Finance Minister John Turner added tax breaks for business and the wealthy to his 1973 and 1974 budgets. This was compounded by the oil crisis of the early 1970s, which set off a dramatic round of inflation. Interest rates rose, but not fast enough to keep up with inflation.

Why don't Canadians know that the largest portion of the deficit was the result of the war on inflation, and that the goal of that war was to protect the assets of bond-holders, even if it meant throwing thousands of people out of work and wreaking havoc with government revenues? And that the second-largest portion of the deficit was the result of tax breaks given to corporations and the wealthy many years ago? And that spending on social programs accounted for only a minuscule proportion of the deficit? With such knowledge available to them, Canadians would surely have favoured a different course of action than the one their elected representatives chose. "If Canadians learned that social spending wasn't really the deficit culprit, they might be less willing to accept the drastic social spending cuts that the government had in mind."[21]

Canadians know little of these facts because of the success of corporate and government propaganda in diverting public attention away from the real causes of the deficit. It is correct to call this effort propaganda because to call it debate, discussion, or persuasion – the hallmarks of democratic discourse – would mean that all sides of the story received equal "air time," and this most certainly was not the case. True, McQuaig did write and publish her book, and it did sell more than 60,000 copies. And other critics of the prevailing wisdom, like Rick Salutin (*Globe and Mail*) and Thomas Walkom (*Toronto Star*), did express their contrarian views in the national media. But these messages were buried under an avalanche of communication designed to spread false information. And while 60,000 is a large number for a Canadian book, it pales in comparison with the 1.7 million Canadians – nearly thirty times more – who watched Malling's New Zealand hippo show. Evidence that contradicted the view that the deficit was caused by overspending on social programs was marginalized.

The option of increasing taxes on the wealthy rather than cutting spending on social programs is no longer mentioned. The current record proves that thousands of jobs have been eliminated, and that those who still have jobs have to work longer hours for lower wages. But the group at the top of the income heap is doing better than ever. There are more wealthy folk than ever before, so there is a lot more rich income to tax. Taxing the rich could make a significant difference to our deficit situation – it could allow some social programs to be brought back to their former level, for instance. And even though every survey that asks the question finds that a majority of Canadians feel the rich don't pay their fair share and should be more heavily taxed, such an option just isn't on the political agenda any more. Chalk up one very successful propaganda campaign.

Deficits, then, were caused not by out-of-control government spending on social programs we can no longer afford, but by other factors – in particular, John Crow's jihad against inflation. When the Bank of Canada backed off slightly from its policy of high interest rates, conditions corrected themselves and the deficit plummeted. Nevertheless, governments continued to make deep, and probably permanent, cuts to social programs, including those that provide public information. If governments had gone after the more important issue of unemployment, public information would have been protected and even strengthened. But by cutting funding for education, health care, libraries, and scientific research, governments made it easier for the information industry to move in and begin taking over these resources. And once the deficit was eliminated, the propaganda machine turned its sights on cutting taxes, to ensure that government would not be able to restore spending on social programs and public information. As author and broadcaster Murray Dobbin wrote, "The call for tax cuts is simply another front in the ideological war on government. Ultimately, slashing taxes means that we will have less revenue for public education, universal medicare and modern infrastructure – the very things that make us competitive."[22]

second myth: information technology will benefit everyone
Investment in information technology will boost jobs and productivity, and ultimately benefit everyone, so it's important to extend information technology throughout society and our economy.

"People have been expecting big productivity gains because of the heavy investment in computers by companies, but it does not look like we've had it yet," remarked Statistics Canada analyst Jean-Pierre Maynard as he released the agency's 1995 and 1996 productivity statistics.[23] The question is, Will we ever have it? Productivity – which is calculated by subtracting all the items that go into the production of goods and services, like labour, machinery, and computers, from the final output – is a closely watched measure of a country's standard of living. The years 1995 and 1996 were supposed to be when Canada finally broke out of the Bank of Canada–induced recession of the early 1990s. Those years, Canadian business spent nearly $50 billion a year on information technology, more than double what it had spent in the mid-1980s, and laid off thousands of workers, yet productivity was up a paltry 0.4 percent. What's going on here?

The Conference Board of Canada, another leading corporate propaganda organization, would have none of the naysaying about information technology and economic growth. Its study came out a month after the Statistics Canada numbers and disputed them, claiming that information technology helps create jobs and boosts the economy. These good things are already happening, the study argues, and by 2015 more than half a million jobs will come from the gains in productivity resulting from IT investments. But that's not even 28,000 jobs a year, less than the margin of error in such estimates, so it's hardly enough to get excited about, given the enormous sums being invested. Worse yet, even these figures are far from certain, Conference Board study co-author Brenda Lafleur admits. Companies often lack skilled workers and do not use information technology properly, she explained when the study was released. "You can't give people a computer and a software training course and expect gains in productivity. You have to adapt your organizational structure and processes to effectively use IT."[24]

Lafleur's study is relevant to an issue of great concern in the IT community: the so-called productivity paradox. Service industries — banking, finance, health care, insurance, telecommunications, advertising, and retail, in particular — spent $860 billion in the U.S. on computers during the 1980s, yet they increased their productivity by a meagre 0.8 percent a year, well below the 2.5 percent they had achieved in previous decades. As MIT's Robert Solow put it, computers could be seen everywhere except in the economic statistics. For corporate propaganda, this fact presents a difficult situation. Citizens might lose confidence in their corporate leaders if they learned that business spent hundreds of billions of dollars and laid off hundreds of thousands of workers with no apparent pay-off to the national economy. Of course, there were pay-offs to individual firms in the form of soaring profits and stock prices, and to corporate executives in the form of obscene compensation packages. But clearly those rewards to a small group of share-owning Canadians and Americans were achieved at significant cost to everyone else. With such a poor performance history, should we be leaving it to IT executives to decide our economic fate?

To prevent this line of thought from taking hold in the public mind, poor productivity performance was downgraded from "crisis" to "paradox," the implication being that it was merely a phenomenon of intellectual curiosity, something only academics would speculate about in the idle hours after the stock market closed and everyone had finished tallying up their gains for the day. It *was* a crisis, though, one representing mismanagement of such a high order of magnitude that heads should have rolled and some form of public accountability should have been imposed on the corporate and government leaders.

There are two approaches to the so-called paradox. The first is to deny that the problem exists. Advocates of this view say that productivity has increased substantially, but we just don't measure it accurately. Because services are generally intangible, they are harder to measure than cars or dishwashers. If we could measure productivity in service industries, the argument goes, we would indeed see that there have been enormous increases. Even the Statistics Canada survey of productivity cautions that its techniques of measuring productivity may under-report gains in the services sector. *Business Week*, a leading corporate propaganda organ, reassures its readers that "as the Industrial Era gives way to the Information Age, new products, new ideas and new technologies are transforming the economy in ways the statistics aren't capturing."[25] Productivity improvement was so evident to the *Business Week* writer — he offered as one example that fax machine prices dropped 28 percent in four years — and the inability of government statistics to measure it so frustrating that he concluded by claiming, "[Economic measures] have always fallen short in dealing with paradigm shifts. We are living in a new era driven by information technologies. The U.S. is a lot stronger than the government numbers are now telling us." Blame the government again — it can't even get its numbers right.

Dozens of academics and economists have beavered away at critiques of the way productivity is measured. The U.S. National Research

Council (NRC) is one establishment agency that has addressed the issue. In a major 1994 study, it concluded that the way productivity is measured makes it incapable of gauging the impact of specific improvements. Productivity, it argued, is usually judged by standards like output (as measured, for example, in dollars) per unit of input (as measured, for example, in work hours), but these measures fail to take into account improvements in quality, response time, and convenience that information technology provides. In the banking industry, for instance, services like electronic funds transfer and automated banking do not show up in productivity statistics, but they have clearly had an impact on industry performance. That observation seems obvious, but the credibility of the NRC study was tarnished by the fact that funding for it was provided by the Alfred P. Sloan Foundation, which is named after the long-time General Motors president who funded the foundation, and Apple Computer, IBM, Digital Equipment Corp., and Xerox (although, as the report notes, the majority of funding did not come from the private sector).[26]

The other approach to the productivity paradox is to admit it is real and to find its causes. This view became compelling when productivity started going up in the 1990s, at least in the U.S. According to the "inadequate measurement" camp, this shouldn't have been happening. Why could we measure these things again? The reason for low productivity, this group claims, is that managers failed to make good use of the technology they spent so much on. The corporate mantra had been "downsize and computerize," but business leaders were short on strategies to incorporate the technology into their operations. This is the Conference Board approach: claim that information technology will increase employment and productivity, but only if management changes its IT practices within the firm.

To a certain extent, managers *could* fix things. They could spend less on computers – many companies had purchased ten times more computing power than they needed. And they could try to keep their workers from using company computers for non-company activities such as surfing the Net, sending personal e-mail, and playing computer games. But most things are not so easily fixable through improved management practices. Ironically, computers may make companies less able to compete. When their major cost was salaries for workers, companies could adjust expenses by reconfiguring the salaries they paid. But companies had become encumbered by less negotiable costs, such as maintaining support staff and upgrading equipment and software. It can cost two to three times as much to maintain a network of PCs as to buy them. Companies may find themselves on a treadmill with no easy way off.

Many of the problems with information technology lie outside the control of management. In the race to be first to market with new software products, quality control often gets left at the starting gate. The Intel Pentium debacle was one highly publicized case, but underlying flaws can be found in most computer software. Some painful examples: compression programs that eat entire hard disks; conflicts between device drivers; and computer crashes. Meanwhile, new software, upgrades, and applications keep coming off the production lines, and business must devote significant employee time and company resources to learn how to use them and integrate them into corporate operations.

Then there's the Year 2000 (Y2K) disaster, which is a direct consequence of a sensational business error that would have provoked a hurricane of criticism if it had occurred only in the public sector. Business saved money in the 1960s and 1970s by not providing full calendar-year information in computer programs. But what did programmers and executives think would happen in 2000? Perhaps they didn't care, given the corporate bias towards short-term financial results. The result is that governments, companies, and individuals are spending more than $1.3 *trillion* in non-productive activities to correct it, lessening further the possibility of productivity increases until well into the twenty-first century (although, perversely, spending on Y2K is counted in the gross domestic product, adding to the nation's economic output).

Productivity did go up in the U.S. in the 1990s, but the gains came from the usual source. During the 1980s, people were replaced by machines under the guise of streamlining. In the 1990s, the mantra was "downsizing, outsourcing, and re-engineering."[27] Translated, these mean: firing workers and replacing them with machines, firing workers and replacing them with cheaper foreign workers, and firing workers and requiring those that remain to work harder. It was a brutal strategy that achieved improved balance sheets.

And those people who are still working have to work longer hours, not only in the office, but also at home. They're the "surviving employees, trying to do more with less." Seventy-hour weeks and a requirement to use the new technology and do tasks that were once the responsibility of no-longer present secretaries are common scenarios. Some companies retain the services of the Institute for Business Technology, which teaches employees how to cope with the mounting workload. Faxes, cellphones, and laptop computers extend the workplace into the car and the home, and even to the vacation spot.

The home office becomes an "effective workplace alternative," with fax, modem, and computer and high-speed telephone lines. An employee can do most everything that is done in the traditional office, except meet face to face, but it's only a matter of time until videoconferencing technology becomes cheap enough and high-quality enough to allow this too. The benefits are obvious. The employee saves by no longer spending an hour or more morning and night in rush-hour traffic. Companies save by needing less office space, fewer parking stalls, and decreased sick leave (assuming workers continue to work from home when sick).

The telecommuting investment is minimal – just a small amount of hardware and software. A company just has to buy additional software licences for employees' home computers. AT&T has allowed 35,000 of its remaining 250,000 employees to telecommute one or more days a week. More ominous is the virtual or mobile office, which uses portable computers and satellite communication devices to enable on-the-go personnel to work wherever in the world they might be.

For most workers, the prospects are bleak. But conditions will improve. "Patience . . . the information technology revolution is like the advent of electricity," some commentators assure their business readers. Thomas Edison designed the first electric station in 1882, but it took thirty or forty years until companies switched from steam and productivity started to rise. According to *Globe and Mail* economics reporter Bruce Little, "If we think now of the 1990s in terms of slow growth and high unemployment, Canadians of the future may look back on the decade as one defined by the rapid shift toward an economy more based on information."[28]

York University professor David Noble, a historian of technology, doesn't buy this line. The information revolution is already forty years old, he argues, and the returns are in.

> People are now working harder and longer (with compulsory
> overtime), under worsening working conditions, with greater anxiety,
> stress, and accidents, with less skills, less security, less autonomy,
> less power (individually and collectively), less benefits, and less pay.
> Without question the technology has been developed and used
> to deskill and discipline the workforce in a global speed-up of
> unprecedented proportions. And those still working are the lucky
> ones. For the technology has been designed above all to displace.[29]

A second return is in too. During the period when the U.S. and Canada spent more than $1 trillion on information technology and productivity remained flat, the average wage declined for most people and rose for the wealthy. The salary for the average American worker declined by 4.6 percent between 1979 and 1995. At the same time, the salary for the top 5 percent of families went up by 29.1 percent. For the top one percent of families, income rose by an astonishing 78 percent. In 1975, the typical chief executive of a large American company earned about forty times as much as a typical worker. In 1995, he earned 190 times as much. That was bad enough, but when productivity started to go up in the U.S. in the 1990s, wages for the average worker continued to fall. Between March 1994 and March 1995, the output per person-hour in the non-farm business sector – in other words, productivity – grew by 3.1 percent, but average wages and salaries fell 2.3 percent. Workers were not sharing productivity gains.

And while most people's real incomes went down during the period of high computer use, a class of obscenely wealthy billionaires was created. There were so many candidates for *Forbes* magazine's 1997 annual list of billionaires (which ranks net worth, or total assets minus liabilities), that it had to raise the cut-off point to $1.2 billion

(U.S.) in order to limit the list to 200. An increasing number of the world's wealthy are information billionaires. Of the 200 on the list, thirty-nine – or nearly 20 percent – had fortunes based on media, computers, or information technology. But that doesn't tell the whole story, since most Asian billionaires became wealthy through real estate and retailing. The true test of IT use is the U.S., which is the nation most emphasizing information products and services. Of the sixty U.S. billionaires on the list, twenty-three, or 38 percent, had fortunes based on IT and media. Americans dominate the list of IT/media billionaires. The list of the twenty top IT and media billionaires is led, not surprisingly, by Microsoft's Bill Gates, who has a net worth of $36.4 billion (U.S.), double what he was worth in 1996. In second place was another Microsoft billionaire, Paul Allen, with $14.1 billion. Third was Canada's own Ken Thomson, with $9.0 billion; he was tied with the Newhouse family (Advance Publications and Condé Nast magazines). Then comes another Microsoft billionaire, Steven Ballmer, worth $7.5 billion. He's followed by John Kluge (Metromedia, film studios, wireless), $7.2 billion; Larry Ellison (Oracle), $7.1 billion; Gordon Moore (5.5 percent of Intel), $6.7 billion; Carlos Slim Helu (controls phone giant Telefonos de Mexico), $6.6 billion; the Bass family (oil and Disney), $6.0 billion; Philip Anschutz (railroads and fibre-optic networks), $5.0 billion; Silvio Berlusconi (media, telecom, digital TV), $4.9 billion; the McCaw family (cable, cellular, digital wireless, satellites), $3.8 billion; Kirk Kerkorian (MGM, Orion Pictures), $3.8 billion; Sumner Redstone (Viacom), $3.4 billion; Dietmar Hopp (SAP, the fourth-largest software company), $3.6 billion; Masayoshi Son (Softbank, a software distributor), $3.5 billion; Edgar Bronfman (Seagrams and MCA), $3.3 billion; and Michael Dell (Dell Computers), $3.3 billion.

After the 1995 U.S. figures on wages and productivity came out showing that, overall, productivity and the salaries of the wealthiest families had gone up while the salary of the average American worker had declined, Robert Reich, Bill Clinton's secretary of labor, blasted Wall Street and America's financial elite for declaring war on workers. He caused barely a ripple in the largest newspapers and received little mention in TV newscasts. In Canada, Deirdre McMurdy, who defends business interests from her post as business columnist at

Maclean's, noted in a 1995 column, when corporate profits were soaring through the roof, that business was not sharing its new-found wealth with its workers because of a "strong whiff of economic uncertainty lingering in the air."[30] Managers wanted growth numbers to "stabilize" before they agreed to wage hikes. But she did not speculate on how long that would take.

The lack of productivity growth is no paradox. While the obscenely wealthy like Bill Gates and Ken Thomson and their corporate underlings sniff the air waiting for "certainty," they continue to get wealthier. Meanwhile, most other people have to work longer hours for less pay and under greater workplace surveillance. Certainly, investing in information technology cannot be sold to the public on the basis that Ken Thomson and Bill Gates will be the prime beneficiaries. But by claiming that there will be productivity gains for everyone, even if they haven't yet occurred, the selling of technology and of the Connecting Canadians programs is made that much easier. We just need to believe that if the private sector builds the network that connects us, we will all benefit . . . someday.

third myth: markets work, governments don't

Governments are incompetent to manage economic affairs and should let business run information networks and the economy.

A third propaganda campaign claims that governments don't know how to manage the economy ("evidence" of this being their wanton spending sprees and accumulated deficits and debt, as detailed by the first propaganda campaign), and so should get out of the way of business and let "the markets work their magic." This campaign was kicked off in the 1970s as a corporate reaction to the interventions of American and Canadian governments over a period that spanned the Great Depression, the Second World War, and the post-war economic boom that sputtered out in the early 1970s. Social programs had gone too far, the argument went; the rich were being taxed too heavily; and the state was intruding too frequently into the affairs of business, extending the scope of environmental protection and product safety, for instance. It was time for a counter-attack.

The key to the strategy was to elevate free enterprise to the status of holy writ. The propaganda triumph – at least in the U.S., where it had greater resonance – was to equate individual freedom with free enterprise and free market. Alex Carey documents the billion-dollars-a-year propaganda campaign launched by the American Advertising Council in 1975 to counter the gains of organized labour and the environmental movement. The results were impressive. A New York firm that specialized in monitoring public opinion for business said, "Between Jimmy Carter's election in 1976 and Ronald Reagan's victory in 1980, the outlook of the American people underwent one of those decisive shifts that historians generally label as watershed events."[31] Within a five-year period, the U.K., the U.S., and Canada had elected reactionary leaders (Margaret Thatcher, Ronald Reagan, and Brian Mulroney), each of whom embarked on concerted and highly successful efforts to roll back the clock. In Canada, thanks to the work of the C.D. Howe and Fraser institutes, what had been radical ideas in the 1970s became conventional wisdom in the 1990s.

The claim that government was incapable of running anything, and therefore should get out of the way, could be found everywhere, including in the rhetoric of the information highway. The Clinton administration's July 1997 "Framework for Global Electronic Commerce" put it this way: "The private sector should lead . . . [because] innovation, expanded services, broader participation, and lower prices will arise in a market-driven arena, not in an environment that operates as a regulated industry."[32]

Not to be outdone, the Information Highway Advisory Council churned out a Canadian version: "In the information economy, success will be determined by the marketplace, not by the government. . . . The private sector should build and operate the Information Highway. Those who make the investments should bear the risks and reap a fair reward."[33] Since the information economy was just getting underway (if it was at all), little hard evidence was available to support claims of the future successes of the market. It was a statement of faith, not fact, and evidence was neither necessary nor forthcoming.

The ascendancy of the market is based on a model assiduously promoted by right-wing economists associated with the University of

Illinois (the so-called Chicago School), the worldwide network of right-wing think-tanks, and the corporate media. The model assumes – erroneously, in the view of progressive and liberal economists – that all human activity behaves like an efficient market. This ignores the easily observed facts that "people help strangers, return wallets, leave generous tips in restaurants they will never visit again, give donations to public radio when theory would predict they would rationally 'free-ride,' and engage in other acts that suggest they value general norms of fairness," argues liberal economist Robert Kuttner. Chicago school economists ignore the fact that there is a civic realm beyond markets, he says. And they ignore the logical outcomes of markets: that 358 billionaires own as much wealth as the bottom 45 percent of the world population. They turn their backs on those who do not have enough income to participate in the market, and they claim that markets work even in areas of human activity with social ends, like health, education, public infrastructure, clean air and water.[34]

So blinded was IHAC by towers of free-market gold, it could not see history and the positive contributions of governments in developing the Canadian economy. One contribution to the economy came from public spending. Military procurement nurtured the computer and electronic industries; National Housing Act and CMHC spending created the land-development industry; highway-building programs developed provinces and the country. Another contribution came from direct government intervention in economic affairs. IHAC could have studied dozens of examples of successful public enterprise. On the Prairies, provincial telephone utilities (Manitoba Telephone System, Alberta Government Telephones, Saskatchewan Telephone Co.) were established by the public sector because the private sector – Bell Canada – refused to connect independent telephone companies to its long-distance lines. Over the years, these systems provided service comparable to the private companies. In fact, the efficiency of Manitoba Tel's operations was "unmatched," says the University of Ottawa's Robert Babe. The same spirit of public enterprise can be seen in Canada's railways and canals, hydro-electric utilities, and public radio and television.

Perhaps IHAC would respond that the future information economy will be so different from the industrial economy that there are no lessons to be learned from the past. This is an erroneous argument likely based on the corporate-sponsored idea that we live in an information age, one that is fundamentally different from the past. (It's erroneous because it is more likely that we live in a corporate age, which is essentially a continuation, and a speed-up, of past trends.)

But even if correct, IHAC's response ignores the easily observed fact that the public sector has already played a major role in the information age. As we've seen, university computing departments and the National Research Council pioneered networking in Canada, successfully establishing and operating CA*net, Canada's Internet backbone, for five years before a private Internet industry even appeared on the scene. In the U.S., the Internet grew out of a network designed to link the National Science Foundation's five supercomputer sites so that researchers working at government agencies and other universities could access these sites remotely. Researchers at one site, the National Center for Supercomputing Applications (NCSA) at the University of Illinois at Champaign-Urbana, developed the first World Wide Web browser, Mosaic. When NCSA released Mosaic to the public domain, some NCSA team members took their taxpayer-created knowledge to California's Silicon Valley, found financial backers, and started a company called Netscape Communications Corp.

With a modest investment, the public sector could have continued to operate the Internet and commanded a major presence in the building of networks. This might have led to a very different kind of information highway, a public network in the mould of our successful public broadcasting system. But politicians and bureaucrats had their thinking so distorted by treetops propaganda that they retreated from this sensible course and gave away the whole candy store. And the public sector continues to make the Internet profitable for the private sector through its investments in education, research, and health care. IHAC says that those who make the investments and take the risks should reap the rewards, so why shouldn't taxpayers benefit? At bottom, IHAC's claim was self-serving rhetoric designed to promote the interests of the big players who dominate the council, companies like Bell Canada, IBM Canada, and Rogers Communications.

Industry still relies on a strong public presence in Internet developments. It needs continued regulation in the form of expanded copyright laws to protect intellectual property on the Net. Microsoft likely wouldn't exist today if the U.S. government had not agreed to the dubious course of extending copyright protection to software programs. Industry needs additional regulation to allow new competitors to piggy-back on the infrastructure of established companies they are trying to displace. Without such regulation mandating fair play, new competitors would be crushed.

Industry still relies on U.S. anti-trust laws, although they've been weakened since the Reagan years, to bring miscreants like Microsoft and Intel to heel. In Canada, industry needs an enforceable competition law to prevent telephone companies from re-establishing monopolies. And it needs government-sanctioned privacy laws to make its electronic-commerce efforts feasible. IHAC and the Clinton administration ignore the crucial fact that supervised deregulation of telecommunications requires discerning public-minded regulation to work. Regulators will not be able to fold up shop and disappear when deregulation is complete because, inevitably, new and unimagined dilemmas will arise. Says Robert Kuttner: "As new products and business strategies appear and markets evolve, so necessarily does the regime of rules."[35]

Kuttner also says, "The grail of a market economy untainted by politics is the most dangerous illusion of our age." It is dangerous because the corporate propagandists have repeated it so frequently over the twenty years the campaign has been in effect that many people have come to see it as an accurate picture of reality, as common sense. It is an illusion because it is false and merely represents what corporate interests want us to believe. Governments have always been positively and productively involved in economic matters, and will continue to be so. Governments have not mismanaged their economic affairs, and many areas of social relations are under their jurisdiction precisely because they cannot be accommodated by market transactions. Nevertheless, governments are turning over to business any activities from which business thinks it can extract profit.

The question has to be this: What is the correct mix of public and private initiative to create information networks that will meet the needs of all citizens? And how can we achieve the mix? The answer to this latter question can be found in the activities of groups that are working to reassert the legitimacy of public and community-based information networks — and to reclaim public information.

reclaiming public information

Corporate-controlled education curriculum, corporate-sponsored
science research, market-oriented libraries — all violate a democratic
society's cherished rights, which centre on freedom of knowledge and
freedom of information. If information and knowledge are distorted
or even removed from public discussion to suit corporate profit and
ideological agendas, then citizens will lose their ability to participate
fully and knowledgeably in the political life of their country.

Such an outcome is not written in the entrails of the Windows
operating system. As Dick Sclove and his Loka Institute demonstrate,

it is possible to challenge corporate control of information and create alternatives that address citizens' real needs. This final chapter surveys and evaluates initiatives that have challenged, or provided alternatives to, commercialized information. It argues that citizens need to continue fighting in the trenches, using networks to stop the next Multilateral Agreement on Investment (MAI), support the Zapatista and other liberation movements, and lobby for universal access to telecommunication services. Librarians, community networkers, progressive academics, socially conscious unions, citizen activists, advocacy groups – all are working to find non-profit and non-commercial alternatives to the information status quo.

But that is only the first step in a more ambitious public-information reclamation project. Eventually, we must change the legal-regulatory-political regime if we are to break the stranglehold of the barons of bandwidth on information policy decision-making. That requires nothing less than the emergence of a strong political force or movement, as Herbert and Anita Schiller argue. The focus of this political activity, I argue, is a new set of human rights for the so-called knowledge society. Civil rights grew out of the eighteenth century, political rights the nineteenth, and social rights the twentieth. What we need now is a set of information rights to equip all citizens to deal with the corporate-inspired, anti-democratic trends of the twenty-first century. Many individuals and groups, either by fighting to provide access to computer networks for all citizens or by using such networks to achieve their goals, have already commenced work on this program.

Of course, there are often large differences among groups working to reclaim public information. Authors and librarians, for instance, share many principles and should be working together towards greater public access to, and use of, written works (and they do cooperate, through programs like author readings in libraries). But they have been split by a seemingly effective strategy spearheaded by multinational information corporations, and they were at each others' throats during the 1996 Copyright Act amendment hearings.

There are also great differences among groups that are using computer networks to achieve their goals. Socially oriented trade unions and environmental groups, for instance, have been forced by corporate propaganda into jobs-versus-environment stand-offs when they should be finding common ground. Creating computer networks that serve community interests is one initiative unionists and environmentalists can share. We need to leave our differences behind. This is the only way non-profit, non-commercial interests can forge alliances that are powerful enough to force government and industry to back off from their Connecting Canadians agenda.

The corporate takeover of public information is neither mysterious nor inevitable. It has been achieved in the same way as every advance in corporate power: by massive corporate spending on public relations and advertising; by lobbying and buying off legislators; by greasing the revolving door (staffing key government offices with corporate executives and providing high-salaried positions for ex-politicians and bureaucrats); by financing think-tanks to spread erroneous news about information technology and markets; by funding sympathetic academics to produce papers authenticating the crucial importance of a privately controlled information economy; by hiring the best lawyers money can buy to argue cases before the courts, courts that are presided over largely by judges who previously lawyered for those same corporations. Information corporations and their propaganda apparatuses have tried to convince us that we have entered an information age, that IT developments are inevitable, and that we have no option but to adjust. This is pure fabrication. The information industry was not expanded by magic. It was advanced by conscious choices made by corporate and political interests and their allies.

The corporate takeover of public information has been validated by the successes of the propaganda machine. It can be dislodged and the public will re-established by rallying public opinion. We have to rethink the reasons for public information. By relating our actions and analyses to the real circumstances of people and their needs for accurate, timely information in their individual lives; in their families; communities, and workplaces; and in their public places, we can overcome corporate propaganda. David Korten's book *When Corporations Rule the World* was a wake-up call for alternative and progressive forces. In it he observes that "each day, more people are saying no to the forces of corporate colonialism, reclaiming their spaces, taking back responsibility for their lives, and working to create real-world alternatives to the myths and illusions [of economic globalization]."[1] In Canada, too, a plethora of groups and people are working in a host of ways to create electronic space and reclaim public information. The most extensive is the community network movement.

community networks

Community-controlled computer networks attempt to reclaim electronic space and could provide a significant challenge to corporate control of information. Freenets, or community networks (as they are usually called in Canada), were set up to enrich their local communities, not return profits to investors. They are non-profit, locally based, locally controlled, and locally owned computer-based communication networks that provide access to community resources and other information. At their high point in Canada, there were thirty-five operating networks with between 250,000 and 600,000 members, according to an estimate advanced in June 1996 by community network activists Garth Graham and Leslie Regan Shade.[2] The networks spanned the country, from Halifax's Chebucto Community Network to Victoria's Telecommunity — Canada's first and the world's eleventh — to Northwest Territories' FreeNet Association. They could be found in every province, in large urban centres and small rural communities.

Graham and Shade defined a community network as a "community 'space' within an 'electronic commons,' whereby members can visit the electronic equivalent of a school, hospital, town hall, post office, citizens' forum . . ."[3] They vary in size, ideology, and governance, but community networks share a desire to provide access to everyone, create local community awareness, and offer essential information about services and programs in non-commercial databases. Non-electronic community information networks are well established and operate through families, neighbourhoods, workplaces, meeting places, sports and social clubs, schools, and churches. They can be found in the "What's Happening" pages of community newspapers, notices on Laundromat bulletin boards, and city hall leaflets delivered to every household. Freenet activists believed their computer networks could enhance those networks and magnify their reach and impact.

But instead of challenging corporate domination, community networks and their national association, Telecommunities Canada, were largely integrated into the corporate-political system, as providers of access to lower-income and rural Canadians, people of little interest to the commercial ISPs that appeared on the scene a year or two after the community networks went on-line. Before ISPs, anyone who wanted access to the Internet and was not connected through CA*net and a university, college, or government agency had to use a community network. But once ISPs were available, community networks were cast in the role of introducing Canadians to the Internet and whetting their appetite for more – at least those who could afford commercial access rates. Industry Canada's view was that Canadians would move from for-free community Net services to for-fee ISP services, a view shared by some in the movement.

National Capital FreeNet chair Dave Sutherland, for instance, said that "Free-Net allows people to try things out for nothing, without any commitment, and decide for themselves if it's something they want to use. For some, the dial-up wait is untenable, so for $15 to $25 a month, it makes a lot of sense to spend the money."[4] When the government of Manitoba and Industry Canada pumped $500,000 into Blue Sky Community Networks of Manitoba, the news release said the goal was not to provide community content, but "to make sure everyone in Manitoba has affordable access to the Internet and the many benefits it can bring."[5] The news release did mention the role of networks in fostering "a sense of community by posting all kinds of local community news," but this came after promoting economic development.

Community networks depend on support from all sectors of society – private, governmental, and non-profit. This is both their strength and their weakness. But although they are not entirely dependent on any one sector, they are placed in a precarious position when two of three sectors combine for ends that run counter to those of non-profit, community-controlled enterprises. A few, like National Capital

FreeNet (NCF) in Ottawa, were able to resist corporate and government pressures. Indeed, NCF became the most successful network in Canada (60,000 registered members and 170 lines by 1997). Jay Weston and George Frakjor of Carleton University's school of journalism heard about the Cleveland Free-Net and decided a similar system should be put in place in Ottawa. They promoted the idea to Sutherland, director of computing and information services at the university, and he helped set up the service in Canada and became the first chair of the network. NCF opened on February 1, 1993, with twenty phone lines that were quickly swamped by users. The network operated out of donated space in Carleton's computer room, with support from the *Ottawa Citizen* and several community organizations. Ontario's New Democratic government provided substantial funding as part of its telecommunications infrastructure program, which allowed NCF to acquire a sizeable pool of modems. In addition, computer companies and Industry Canada donated equipment and contributed support. NCF relied on FreePort software from Case Western University, which came with the Cleveland Free-Net system, and added bilingual menus. The freenet grew quickly, becoming the second-largest community network in the world. Why was it so successful? NCF organizers at Carleton University and others spent a year planning the network before the launch, and then ensured that it was democratically run. All decisions of importance are made in public, with voting occurring on-line. The annual meeting, which sets policy for the coming year, is also held on-line and is open to all members, many of whom actually participate. In 1996 it moved to a Web-based system, which boosted the network's accessibility for organizations and individuals in the region.

Toronto Freenet (TFN), by contrast, violated both principles of community networks as enunciated by Garth Graham: to remain independent of government and to not become commercial.[6] It started with a million dollars – half in cash from the provincial New Democratic government over three years and half in funding and support from Rogers Cablesystems, Canada's largest cable-system operator.

But the money wasn't the problem. All networks rely on government or industry financial support. TFN, however, operated out of

Rogers's Markham, Ontario, technical operations centre. "Little is known about the precise nature of this arrangement because the contract with Rogers stipulates that no information about the deal could be made public," writes Vancouver CommunityNet organizer Neil Guy,[7] and this makes many in the Canadian networking community uncomfortable. Guy could learn little about TFN because no one with the organization would respond to his e-mail queries. TFN signed a confidentiality agreement with Rogers that covered both the dollar value donated and the terms of the agreement itself. Yet that didn't seem to bother executive director Rick Broadhead, who called the agreement "standard business practice." At a 1994 community networks conference, Broadhead defended his actions. "There can be a real conflict between the democratic values of the freenet movement on the one hand and professionalism on the other," he said, "and we are trying to run a professional organization here."[8]

Following the model of its public library, the Edmonton FreeNet came on-line in October 1994 with a mandatory twenty-five-dollar membership fee. Calgary Free-Net followed Edmonton's lead. Low-income individuals could request a fee waiver, but every other individual and organization desiring access must pay the fee. This has allowed the network to hire three paid staff members for its 11,000 members and 106 dial-up lines.

Halifax's Chebucto Community Net uses cable-system access for part of its data transmission. It gained early support and exposure through an alliance with the *Halifax Daily News*, and its technical facilities were run through Dalhousie University's computing science department. Chebucto has produced a standardized set of software, called the Chebucto Suite, which is based on the Lynx text-only World Wide Web browser and can be used by other community networks – indeed, many other networks *have* picked it up.

Libertel Montreal received strong support from the Quebec government, largely because of the lack of commercial Internet providers and the paucity of French-language Internet content in the province. But despite provincial government support, Libertel took several years to launch and died after only four months, on November 30, 1996, having drawn only 2,800. In 1993, Libertel was promised a government grant of $600,000, but it did not receive the first $125,000 until 1995 and then received a further $225,000 in May 1996. "They were the envy of everyone," recalled Lisa Donnelly, the executive director of Ottawa's National Capital FreeNet. "We would have loved to have a third of what they got. But it just came too late."[9] Why did it come so late? Some, like Montrealer Matthew Friedman, who wrote a book on the new technologies, believe Libertel was a low priority with the Parti Québécois government because it did not promote French. Hugo Seguin, aide to Louise Beaudoin, Quebec's minister of culture, communications, and language, blames the failure on the local organizers, who he says did not obtain enough additional support in the community. He admitted, though, "that for us there is a cultural component at stake. We want to create Quebec sites so that when Quebeckers are online they are offered an international content but also one in French."[10]

A different model in Canada was provided by Manitoba's Blue Sky Community Networks. It started in November 1994 in Winnipeg, taking advantage – like the other large urban community networks – of the large population base within the local calling area and the support of community colleges and universities. But Blue Sky moved almost immediately to help provide services to widely dispersed rural communities around the province. The Winnipeg node has ninety-six dial-up lines with 104 terminals in public libraries and twenty-five terminals in city drop-in centres. Blue Sky also hosts networks for rural communities on the main Winnipeg-based system.

By 1996, the umbrella organization consisted of twenty-seven community networks. Manitoba's rural libraries were also scheduled to join Blue Sky in a partnership, and the network has also worked closely with the province's sixty-one First Nations bands and the Assembly of Manitoba Chiefs to help bring community networks to reserves across the province. An Aboriginal system named People First Net was started by Blue Sky with some federal seed funding. Blue Sky was also helped by a $500,000 grant under the Canada-Manitoba Infrastructure Works Agreement, proving that there is always money available if government wants to support particular initiatives. This funding allowed the organization to add new community networks, expand the core computer system, add fifty new terminals for free public access, and increase from twenty-five to one hundred the number of telephone lines.

Vancouver Regional FreeNet (VRN) was formed in 1993 following the well-publicized successes of Ottawa and Victoria. From the beginning, the organizers were torn between taking political or corporate approaches to community networking. Many of the key early organizers were activists who believed the purpose of community networking was to promote democratic communication – "anything that had the slightest tinge of commercial value was frowned upon and met with outright hostility."[11] They were interested in capitalizing on grassroots volunteer participation, rather than utilizing institutional support for building the organization. Also, several key participants, like Brian Campbell, came from a public library background and saw the key issue as making information accessible to the general public. Consequently, VRN was not supported by large institutions to the same degree as other community networks. Neither UBC nor SFU would back the Vancouver community network, and support was not forthcoming from the community colleges (which had limited computing resources at the time).

Financing is clearly an ongoing concern, though, especially with the tendency of governments to limit their contributions to start-up seed funding. Organizers have estimated that to run the network costs about eight dollars (U.S.) per member per year, mainly for phone-line charges. That may not seem like much, but for an organization with 50,000 members like NCF, it adds up to $400,000 a year. Edmonton FreeNet believes it is not unfair to charge users ten to twenty dollars a year while allowing a fee-waiver for low-income users. Most community networks cover these costs through voluntary donations from users and other fund-raising activities.

Meanwhile, community networks have been denied charitable status by Revenue Canada since the Victoria Community Network applied for it in 1993. The refusal partly stems from their own constitutions, which have not satisfied Revenue Canada's strict definition for charitable status. Also, because community networks are new, there are no precedents that could guide Revenue Canada's interpretation of the law regarding charitable organizations. This was a blow to community networks because funds given to their organizations could not qualify the donors for tax deductions. VCN fought this ruling in the courts, using the West Coast Environmental Law Association. In July 1996, the Federal Court of Appeals decided in VCN's favour, ruling that "there is absolutely no doubt . . . that the provision of free access to information and to a means by which citizens can communicate with one another on whatever subject they may please is a type of purpose similar to those which have been held to be charitable in the past."[12]

cleveland free-net and telecommunities canada

Few Canadian freenets call themselves freenets. Ironically, the term is a trademark owned by the U.S.-based National Public Telecomputing Network. The first freenet was started in Cleveland, Ohio, in 1984 by Tom Grundner of Case Western Reserve University. He set up an experimental medical-information system that would allow members of the public to leave on-line specific health questions, which would be answered within twenty-four hours by a health professional.

It was low-tech, as befitted the time, but St. Silicon's Hospital and Information Dispensary, as it was jokingly called, convinced Grundner there was potential in electronically disseminating important community information. He worked with his university to set up the first freenet in Cleveland in 1986, tying a public community information system to personal electronic-mail accounts. The service was wildly successful and drew tens of thousands of registered users.

Grundner left to set up the National Public Telecomputing Network (NPTN), an organization launched to develop and coordinate freenets across the country. NPTN was also successful, and had dozens of affiliated community networks and nearly 500,000 users country-wide. One of Grundner's goals for NPTN was cyber-casting; the idea was for local freenets to produce their own content, which would then be distributed across the entire network in much the same way that the Public Broadcasting System's non-commercial programming originates with affiliates and is distributed to all stations. Grundner's prime cyber-casting focus was educational material,

reclaiming public information > 267

which was produced under the umbrella of Academy One. But by the mid-nineties NPTN faltered, and its highly organized and centralized model was being questioned by many activists who desired more local control.

In 1991 and 1992, when organizing committees in Victoria and Ottawa began discussions about establishing freenets in their cities, NPTN was there to help. Unknown to the Canadians, NPTN had trade-marked the words "FreeNet" and "Free-Net," and then argued that any organization calling itself a freenet should conform to basic standards of service so that consumers would have access to what NPTN con-sidered to be a uniformly high-quality product. NPTN required the word "freenet" to be hyphenated (Free-Net) and charged membership fees, which in 1995 were increased to $2,000 (U.S.) a year, a sig-nificant amount for smaller networks. Canadian networks were also required to carry Academy One, which included information on American presidents and the U.S. Constitution, but nothing on Canadian subjects. NPTN executive director Peter Harter was quoted as saying in 1995 that "one thing Free-Net does not represent is free-loading." That was not the view of Canadian networkers like Michael Gillespie, vice-president of Blue Sky, for whom "free" meant "free of toll charges, free of usage charges, free of hassle, free of intimidation, free of red tape, free of timetables, free of censorship." Victoria and Ottawa joined NPTN, but other Canadian community networks, wary of Grundner's approach to community networking – some called it free market, not free access – decided to establish an alternative umbrella organization called Telecommunities Canada.[13]

In August 1993, National Capital FreeNet hosted the first national conference on community networking at Carleton University. The con-ference was convened to discuss a national strategy. More than forty up-and-running networks and organizing committees recommended establishing a national organization to promote local community net-work initiatives, and to represent the Canadian community networking movement at national and international levels. An informal structure and interim board was set up at a second Ottawa conference in 1994, and a formal board was elected and structure adopted the next year in Victoria. TC members are community network organizations. They must be non-profit, provide membership and equitable access to every citizen in their community, and have as their goals to encourage "exchange, publication and access to the broadest range of information of interest to the community, endeavour to create connections with other computer-based networks, and allow the free and interactive flow of information among communities."[14]

TC is the voice of community networks in Canada, although given the diverse origins and goals of individual networks, it is a confused and muffled voice. TC was late in starting – CANARIE, for example, was first discussed in 1988, six years before TC – and it suffers from limited resources. Its members are scattered across Canada, and are more active in their local networks than in national activities. They collaborate mainly by e-mail, which is good for some things, but not collective decision-making. Its formal organization consists of seven elected volunteer board members. It has no office, no staff, and most important, no consistent sources of funds, except for project grants for administrative overheads, the residuals from the annual conferences, and Industry Canada funding for the conferences. This money pays only for four annual face-to-face meetings.

However, there were several common issues faced by the burgeoning community networks. One was how to deal with NPTN, and the two organizations finally reached an agreement in 1996. TC members were given permission to use the name Free-Net, in exchange for paying a nominal amount to NPTN. As regards Academy One and other American-oriented content, by 1996 NPTN's cyber-casting initiative was in disarray, having been overtaken by the explosive growth of the World Wide Web, so it was no longer a problem. Few Canadian community networks went back to the name, however. Many had already changed to some variant of community network. The word "freenet" was pleasant-sounding and meaningful, but what it meant for many was that nobody had to pay – and as a result, donations, the essential source of funding for all freenets, suffered.

what industry canada wants (supping with the devil)

A second issue faced by all community networks was the need to lobby the federal government – Industry Canada, in particular – for financial support for networks that were just starting and for ongoing support once they got off the ground. TC has failed to move Industry Canada. The federal government is clearly not interested in the sustainability of the community networking movement and has rebuffed TC's efforts for support. The problem is that Industry Canada has its own model of community networking, called the Community Access Program (CAP), which we discussed in Chapter 2. It views this initiative as a seed program, designed to kick-start public demand for commercial services in areas of the country not yet served by ISPs. Notes Neil Guy, a founder of the Vancouver Community Network, "TC, with its interest in seeing community networks nationwide become self-sustaining and well-supported, has a fundamental ideological conflict with . . . Industry Canada."[15] For Industry Canada, community networks are simply another ingredient in the Connecting Canadians witches' brew, an interim stage to be tolerated until commercial interests can take them over. For networkers, however, the networks are important in themselves. CAP provides access, period. Community networks, by contrast, are fundamentally interested in developing public space and providing community-generated content.

There was palpable tension and animosity between the two. TC was frustrated with Industry Canada's total refusal to promote the development of community-controlled public space, along with its failure to provide ongoing grant monies and institutionalized support so that the newly born community networks would not die within a year or two of their formation. Industry Canada, for its part, is frustrated with what it sees as a small group of ideologues trying to interfere with the smooth running of its program by altering the terms of its mandate. In Industry Canada's vision of cyberspace, as Parke Davis told the 1994 Ottawa conference, community networks are there to help achieve the federal goal of ensuring that as many people as possible have access to the budding information highway at an affordable price.[16]

TC cannot afford to give up all communication with Industry Canada, given the agency's pervasive role in all things networky, but it has turned its attention to provincial networking initiatives by setting up organizations in some provinces that lobby provincial governments. In the summer of 1997, the two organizations hammered out a so-called framework for cooperation to enhance the ability of Canadian communities to utilize electronic public space.

Rural Canada was the primary battleground between the two competing visions. Provinces like Manitoba, British Columbia, and Nova Scotia experienced a rapidly growing base of small networks outside their major urban centres. And to the extent that networks in those provinces have tried to move the provincial governments, they have usually come up against the same interests that control Industry Canada. In B.C., organizers formed B.C. Community Networks in December 1993 to serve as a unified voice for the various organizing committees and operating networks. Its goal was to lobby the provincial government for funding and negotiate with corporations for community network support.

does community networking have a future?

It is too early to judge the impact of community networks on the broader networking picture in Canada, but it is clear they never became the social movement their organizers hoped for. The implacable opposition of Industry Canada and the provincial governments, even the social democratic ones, guaranteed this outcome. In the minds of most, community networks had a limited and temporary role to play in getting Canadians on-line. Then they were supposed to wither away. Indeed, community networks did get people on-line, but they failed to create a critical mass of public, non-profit, community content. There was a simple reason for this. Often, the creation of local content was an outcome of designated grants. When the grants ended, there was no money to update the information, which soon became stale and out-dated. And the networks were too dependent on key players in the information industry. Funding was usually provided by Industry Canada, which wanted community nets to become

part of its Community Access Program, and by provincial governments, which saw the community nets playing a role in provincial
economic development.

Even the universities that hosted some community network facilities, like Carleton and UBC, were not entirely committed to the vision.
They were active participants in CANARIE from the beginning and
must have held a different view of the direction computer networks
should take in Canada, one of high-speed networks and commercial
applications and services. The telcos, meanwhile, simply pretended
community nets didn't exist. Stentor, for instance, defined content
creators as "independent film and television producers, production
houses, as well as private and public broadcasters." By excluding
community networks from content creation, their work as information providers was marginalized.

The mixed motives of the organizers, who ranged from communi-
tarian visionaries to bread-and-butter chamber-of-commerce types,
made collective action difficult. Acceptable-use policies that were in
effect in many freenets did not allow corporate advertising, corporate
accounts, or overt buying and selling. On the other hand, some nets
made openings for commercial use of their networks by establishing
paid-for higher levels of membership or sponsorships. In the passive
consumer model pushed by CANARIE and the corporate interests that
ran it, there was marginal space only for non-profit community content. Freenets help achieve a federal goal of ensuring that as many
people as possible have affordable access to the information highway.
With so many foes in government and industry, community networks
could not create the critical mass of public content needed to capture
the attention and imagination of Canadians.

But there's a more fundamental reason for the lack of success of
the networks. To some extent, they fell victim to the same myth that
many others did: technology could, by itself, change society. This is
the myth of technological determinism, the "build it and they will
come" scenario, once again. If they merely created the networks,
some community network activists seemed to believe, that would help
build communities. The literature is replete with examples of this
thinking. Although most books don't say that computer networks

create communities, they imply something similar. Doug Schuler, whose book on community networks is the authoritative source, wrote that "new computer-based community networks are intended to help revitalize, strengthen and expand existing people-based community networks."[17] Neil Guy writes that

> some in the community networking movement [hope] that the networks can serve as a sort of technical fix to many of our society's problems; that the installation of computer-mediated discussion systems is somehow going to enhance the vibrancy of community life and solve deeply rooted social problems. This belief is looking increasingly naive.[18]

Computer networks cannot create communities, nor can they foment resistance to corporate control, but they can assist groups already working for social change.

a progressive global network

Progressive people around the world were communicating with each other in electronic networks – computer, fax machine, telephone, radio, satellite, VCR, video camera, and community TV – long before the Internet blazed onto the scene. They operated independently of commercial media networks; they were also decentralized and egalitarian, even though each medium had long been dominated by large corporations. According to Howard Frederick's optimistic assessment, "for the first time in history, the forces of peace and environmental preservation have acquired the communication tools and intelligence-gathering technologies previously the province of the military, government, and transnational corporations."[19] Frederick credited one organization in particular for these developments: the Association for Progressive Communications, which was born in 1984 when four Silicon Valley organizations created PeaceNet, the world's first computer network dedicated exclusively to serving the needs of the peace, human-rights, and social-justice movements. PeaceNet became a division of the San Francisco–based Tides Foundation, a charitable foundation that formed the Institute for Global Communications (IGC) to direct and support its activities.

The same year, with seed money from Apple Computer, EcoNet was created to advance the cause of planetary environmental protection and sustainability; it joined IGC in 1987. A third network, ConflictNet, dedicated to serving non-violent conflict resolution, was added in 1990. IGC had already been collaborating with a similar network in England called GreenNet. In 1987, IGC donated software to GreenNet, and they began sharing e-mail and conferences through a transatlantic link, a partnership that was so successful that IGC helped establish five more networks in Sweden, Canada, Brazil, Nicaragua, and Australia. With the help of the United Nations Development Program and some charitable foundations, the seven networks founded the Association for Progressive Communications (APC) in 1990. The original text-based system provided e-mail and conferencing on inexpensive microcomputers, with software available to partners at no charge. The system was low-cost and low-tech, an appropriate configuration for countries where the telecommunications infrastructure was poor. The conferences carried the world's important alternative news sources, including InterPress Service, the Third World's largest news agency; Environmental News Service; Alternet; and the New Liberation News Service. APC subsequently added LaborNet and WomensNet, and today has twenty-five member networks and more than 50,000 members, making it a small but significant alternative to the corporate-dominated Internet. As the following list demonstrates, APC and other NGOs have been effective in using the Internet and other media in major struggles over the decade.

- After the Chinese government massacre in Tiananmen Square in Beijing in 1989, students transmitted detailed, vivid reports instantly by fax, telephone, and computer networks to activists around the world. The impact of these reports was so immense and immediate that the Chinese government tried to cut telephone links to the outside world and monitored the USENET computer conferences where much of this activity was taking place.
- During the attempted coup in the Soviet Union in 1990, APC

partners used telephone circuits to circumvent official control, sending news dispatches by local phone calls to Baltic states, then to NordNet Sweden, and from there to London-based GreenNet and on to the rest of the APC.

- During the Gulf War, APC networks carried accurate reports of the effects of the war on the Third World, Israel, and the Arab countries, while the official media willingly complied with U.S. government censorship.

- APC provided communication services for environmental and non-governmental organizations and citizen activists before, during, and after the 1992 United Nations Conference on Environment and Development in Rio de Janeiro.

- In the U.S. and Canada, through EcoNet, high-school students monitored water quality in local rivers. In one project, students from different schools located in the same watershed, some upstream and others downstream from a pulp mill, provided each other with reports on water conditions in their part of the system.

- In 1994, the Native Forest Network, a group of environmental and social activists, worked with Cree and Inuit communities in northern Quebec, using computer networking to organize international actions against Hydro-Québec's Great Whale Hydroelectric Project. APC networks helped co-ordinate protests in sixteen cities on three continents. These and other APC-coordinated actions were a factor in the cancellation of the project in late 1994.

- The Zapatista rebels of southern Mexico inaugurated a new form of social struggle, which has been dubbed "Net War" by U.S. national security specialists. With few weapons and fighters, they levered their links with media and NGOs to create trans-border coalitions that were highly connected and coordinated through the Internet. And they used the Internet to spread information about the conflict. Observers expect more such Net wars in the future.[20]

- The Multilateral Agreement on Investment, a charter of rights for global capital, was framed as the first Internet negotiation. The deal was supposed to sail through in relative obscurity, the same way the Internet copyright treaty did at WIPO in Geneva in 1996. But U.S. consumer advocate Ralph Nader put a draft of the MAI on one of his

Web sites, and dozens of other groups in scores of countries quickly picked it up and spread the news. As soon as Canada's Council of Canadians received a draft, it posted it on its Web site and alerted its allies internationally. Once again, as in the success of the Zapatistas, NGOs around the world were key in disseminating information and in coordinating their efforts to defeat the deal. By the time of the MAI's demise, 600 groups in seventy countries had signed on to oppose it.[21]

APC is engaged in scores of lower-profile communications actions as well. A coalition of fair-trade organizations e-mails notices asking consumers to boycott companies using sweatshop labour; a team of women's organizations learns Web site skills and builds a clearing-house of information for South African women; an AIDS research organization in the U.S. puts a full-text database of bibliographies, abstracts, and documents on a Web site for public access and searching. As these examples indicate, the APC and its sister NGOs are truly alternative, since they exist to facilitate local and global social change and to challenge dominant systems. APC is also active at the international level. Since 1992 it has provided telecommunications services for NGOs and other delegates for UN world conferences; it was awarded consultative status to the Economic and Social Council of the UN in 1995.

canada's web networks

APC services are available in Canada through Web Networks, Canada's APC member network. Founded in 1987 as Web, or web.net, as it was then known, and based in Toronto, it serves 3,500 non-profit organizations and progressive Canadians. According to the Web Networks welcome page,

> Web Networks members are more diverse than ever. They're women's advocates, environmentalists, and human rights activists. They're unions, human service agencies, and arts organizations. They're First Nations people, and they're gays and lesbians. They're inter-faith visionaries, and they're alternative health practitioners. And [they are]

a whole host of others who share a commitment to making their world a more just and humane place.

Web Networks is Canada's only national non-profit ISP, and its employees are members of the Communications, Energy and Paperworkers' Union of Canada. An overt commitment to social change infuses its Web pages, where it is described as:

- providing alternative news feeds for members, including Inter-Press Service, Human Rights Information Network and environmental and labour news;
- helping member groups organize campaigns for social and environmental justice;
- assisting non-profit groups wanting to create an on-line presence; and
- providing a home for over 1,000 progressive conferences on a wide array of social justice subjects. The conferences are similar to Usenet newsgroups but are insulated from commercial messages that have turned Usenet into a barren wasteland. Conferences are open only to Web Networks members.

Until 1996, web.net was operated by the NirvCentre, a non-profit organization that assisted other non-profits in using IT. By then, web.net had found itself competing with commercial ISPs for customers and had gone into debt. To remain viable, NirvCentre sold its equipment and computers to Waterloo-based Open Text. Corp. (with which it had a long-term relationship), merged with web.net to become Web Networks, put the profits from the sale into non-profit services, and began charging a fee for service. Says Web Networks communications director Tonya Hancherow, "We charge for services, but we subsidize community organizations. We can put our resources where we believe they will do the most good."[22]

One high-profile Web Networks campaign in 1997 was Citizens for Local Democracy, or C4LD, which fought, unsuccessfully, the Harris government's plan to forcibly amalgamate the six cities of Metro Toronto. C4LD called on community organizer Liz Ryckert, who had co-authored a book about on-line organizing, to develop the group's strategy. She turned the C4LD Web site into a "hive of debate, news and strategizing" that received 17,000 hits, or visits, a week during the winter of 1997. *Toronto Star* columnist Michele Landsberg called it a "cyberspace Democracy Wall."[23] She argued that the small core group of C4LD – no more than 400 members – was more effective than its numbers would indicate, because it used the Net to share information, empower its members, many of whom had never participated in citizen protest before, and develop strategies.

organizing and circuit riding

So the Net can be an effective tool in helping citizen groups organize to achieve their goals even if, as in the case of C4LD, they are not ultimately successful. One mission of Web Networks and APC is to help progressive and alternative groups develop their capability to use IT and computer networks. Founded in 1996, NetAction is a nonprofit organization, supported by the Tides Foundation of San Francisco, which also backs the American APC network, informs citizens about technology-based social and political issues, and helps activists learn how to use the Internet as a tool for organizing, outreach, and advocacy. NetAction publishes two newsletters, including a valuable one called the *Micro$oft Monitor*, and has published several white papers on Microsoft's threat to a healthy, competitive networking environment. Some APC endeavours provide information rather than technical assistance. Corporate Watch is an essential source for information on transnational corporations. It provides links to hundreds of alternative and progressive sites, covering topics such as advertising-greenwash, energy-alternative technology, consumer activism/boycotts, chemical industry toxics, and Internet activism. Corporate Watch has published studies on organizing Silicon Valley workers and the future of the Internet. It is sponsored by the IGC and the Transnational Resource and Action Center.

In the environmental movement it's called capacity building, and on the West Coast dozens of environmental organizations are using computer networks in their work, thanks to the strategic investments of a clutch of progressive American charitable foundations. Seattle-based ONE/Northwest (Online Networking for the Environment), according to its Web site, helps the West Coast environmental community "protect the environment through the effective use of electronic networking technologies." Formed in 1995, the foundation has assisted more than seventy-five British Columbia organizations by setting up e-mail lists, providing detailed assessments of their technological and communications needs, giving presentations and workshops around the province, and providing on-site services where ONE/Northwest staff install modems and network computers, train staff, and solve problems.

ONE/Northwest is the brainchild of West Coast native Paul Brainerd, who made his fortune as the founder of Aldus Corp., the developer of PageMaker software. Brainerd sold the company in 1995 and established a foundation in Seattle with a $50-million endowment to promote environmental stewardship by providing funding to hundreds of environmental groups in the U.S. Pacific Northwest, British Columbia, and Alaska. One Brainerd program, called Communications and Capacity Building, was the starting point for ONE/Northwest.

In 1995 Brainerd and the Bullitt Foundation, another Seattle-based environmental foundation with a capacity-building program, undertook a study of how environmental groups were using electronic networking tools and concluded that one way to increase the networking capabilities of the community was to start a non-profit organization focused solely on providing technical assistance. They pooled resources and brought in additional funders. Seattle is Microsoft country, and several Microsoft executives became participants and contributors to ONE/Northwest. Steve Albertson, a six-year Microsoft veteran, was hired as the foundation's first executive director in 1995.

But acquiring technical expertise in computer communications is not an end in itself for any organization. Brainerd looks for the strategic benefits of electronic networking, and for how providing technical expertise can help a group further its work. The W. Alton Jones Foundation, based in Virginia, is a major funder of environmental groups working on West Coast rainforest issues. This foundation developed a "circuit rider" program to help non-profit organizations (NPOs) make better use of communication and information technologies. It has found that many non-profits were underachievers in the IT world. Circuit riders are talented individuals who provide hands-on, technical consulting and education in the use of computer communications to the NPOs. A small investment in a circuit rider enhanced the impact of other grants the foundation made.[24]

Women's groups are also using computer networks in their organizing work. Feminists began communicating electronically in the early 1980s through newsgroups such as Net.women, mailing lists (Femail) like mail.feminist, and the Women's Bulletin Board System. With the development of the World Wide Web, many women's groups have created homepages to publicize their services and communicate with other organizations. Web Networks has Women'sWeb, which it advertises as "Canada's first Internet-based service and support program for women." Women'sWeb operates on the same model as other Web networks, providing technical services and training and assisting in integrating computer communications into campaigns.[25]

While women's and environmental movements are making effective use of computer networks, the trade union movement, which should be playing a leading role in resisting the commercialization of public information and networks, lags behind. Some unions are finally recognizing the strategic importance of networking. Web Networks hosts UnionNet, which calls itself an "online home for Canada's labour movement." It isn't quite that, but UnionNet does host thirty conferences on topics of interest to working people, such as labr.privatiza (privatization), labr-mexico (Mexico, NAFTA), labr.maritime (maritime workers), and women.labr (women and labour issues). UnionNet also provides labour news from around the world, and is a Web presence for some of Canada's largest unions – the Canadian Auto Workers (CAW), the United Steelworkers, and the Communications, Energy and Paperworkers – as well as some smaller unions like Pulp and Paper Workers of Canada, the Power Workers Union (which represents Ontario Hydro workers), and the Canadian Union of Public Employees' Ontario division (which is an umbrella group for CUPE locals and district councils in Ontario). The Canadian Labour Congress, the labour central for most unions in Canada, also has a Web Networks site.

The CAW launched its Web site in December 1995, adding to the union's channels for communicating internally with its members, locals, and leaders, and externally with activists in other unions, the media, the public, and industry. The site offers weekly newsletters, major policy documents, news releases, bargaining updates, and electronic clipping services. Some locals developed their own homepages, with links to the national site. During negotiations and strike actions, the Net replaced fax machines as the technology of choice for internal communications and for reaching the media and the public. Journalists had direct access to press briefings, even if they were unable to attend. During CAW's strike against the auto industry in 1996, the number of visits to the homepage jumped from 2,000 to 40,000 a week. Many unions recognize that the Internet can never replace the main instruments of collective action – face-to-face communication and group interaction. They have also long understood that the mainstream corporate media present a biased and distorted picture of the trade union movement. The Internet allows unions to bypass the media and communicate directly with the public. And social unions like the CAW, which has a mandate written into its constitution to "work for social justice and contribute to world peace," are using the Net to reach out to like-minded individuals and groups concerned with issues like housing, education, health care, and the environment.

The Internet's most promising use for trade unions may be its ability to reach and mobilize support for union issues worldwide. The locked-out Liverpool dock workers successfully mobilized international support for their struggles on-line in a campaign they called "The World Is Our Picket Line." Dock workers everywhere are fighting "casualization," another business-school term that means fewer workers working harder with fewer benefits and no job security. Casualization means being on call twenty-four hours a day and, once on the job, working until it is finished, often in twelve- or fourteen-hour shifts. In January 1997, dock workers in thirteen countries shut down shipping operations for twenty-four hours, thanks to a long process of solidarity building that used phone, fax, Internet, and videos.

The Korean Confederation of Trade Unions (KCTU) used the Internet to make Korean strikes one of the best-covered labour struggles in Asia. The KCTU distributed its strike bulletins (which appeared as frequently as daily) almost instantaneously in English to hundreds of supporters around the world, starting with e-mail in the early 1990s and moving to the World Wide Web later. Unions and supporters in many countries established links with the KCTU site, and then spread the news to other e-mail lists and Web sites. KCTU supporters could post messages of support and could also find out who else was reading and sending messages, fostering a sense of transparency and solidarity. Notes one supporter, "Without computer communications, some – perhaps many – supporters outside of Korea likely wouldn't have known enough about the struggle in time to offer solidarity."[26]

The International Federation of Chemical, Energy, Mine and General Workers Union (ICEM) used the Internet in its 1996 campaign against multinational Bridgestone Corp., the Japan-based tire maker, over its sacking of 2,300 striking workers at Firestone, its U.S. subsidiary. This was one of the first attempts by a union to mobilize worldwide support for its issues.

a public information coalition

Women's, environmental, and social-justice groups, trade unions, and organizations in many other fields are doing important work for their constituencies using the Internet to broaden their reach and make their efforts more effective. For them, the Internet and IT are secondary tools to help them achieve their goals. Many other individuals and groups see access to the Internet as an end in itself, and like community networkers they are working to create public, non-commercial electronic space. For instance, the individuals and collectives that make up Tao Communications of Toronto are actively working to create public space on the Internet. As a Tao brochure states: "We organize networks as a means of defending and expanding public space, exercising the right to self-determination. We create knowledge through independent public interest research, and distribute it freely through participatory education."

Meanwhile, as a result of Industry Canada's Connecting Canadians strategy, public information is increasingly being colonized and the Internet comes under greater commercial control. The power of the Industry Canada/CANARIE/Bell Canada juggernaut can be resisted only by the formation of a coalition of *everyone* who sees a public, non-commercial role for the Internet. In this coalition, librarians will be a core constituency. They have already played a central role in establishing and supporting community networks. The Vancouver Public Library was a sponsor of Vancouver CommunityNet. In Manitoba's Blue Sky network, most public access terminals (PATs) were placed in Winnipeg public libraries. Public libraries create non-commercial portals that users can log onto, confident that all information and links have been chosen by professional librarians on the basis of the quality of the resources, not commercial consider-ations. To achieve this laudable goal, librarians need to form political alliances with all those individuals and groups in society concerned with the role of libraries in providing public information. Teachers' unions are another obvious constituency that should be involved from the beginning, as are progressive academics and their unions. Unions that represent workers in the telecommunications industry are creating alliances with consumer and community groups "to advo-cate a socially responsive vision of a non-market telecommunication system,"[27] and are also key in the coalition.

Environmental groups, other trade unions, women's groups, and all organizations that use networks as a tool in their work need to make democratic communications a priority. Robert McChesney's admonition, quoted at the beginning of this chapter, about the need for progressive forces to focus on the media applies to the Internet as well.[28] Whatever an organization's first goal might be – achieving equality of opportunity for women, saving old-growth rainforests, fighting for basic workers' rights – the creation of a public Internet and reclamation of public information should be its second goal.

Harvard Law School professor Andrew Shapiro suggests that the burgeoning use of the Internet gives advocates of public, democratic media an opportunity to expand the reach of their views. On the Internet, the problem is not channel and frequency scarcity, as was the case with broadcasting media, but abundance. There is so much material on the Internet that the sheer magnitude creates a dearth of attention. Television-viewing couch potatoes will eventually stumble on community programming as they flip channels sequentially. But the same cannot happen on the Internet, since most users access Web sites through portals and search engines biased towards sites that have paid for prominent positioning.[29] Activists cannot challenge the marketing power of a Microsoft, Disney, or Yahoo!, but by working more closely together they can connect their Web sites and create portals for alternative access. For instance, the San Francisco–based Economic Security Project has created what it describes as a "quasi-Web portal for people with a humanistic, progressive point of view."[30]

But creating alternative portals is not enough. People concerned about reclaiming information resources need to move from technology to the political arena and challenge corporate power and propaganda. Corporate-sponsored futurists like Nicholas Negroponte and Don Tapscott claim we are moving into a knowledge society because of greater use of information networks and technology. Once again this is the old technological determinism argument. The reality is that we are still in the same corporate-dominated society, only this time the domination is greater because of the surveillance capabilities of computer networks.

a charter of information rights

Progressives cannot rely on governments to deliver the information services citizens need. Even if social movements and community networks form broad and powerful alliances to pressure sympathetic governments to strengthen access to information, privacy protection, and other rights, there is little to prevent backsliding once the heat is removed. Bureaucrats do not enjoy having their actions held up to public scrutiny, and industry lobbyists are ever present, pressuring governments to change the rules in industry's favour. Along with citizen activism, we need legal guarantees and protections for a new set of human rights, which are essential in an IT-dominated society. Only when citizens have obtained these rights will they be able to regain control over public information resources.

Modern struggles for human rights began in the eighteenth century. The War of American Independence and the French Revolution sought basic civil rights, such as freedom of thought, religion, speech, and assembly; the right to own property; and the right to justice. In the nineteenth century, struggles focused on citizens' rights to hold public office; to elect local and national representatives who participate in passing laws and formulating policies; and to join trade unions, which represent their interests in the workplace. Some groups, notably women, didn't achieve such political rights until the twentieth century, when the focus shifted to social rights, which include the rights to basic standards of living, housing, health services, and education. And as we enter the twentieth-first century, we need a new set of rights of citizenship, called information rights. Much work on achieving these rights has already been done at the national and international levels. The task now is to create public awareness about the threats to public information and the need to protect citizen interests.

right to privacy

Classical Greece and ancient China recognized the need for a balance between public and private worlds, but it wasn't until the emergence of newspapers in the late-nineteenth century that a separate right to privacy was first proposed. Two Harvard law professors, Louis Brandeis and Samuel Warren, worried about the undue amount of newspaper publicity given to Warren's wife and his family's Back Bay social activities. They wrote a famous article decrying the yellow journalism of the day and, for the first time, outlining a legal definition of the right to privacy. For them, each individual had the right to determine to what extent his thoughts, sentiments, and emotions would be communicated to others. Today, media invasion of privacy remains a concern, but the issue faced by most citizens is protection of personal information – name, address, telephone number, social insurance number, supermarket and electronic-commerce purchases, medical records, video-store rentals, and so on. Public- and private-sector organizations collect huge amounts of information about individuals and face enormous pressures to use the information for purposes other than why it was collected. A health-insurance company obtains information about a person's drug prescriptions, for example, and refuses coverage on that basis. A politician rents pornographic videos and the information is obtained by a rival political party. A person flies to Vail, Colorado, at Christmas and the information is passed on to ski-equipment dealers.

The idea of data privacy grew out of these potential threats. It maintains that personal information should be collected only when truly warranted, used only for the purposes set out beforehand, disclosed only in narrowly defined circumstances, and be accessible to the individual it concerns. Federal and provincial privacy laws apply to the information practices of governments, but even here grey areas exist (data-matching, for example, allows information in federal employment-insurance files, say, to be matched with provincial government social-assistance records to find suspected welfare cheats). John Manley's Bill C-54 is intended to apply a right to information privacy to the private sector, but it contains large gaps, the most significant being that the federal privacy commissioner can make recommendations only, not binding orders, which means that a recalcitrant corporation cannot be compelled to comply with the law. While these existing and proposed laws do give citizens some protections in specific areas of information-gathering, Canada has not progressed far towards the goal of recognizing privacy as a basic human right. Few laws apply to privacy rights in the workplace, for instance, where electronic monitoring of worker performance is endemic. Section 8 of the Charter of Rights and Freedoms stipulates that "everyone has the right to be secure against unreasonable search and seizure," but this is of limited use when we are facing the information practices of Web site operators.

A right to privacy must be enshrined in the Charter of Rights and Freedoms, but it must be done carefully or Canadians may actually end up with fewer information rights. This is because privacy laws are usually connected to laws that provide for access to information in government files. The two laws work together. Access-to-information laws make availability of government files a right of citizenship, but because so much of this information concerns individuals, privacy laws must also come into play. The Mulroney government had a well-known hostility to freedom of information. When the government-sponsored Beaudoin-Dobbie Special Joint Committee on a Renewed Canada issued its report in 1992, the government appended to the section on the Charter a recommendation that a right to privacy be added. This item appeared from nowhere and had not been discussed by the committee. Opposition members feared that the Tory government was attempting an end run around access. Enshrining a right to privacy without a right of access would mean that privacy would take precedence over access and the government would be able to reject access requests on the grounds that they violated somebody's privacy. Was a conspiracy afoot? The privacy right was promoted by Bruce Phillips, Canada's privacy commissioner, who also happened to be Mulroney's former press secretary. Access commissioner John Grace was not even informed that the privacy clause was added to the report.[31] Privacy protection must be added to the Charter, but it must be accompanied by a right of access to information.

right of access to information

Freedom-of-information laws have made the greatest advances of all information rights. The federal Access to Information Act was passed, along with the Privacy Act, in 1983 by the Trudeau government. All provincial governments have since passed similar laws. Worthwhile access laws are based on three principles: 1) citizens have a right of access to information in government files; 2) necessary exceptions from the right of access must be limited and specific; and 3) decisions on disclosure must be reviewed independently of government. The federal government says its law follows these principles, but there are so many exceptions, and they are so vague, that the law's effectiveness – and citizens' basic rights – are seriously compromised. Government bureaucrats have many ways to hide information, delay requests, and generally frustrate the right of access.

Some critics, like Ottawa's Ken Rubin, claim the act is a failure and in some ways a step backwards. One particularly dangerous provision is the innocuous-sounding Section 68, which stipulates that any records that have been published, or are likely to be published, within ninety days are excluded from the act altogether. At first glance, this seems reasonable; if the information is already available, or soon to be available, in libraries, the government should not be required to collect it again. But the problem is that governments are increasingly licensing commercial vendors to "publish" records in expensive databases. Once these have been published, the government no longer has to provide access under the act. And since all government information is being produced in electronic formats – as CD-ROMs or posted on Web sites, where fee-paying services will soon come into effect – access may be restricted. Citizens must have a right of access to information in government files enshrined in the Charter along with a right to privacy.

right of access to information services and advice

Government information is well organized and usually reliable. The same cannot be said for most information available on the Internet. Citizens face an overwhelming deluge flooding over them from myriad sources. Few have the time, skills, and experience to find, collect, analyze, and interpret all the information available on a subject.[32] To overcome this obstacle, we need a network of easily accessible information services to help us perform these tasks. These services would collect information Canadians need as citizens, make it readily available, and ensure that it is up to date. Citizens also need advice to help them interpret the information they collect, tailor it to their specific circumstances, and decide on specific courses of action.

In an age dominated by the information industry, citizens must have a right to access such services. This right, seemingly new, is merely a codification of existing services, such as the free public library. Librarians play a crucial role in making information accessible to patrons. People also receive information advice from a variety of governmental and non-governmental sources: unions provide members with information on the risks of cancer associated with workplace hazards; government labs provide information on research into product safety; social-service agencies provide information on programs and services; high-school and college counsellors provide information on jobs and careers; consumer associations produce easily accessible magazines and other publications that evaluate product performance; community legal clinics provide general legal advice for some citizens; government telephone networks direct callers to appropriate departments to have their information requests answered. This right recognizes the crucial nature of these services and the fact that they will grow in importance as the glut of information makes it increasingly difficult for citizens to separate the valuable from the junk.

right to benefit from intellectual and artistic works

A most pressing information need for citizens is a recalibration of the balance between the rights of society and the rights of authors and inventors over works of the mind, so-called intellectual property. The original purpose of IP laws, as I've argued, was to balance the rights of society and the rights of creators so they could each benefit from new works and inventions. I've also argued that this balance has been destroyed, and that because of the continuing expansion of IP rights society receives few benefits from new works. Society seems willing to allow copyright monopolies to exist because of the myth of the author as creative genius. But when that myth is used to buttress huge storehouses of intellectual property accumulated by Disney, Thomson Corp., and News Corp., and when most works borrow freely from the common pool of information developed by society over centuries, it's time to rethink the purpose of copyright. Authors, songwriters, poets, and painters must be compensated for their works. That's a given. But society's rights must also be protected. It's time to bring an end to the view expressed by Industry Minister John Manley and Canadian Heritage Minister Sheila Copps when they introduced amendments to the Canadian Copyright Act in 1996. The proposed law, they wrote, would "achieve a fair balance between the rights of those [who] create works and the needs of those who use them." Users — or, better, citizens — must have rights and not just needs. As the 1948 United Nations Universal Declaration of Human Rights proclaimed:

27 (i) Everyone has the right freely to participate in the cultural life of the Community, to enjoy the arts and to share in scientific advancement and its benefits.

27 (ii) Everyone has the right to the protection of the moral and
material interests resulting from any scientific, literary or artistic
production of which he is an author.

right to communicate

The right to communicate originated from the communication imbal-
ances and inequalities that faced the world after the Second World
War. Article 19 of the United Nations Universal Declaration of Human
Rights states that "[e]veryone has the right to freedom of opinion and
expression; this right includes freedom to hold opinions without inter-
ference and to seek, receive and impart information and ideas through
any media and regardless of frontiers." The International Covenant on
Civil and Political Rights (1966) stipulates that the right to freedom of
expression "comprises the freedom to seek out, to receive and to communicate information and ideas of all kinds, regardless of frontier,
whether in oral, printed or artistic form, or by any other means of the
individual's choice." The development of American-controlled, direct-
broadcast, satellite-transmission systems in the 1960s meant that only
one aspect of the principle, the right to receive information – mainly
U.S.-originated information – was achieved, while rights to seek and
to impart or communicate information were ignored.

The right to communicate was inspired by the Non-Aligned
Movement of Nations at the United Nations Educational, Scientific,
and Cultural Organization (UNESCO) in the 1970s. This right was
encompassed within what was called the New World Information and
Communication Order (NWICO). The right to receive information and
ideas – the free-flow-of-information doctrine – was the clarion call
for the emerging global information industry, which was represented
at the UN by the Reagan and Thatcher governments. During the 1980s,
UNESCO was split by the right-to-communicate and free-flow-of-
information camps. In 1985, Reagan pulled the U.S. out of UNESCO,
and a year later Thatcher followed suit. Since these two countries
paid the lion's share of UNESCO's bills, the organization was under
enormous pressure to drop its support for NWICO, which it did several
years later with the election of the American-backed Frederico Mayor
of Spain as director-general of UNESCO. Within several years, all

mention of NWICO disappeared from official discourse and the Disney Channel could get on with colonizing the world.

To be free, free-flow must be two-way. The Internet promised to provide greater opportunities for two-way communication than other media had done. As the information industry solidifies its grip on the Internet, however, that promise recedes. Nevertheless, the right to communicate remains alive as a movement at the international level. Member organizations in the Association for Progressive Communication and hundreds of NGOs (especially in non-OECD countries) are working for a greater right to communicate. In September 1998, more than 200 organizations and individuals sponsored an international forum on communication and citizenship in El Salvador; the forum urged the United Nations to convene a world conference on communication.

The right to communicate is especially relevant to the Canadian experience. For decades, we have faced the onslaught of American television programming and Hollywood films, and are denied access to Canadian programs and films that would express our own viewpoints and concerns. Every time the CBC closes an international bureau because of budget cuts, Canadians end up relying more heavily on American reports and an American perspective on the world. The Charter of Rights and Freedoms does contain a provision for "freedom of thought, belief, opinion and expression, including freedom of the press and other media of communication," but as William Birdsall points out, this right reflects the traditional one-way communication of the free-flow-of-information doctrine.[33] The Charter should be amended to reflect the right to seek, receive, and convey information.

Only when citizens have obtained these rights and faced down John Manley's propaganda campaign will we regain control over public information resources. And only then will we move forward into a genuine knowledge society.

endnotes

Introduction

1. See Herschell Hardin, *The Privatization Putsch* (Halifax, NS: Institute for Research on Public Policy, 1989), for a spirited defence of Canada's record of public entrepreneurship.

Chapter 1: Connecting Canadians . . . to What?

1. David Aikin, "Canada 10th on Information Highway: Study," *National Post*, 6 Apr. 1999, A1.
2. Peter Watkins, "Just Logging On Won't Win the War of the Net," *National Post*, 7 Apr. 1999, C7.
3. Industry Canada, "Speaking Notes for the Honourable John Manley, Minister of Industry, Vancouver Board of Trade, Connecting Canadians," Vancouver, 17 Dec. 1998, 4.
4. Industry Canada, Task Force on Electronic Commerce, "Canada Moves to Promote E-Commerce," Ottawa, 1 Oct. 1998.
5. Canada, "The Canadian Electronic Commerce Strategy" (Ottawa, 1998), 25.
6. Ibid., 4.
7. Ibid., 38.
8. James Love, "Notes from the OECD October 7-9, 1998, Ministerial Meeting on Electronic Commerce at Ottawa, Ontario, Canada," Consumer Project on Technology, Info-Policy-Notes, 19 Oct. 1998.
9. Sid Shniad, "An Excerpt from Comments Made by IBM President Louis Gerstner, Jr., at the OECD Ministerial Conference on Electronic Commerce, Ottawa, Ontario, Canada," Universal Access Canada, 8 Oct. 1998.
10. Information Highway Advisory Council, *Connection Community Content: The Challenge of the Information Highway* (Ottawa, 1995), 162.
11. National Library of Canada, Task Force on Digitization, "Towards a Learning Nation: the Digital Contribution," Ottawa, 31 Dec. 1997.

12. Tyler Hamilton, "Ottawa Chooses Mpact for E-commerce Service," *Globe and Mail*, 27 Nov. 1998, B7.

13. Eric Beauchesne, "Cuts Rob Canadians of Information," *Vancouver Sun*, 20 June 1990, A8.

14. Ronald C. McMahon, "Cost Recovery and Statistics Canada," *Government Information in Canada* 2, no. 4 (Spring 1996).

15. Denis DesJardins, "StatsCan Not Out for a Profit," *Vancouver Sun*, 24 Nov. 1992, A12.

16. Vincent Mosco, *The Pay-per Society* (Toronto: Garamond Press, 1989), 67.

17. Robert Babe, "Convergence and the New Technologies," in *The Cultural Industries in Canada*, Michael Dorland, ed. (Toronto: James Lorimer, 1996), 304.

18. Graham Norgate, "Should Information Be Free? Or Is It Like Water?" *Feliciter*, May 1995, 11-14.

19. Industry Canada, "Building the Information Society: Moving Canada Into the 21st Century" (Ottawa: Minister of Supply and Services Canada, 1996).

20. Information Highway Advisory Council, *Preparing for a Digital World: Final Report of the Information Highway Advisory Council* (Ottawa, 1997).

21. Herbert S. Dordick and Dale Lehman, "Information Highways: Trickle Down Infrastructure," in *The People's Right to Know*, Frederick Williams and John Pavlik, eds. (Hillsdale NJ: Lawrence Erlbaum Associates, 1994), 174.

22. Ibid., 175.

23. Ibid., 176.

24. Ibid.

25. Paul Luke, "Literacy Skills Pad Salaries," *The Province* (Vancouver), 13 May 1997, A33.

26. Southam News, "Westerners 'More Literate' Than Easterners," *Vancouver Sun*, 1 Sept. 1996, A3.

27. Information Highway Advisory Council, *Connection Community Content*, 58.

Chapter 2: The Information Industry Targets the Public Library

1. Heather Menzies, *Whose Brave New World: The Information Highway and the New Economy* (Toronto: Between the Lines, 1996), 148.

2. Herbert Schiller and Anita Schiller, "Libraries, Public Access to Information, and Commerce," in *The Political Economy of Communication*, Vincent Masco and Janet Wasks, eds. (Madison: University of Wisconsin Press, 1988), 147.

3. Quoted in Karl Nyren, "Information Entrepreneurs Stake Claims at LACUNY," *Library Journal*, 1 June 1979, 1200.

4. Herbert Schiller, *Information Inequality: The Deepening Social Crisis in America* (New York: Routledge, 1996), 36.

5. Stan Skrzeszewski, "Report on the Library Consultation Meeting," Science Promotion and Academic Affairs, Industry Canada, 19 Apr. 1996. Accessed on the SchoolNet Web site at www.schoolnet.ca/ln-rb/e/about/meeting.html

6. Stan Skrzeszewski and Maureen Cubberley, "Introducing LibraryNet: A Concept Paper," Industry Canada, 23 May 1996. Accessed on the SchoolNet Web site at www.schoolnet.ca/ln-rb/e/about/concept.html

7. ASM Consultants, "Session Abstracts, Libraries as Leaders in Community Economic Development," Victoria Conference Centre, British Columbia, 16-17 June 1998. Accessed on the ASM Web site at www.asmconsultants.com/abstract.html

8. Vicki Whitmell, "Fee-based Information Services as an Important Tool in Enhancing Community Economic Development," Victoria Conference Centre, British Columbia, 16-17 June 1998. Accessed on the ASM Web site at www.asm-consultants.com/abstract.html

9. Industry Canada, "Welcome to LibraryNet." Accessed on the SchoolNet Web site at www.schoolnet.ca/ln-rb/e/index.html

10. Ekos Research Associates, "Canadians, Public Libraries and the Information Highway: Final Report," October 1998. Accessed on the SchoolNet Web site at www.schoolnet.ca/ln-rb/e/ekos/ekos4.html

11. Cal Millar, "Oakville Opens Virtual Library," *Toronto Star*, 6 Apr. 1998, F2.

12. Canada's SchoolNet, "Industry Canada and Avita Technologies Announce the Launch of an E-commerce Application for Public Libraries," *@SchoolNet Today*, 18 Dec. 1998. Accessed on the SchoolNet Web site at www.schoolnet.ca/today/press/1053.html

13. Gates Library Foundation, "About GLF." Accessed on the GLF Web site at www.glf.org/about/default.html

14. Steve Lohr, "Gates to Aid Libraries, in Footsteps of Carnegie," *New York Times*, 24 June 1997, D1.

15. "ALA, Microsoft Launch 'Libraries Online!'" *American Libraries* (Jan. 1996): 7.

16. "Microsoft Announces Initiative to Bring Libraries Online! to 41 Communities," *PR Newswire*, 9 Oct. 1997. Accessed on www.webtechniques.com/news/101096c.shtml

17. "Microsoft Expands Libraries Online! to Canada," News Release, 25 July 1996. Accessed on www.librariesonline.org/press/canada1.html

18. Jenny Lee, "Microsoft Makes Donation to VPL," *Vancouver Sun*, 24 Jan. 1997, D1.

19. Microsoft Canada and Hill & Knowlton, "Unique Partnership to Provide Access to Technology to Local Families," News Release, 3 Dec. 1996. Accessed on www.opl.ottawa.on.ca/english/new/press.html

20. Susan Riley, "Corporate Money Not the Real Threat to Public Libraries," *Ottawa Citizen*, 28 Oct. 1996, D5.

21. Geoffrey Nunberg, "Digital Dilemmas," *Vancouver Sun*, 16 Feb. 1999, A17.

22. Quoted in Violet L. Coughlin, *Larger Units of Public Library Service in Canada* (Metuchin, NJ: Scarecrow Press, 1968), 33. This section is based on Coughlin's account.

23. Ibid.

24. Ibid., 52.

25. Joseph Frazier Wall, *Andrew Carnegie* (Oxford: Oxford University Press, 1970), 815. This section relies on Wall's extensive biography. See also George Swetnam, *Andrew Carnegie* (Boston: Twayne, 1980), 149-52.

26. Diane Mittermeyer, "The Public Library Boards of Trustees Versus the Committees of City Council: A Power Game," *Canadian Journal of Information and Library Science* 19, no. 1 (Apr. 1994): 3.

27. Charles Mandel, "User Fees for Edmonton Public Library," *Quill & Quire* 59, no. 12 (Dec. 1993): 19.

28. Elizabeth Aird, "As Readers Languish, the Library Motors Along," *Vancouver Sun*, 3 Jan. 1998, C3.

29. John McCallum, "Libraries & Librarians at the Crossroads," *CAUT Bulletin*, Nov. 1996, 8.

30. Schiller and Schiller, "Libraries, Public Access to Information, and Commerce," 149.

31. John Haar, "The Politics of Electronic Information: A Reassessment," in *Critical Approaches to Information Technology in Librarianship*, John Buschman, ed. (Westport, CT: Greenwood Press, 1993), 199.

32. Guy Lamolinara, "Metamorphosis of a National Treasure," *American Libraries*, Mar. 1996, 32.

33. Ibid., 31.

34. Wayne Kondro, "Ottawa Undertakes Review of National Library and National Archives," *Perspectives* 2, no. 3 (May 1998). Accessed on www.hssfc.ca/Pub/PublicationsEng.html

35. Lamolinara, "Metamorphosis," 31.

36. Michael Lesk, "Going Digital: Electronic Libraries Will Make Today's Internet Pale by Comparison, But Building Them Will Not Be Easy." Accessed on www.sciam.com/0397issue/0397lesk.html

37. LaMolinara, "Metamorphosis," 32.

38. The White House, *The National Information Infrastructure: Agenda for Action*, Washington, D.C., 15 Sept. 1993.

39. Canadian Initiative on Digital Libraries, "What's New: September Update." Accessed on the National Library of Canada Web site at www.nlc-bnc.ca/cidl/newe.html

40. Kondro, "Ottawa Undertakes Review."

41. Howard Wactlar, "Informedia Digital Video Library," *D-Lib Magazine*, July/Aug. 1996. Accessed on www.dlib.org/dlib/july96/07wactlar.html

42. Carnegie-Mellon University, "The NetBill Project," 11 Apr. 1997. Accessed on the Carnegie-Mellon University Web site at www.ini.cmu.edu/NETBILL/

43. Carnegie-Mellon University, "The NetBill Overview." Accessed on the Carnegie-Mellon University Web site at www.ini.cmu.edu/NETBILL/pubs/CompCon_TOC.html

44. Ibid.

45. Carnegie-Mellon, "The NetBill Project."

46. Canadian Library Association, "1995 Conference, Agenda 16, Resolution 1," *Feliciter*, Jul./Aug. 1995, 14-15.

47. Brian Reynolds, "Public Library Funding: Issues, Trends, and Resources," *Advances in Librarianship* 18 (New York: Academic Press, 1994), 171.

48. Canadian Press, "Albertans Shell Out for Library Cards," CP newswire, 3 June 1995.

49. Brian Campbell, "Forming and Implementing a National Information Policy," *Canadian Library Journal*, Feb. 1992, 13.

50. Nick Moore, "Rights And Responsibilities in an Information Society," *Journal of Information, Law and Technology*, no. 1 (1998). Accessed on elj.warwick.ac.uk/jilt/infosoc/98_1moor/

Chapter 3: The Private Government of Connected Canada

1. Communications Canada, "Communications for the Twenty-First Century: Media and Messages in the Information Age" (Ottawa, 1987), 5.

2. Robert Babe, *Telecommunications in Canada* (Toronto: University of Toronto Press, 1990), 6.

3. Ibid., 7.

4. Ibid., 8.

5. Information and Technology Access Office, "British Columbia's Electronic Highway" (Victoria, B.C.: Ministry of Government Services, n.d.), 1.

6. David Johnston, Deborah Johnston, and Sunny Handa, *Getting Canada OnLine* (Toronto: Stoddart, 1995), 211-12.

7. Industry Canada, "Speaking Notes for the Honourable John Manley, Minister of Industry, Vancouver Board of Trade," Vancouver, 17 Dec. 1998, 3.

8. Keith Spicer, quoted in Robert Babe, "Convergence and the New Technologies," in *The Cultural Industries in Canada*, Michael Dorland, ed. (Toronto: James Lorimer, 1996), 295.

9. Ibid.

10. Andrew Bjerring, "Research Networking in Canada: CA*net and CANARIE." Posted on uwo.newsletters, USENET, University of Western Ontario, London, 9 Nov. 1992.

11. A. Paul Pross, *Group Politics and Public Policy*, 2d. ed. (Toronto: Oxford University Press, 1992), 119-21. See also David Firman, "Connection Community Control: An Analysis of the Information Highway Policy Community," CMNS 482-4, School of Communication, Simon Fraser University, 21 Apr. 1997.

12. Gary Chapman, "Microsoft Trial Obscures Larger Inequality Issues," *Los Angeles Times*, 2 Oct. 1998.

13. Laura Eggertson, "Manley Advocates Aerospace Funding," *Globe and Mail*, 12 June 1997, B4.

14. Giles Gherson, "Chrétien's New Cabinet Ignores Thriving Left Wing," *Vancouver Sun*, 13 June 1997, A4.

15. Edward Greenspon and Anthony Wilson-Smith, *Double Vision: The Inside Story of the Liberals in Power* (Toronto: Doubleday, 1996), 203.

16. Hugh Winsor, "Contract Dispute Raises Lobby Issue," *Globe and Mail*, 4 Dec. 1995, A1.

17. Ibid.

18. Industry Canada, "Lobbyists Registration." Accessed on the Strategis Web site at strategis.ic.gc.ca

19. Hugh Winsor, "Lobby Group's Contract with Ottawa to Go Ahead," *Globe and Mail*, 15 Dec. 1995, A14.

20. For a history of CANARIE and early networking developments in Canada, see Leslie R. Shade, "Computer Networking in Canada: From CA*net to CANARIE," *Canadian Journal of Communication* 19, no. 1 (Winter 1994): 53-69.

21. Accessed on CANARIE Web site at www.canarie.ca

22. Accessed on CANARIE Web site at www.canarie.ca/eng/appdev/comp/compmain.html

23. CANARIE, "Director Biographies." Accessed on CANARIE Web site at www.canarie.ca/eng/org/directors/

24. CANARIE, "Technology and Applications Development Projects 1997." Accessed on CANARIE Web site at www.canarie.ca/eng/outreach/publications/press/TADbackgrounder.html

25. Newbridge Networks, *Annual Report to Shareholders 1997*, 50.

26. Newbridge Networks, *Annual Report to Shareholders 1998*, 63.

27. CANARIE, "Director Biographies."

28. Atlantic Institute for Market Studies, "The Coming Upheaval in Higher Education." Accessed on AIMS Web site at www.aims.ca/upheaval.html

29. The 21st Century Learning Initiative Canadian Working Group, "Shared Values and Beliefs." Accessed on their Web site at www.21learn.org/innov/canadatxt.html

30. Ken Fockler, "Historic Day." Posted on private distribution list, and reported on can.infohighway, USENET, 1 April 1997.

31. Search of *Canadian News Disk* database, 12 Aug. 1998.

32. Jim Carroll and Rick Broadhead, *Canadian Internet Handbook*, 1995 edition (Scarborough, ON: Prentice-Hall Canada, 1994), 56-57.

33. Elizabeth Angus and Duncan McKie, "Canada's Information Highway: Services, Access and Affordability," New Media Branch and Information Technologies Industry Branch, Industry Canada (May 1994), 94-96.

34. CANARIE, "ONPS Project List." "Descriptions, 1996." Accessed on the CANARIE Web site at www.canarie.ca/frames/startappdeve.html

35. Mark Evans, "PSINet Plans $100-Million Network," *Globe and Mail*, 21 Jan. 1999, B5.

36. Worth Johnson, "CA*net II: The Next Generation Internet in Canada," *Focus* (Simon Fraser University, Fall 1997), 1.

37. Robert McChesney, "The Global Struggle for Democratic Communication," *Monthly Review* 48, no. 3 (July-Aug. 1996): 11.

38. Reprinted in *Focus* (Simon Fraser University, Fall 1997), 7.

39. "Prime Minister Honours University Staff," *Focus* (Simon Fraser University, Fall 1997), 6.

Chapter 4: Telephone Companies Enter the Content Business

1. Atlantic Institute for Market Studies, "AIMS." Accessed on AIMS Web site at www.aims.ca

2. Atlantic Institute for Market Studies, "AIMS – Annual Report," 1997. Accessed on AIMS Web site at www.aims.ca/annualreport/1997/arenglish.html

3. Ibid.

4. Atlantic Institute for Market Studies, "The Coming Upheaval in Higher Education." Accessed on AIMS Web site at www.aims.ca/upheaval.html
5. Atlantic Institute for Market Studies, "AIMS — Annual Report," 1997.
6. Maritime Telephone & Telegraph, "MT&T's Virtual Learning Centre." Accessed on MT&T Web site at www.mtt.ca/MTTU/VirtualLearningCentre/
7. Robert Babe, *Telecommunications in Canada* (Toronto: University of Toronto Press, 1990), 95.
8. Ibid., 99-100.
9. Edward Greenspon and Anthony Wilson-Smith, *Double Vision: The Inside Story of the Liberals in Power* (Toronto: Doubleday, 1996), 97.
10. Robert L. Simison, "OECD Panel Urges Focus on Shareholder Value," *Globe and Mail*, 2 Apr. 1998, B14.
11. Lawrence Surtees, "BCE Hires Gourde for Satellite Arm," *Globe and Mail*, 1 Apr. 1998, B4.
12. Lawrence Surtees, "Former Competition Bureau Chief Joins Telus," *Globe and Mail*, 5 July 1996, B3.
13. Industry Canada, Competition Bureau, "Director Announces Results of Competition Act Review of Stentor," *Backgrounder* 57 (22 Feb. 1996), 7.
14. Scott Feschuk, "Addy to Step Down from Competition Bureau," *Globe and Mail*, 6 June 1996, B4.
15. Hudson Janisch, "Recasting Regulation for a New Telecommunications Era," *Policy Options*, Sept. 1994, 20.
16. Stentor Telecom, "The Information Highway: Canada's Road to Economic and Social Renewal, A Vision Statement," Ottawa, 1993.
17. Ibid.
18. Ibid., 8.
19. Ibid., 10.
20. "Value-Added Services Key to Successful Telecommunications," *Globe and Mail*, 9 Dec. 1994, C4.
21. David Smith, "Broadband Information Highway Just Around the Corner," *Vancouver Sun*, 6 Apr. 1994, A1.
22. Industry Canada, "The Canadian Information Highway: Building Canada's Information and Communications Infrastructure" (Ottawa: Supply and Services Canada, 1994), 21-32.
23. Ian Austen, "Federal Advisers on Information Highway Taking a Secret Route," *Vancouver Sun*, 17 Mar. 1994, D7.
24. Ibid.
25. Information Highway Advisory Council, *Connection Community Content: The Challenge of the Information Highway* (Ottawa: Supply and Services Canada, 1995), 92-93.
26. Philip DeMont, "BC Tel's Special Status Key to Cable Battle," *Financial Post*, 6 Aug. 1996, 5.
27. John Rainford, "Inside the High-Powered Telecommunications Lobby," *Hill Times*, n.d.
28. John Sawatsky, *The Insiders: Power, Money and Secrets in Ottawa* (Toronto: McClelland & Stewart, 1989), 61.

29. Industry Canada, "Consultant Lobbyist Detail Report." Accessed on Strategis Web site at www.strategis.ic.gc.ca

30. Capital Hill Group, "Our Public Affairs Team." Accessed on Capital Hill Group Web site at www.capitalhill.ca/e_index.html

31. Alex Carey, *Taking the Risk Out of Democracy: Corporate Propaganda versus Freedom and Liberty* (Urbana, IL: University of Illinois Press, 1997), 88-90.

32. For an account of the campaign, see William Boei and Peter O'Neil, "Lines Cleared for Competition in Cable TV, Phone Service," *Vancouver Sun*, 7 Aug. 1996, A1; Robert Williamson, "BC Tel Fights Foreign Ownership Move," *Globe and Mail*, 24 June 1995, B3; William Boei, "Victoria Asks Feds to Drop BC Tel Rule for Ownership," *Vancouver Sun*, 20 Dec. 1995, D1.

33. John Graham, "Bell's E-commerce Strategy Emerges," *National Post*, 5 Apr. 1999, C16; Tyler Hamilton, "BCE Emergis Becomes a Heavy Hitter," *Globe and Mail*, 18 Feb. 1999, T4.

34. Lawrence Surtees, "Telus Geomatics Plots Software Success," *Globe and Mail*, 8 Oct. 1998, C4.

Chapter 5: Enclosing the Information Commons

1. Simon Chester, "A $100 Million Fight — Copyright on the Infobahn," *Playback*, 7 Oct. 1996, 20.

2. David Vaver, *Intellectual Property Law* (Toronto: Irwin Law, 1997), 271.

3. Jim Carroll, "One Author's Vigilance," *Media* 3, no. 3 (Fall 1996): 8.

4. Ann Diamond, "The Year of the Rat," *Canadian Forum*, Oct. 1996, 23.

5. Periodical Writers Association of Canada, "Copyright Hall of Shame." Accessed on the PWAC Web site at www.cycor.ca/PWAC/offend.html

6. Periodical Writers Association of Canada, "TERLA Contracts Coming Soon," *Contracts Alert*, no. 10 (Oct. 1998). Accessed on www.web.net~pwac

7. Charles Mann, "Who Owns Your Next Good Idea?" *Atlantic Monthly*, Sept. 1998, 66.

8. Gillian Davies, *Copyright and the Public Interest* (Munich: Max Planck Institute for Foreign and International Patent, Copyright and Competition Law, 1994), 2.

9. Mann, "Who Owns," 66.

10. The copyright clause is in Article I, Section 8.

11. *Hansard: Parliamentary Debates*, vol. 56, no. 5 (Feb. 1841), 346.

12. Quoted in Association of Universities and Colleges in Canada et al., "Education and Library Groups Reject Copyright Bill," *Communiqué*, Ottawa, 14 Mar. 1997.

13. Vaver, *Intellectual Property Law*, 23.

14. Anne Wells Branscombe, *Who Owns Information?* (New York: Basic Books, 1994), 1.

15. Thomson Corp., *Annual Report 1996*, 6-7.

16. Ibid., 38.

17. Ibid., 9.

18. Ronald Bettig, *Copyrighting Culture: The Political Economy of Intellectual Property* (Boulder, CO: Westview Press, 1996), 49.

19. Mann, "Who Owns," 58.
20. Garry Blackwell, "Mine! Mine! Mine!" *Home Computing & Entertainment*, n.d., 46
21. Robert Allen, *Enclosure and the Yeoman* (Oxford: Clarendon Press, 1992).
22. Ibid., 18.
23. J.M. Neeson, *Commoners, Common Right, Enclosure and Social Change in England, 1700-1820* (Cambridge: Cambridge University Press, 1993), 12.
24. Allen, *Enclosure*, 21.
25. Myra Tawfik, "The Secret of Transforming Art into Gold: Intellectual Property Issues in Canada-U.S. Relations," *Canadian-American Public Policy*, no. 20 (Dec. 1994): 3.
26. World Intellectual Property Organization, "What Is WIPO? Accessed on the WIPO Web site at www.wipo.org/eng/main.html
27. Tawfik, "Transforming Art into Gold," 18-19.
28. Ibid., 15.
29. Ibid., 16.
30. Ibid., 11-12.
31. Ibid., 8.
32. James Boyle, *Shamans, Software and Spleens: Law and the Construction of the Information Society* (Cambridge, MA: Harvard University Press, 1996), 123, fn. 9.
33. Jonathan Manthorpe, "Piracy No Longer the Stuff of Old Movies," *Vancouver Sun*, 16 Feb. 1998, A14.
34. *Webster's New Collegiate Dictionary* (Springfield, MA: G.&C. Merriam Co., 1981).
35. *The Compact Edition of the Oxford English Dictionary*, vol. 2 (Oxford: Oxford University Press, 1971).
36. Vaver, *Intellectual Property Law*, 297.
37. Tawfik, "Transforming Art into Gold," 5, fn. 13.
38. David Aikin, "Software Piracy Shocking, Costly," *Vancouver Sun*, 17 June 1998, D2.
39. Canada Newswire, "Microsoft and Canadian Authorities Stop Alleged Software Piracy Operation," 3 Oct. 1996. Accessed on Newswire Web site at www.newswire.ca/releases/October1996/03/c0604.html
40. Canadian Alliance Against Software Theft, "The Contribution of the Packaged Software Industry to the Canadian Economy." A study conducted by Price Waterhouse Coopers, commissioned by the Business Software Alliance (BSA), Oct. 1998. Accessed on the CAAST Web site at www.caast.org/resource/news/10221998-a.asp
41. Pamela Samuelson and John Browning, "Confab Clips Copyright Cartel: How a Grab for Copyright Powers Was Foiled in Geneva," *Wired* 5.03, March 1997. Accessed on the *Wired* magazine Web site at www.wired.com/wired/5.03/netizen_pr.html
42. "Copyright Rules Updated for the Net," *InfoWorld Canada* 22, no. 2, Feb. 97, 12.
43. Peter Lewis, "Digital Age Forces New Look at Copyright," reprinted in *Vancouver Sun*, 4 Dec. 1996, D16.

44. Wendy Lubetkin, "New Treaties Would Update Copyright Law for the Digital Age," *USIS Geneva Daily Bulletin*, 5 Dec. 1996. Posted to info-policy-notes@essential.org on 6 Dec. 1996.

45. International Federation of Library Associations, "Comments on the Proposed New Treaties in the Copyright Field Under Discussion Within WIPO," Nov. 1996. Posted on Diglib@infoserv.nlc_bnc.ca, 15 Nov. 1996.

46. Ibid.

47. "Copyright Law Imperiled by New Treaties," *Financial Post*, 30 Nov.-2 Dec. 1996, 1-2.

48. Information Highway Advisory Council, *Connection Community Content: The Challenge of the Information Highway* (Ottawa, Supply and Services Canada, 1995), 115.

49. Ibid., 114.

50. "Letter to President Clinton," 10 Dec. 1996. Posted on info-policy-notes@essential.org on 11 Dec. 1996.

51. James Love, "A Primer on the Proposed WIPO Treaty on Database Extraction Rights That Will Be Considered in December 1996," *Consumer Project on Technology*, 10 Nov. 1996. Accessed on www.essential.org/cpt/ip/cpt-dbcom.html

52. Michael Bloomberg, "Letter to Carmen Guzman Lowrey, U.S. Patent and Trademark Office," 22 Nov. 1996. Posted on info-policy-notes@essential.org on 10 Dec. 1996.

53. James Love, "Government Proposed New Regulation of Sports Statistics and Other Facts," *Info-Policy-Notes*, 10 Nov. 1996. Posted by love@tap.org

54. Love, "Primer on the Proposed WIPO Treaty."

55. Alex Fowler, American Association for the Advancement of Science, "Letter to Vice President Albert Gore, Jr.," 25 Nov. 1996. Posted by love@tap.org, on 25 Nov. 1996.

56. Love, "Primer on the Proposed WIPO Treaty."

57. Casey Mahood, "U.S. Acquisition Opportunities for Thomson," *Globe and Mail*, 30 Aug. 1995, B8.

58. Casey Mahood and John Saunders, "Thomson Buys U.S. Giant," *Globe and Mail*, 27 Feb. 1996, B1, B8.

59. Robert Howell, "Database Protection and Canadian Laws (State of Law as of June 15, 1998)." Prepared for Industry Canada and Canadian Heritage, Oct. 1998, 89-90. Accessed on the Strategis Web site at strategis.ic.gc.ca/SSG/it04771e.html

60. Industry Canada, "The Canadian Electronic Commerce Strategy" (Ottawa, 1998), 31.

61. Boyle *Shamans, Software and Spleens*, xiii.

62. Keith Porterfield, "Information Wants to Be Valuable." Accessed on www.netaction.org/articles/freesoft.html

63. Ross Laver, "Bill Gates Besieged," *Maclean's*, 15 Mar. 1999, 30-35.

64. Gene Wilburn, "The Cathedral, the Bazaar and the Netscape Factor," *Computing Canada*, 16 Feb. 1998, 9.

65. Ibid.

66. Leander Kahney, "Open Software Wins in Mexican Schools" *Wired*, 11 Dec. 1998.

Chapter 6: Academics Build Their Intellectual Property Portfolios

1. Bill St. Arnaud, "Network Developments," Presentation to Access 96: Innovative Technology in Libraries Conference, Simon Fraser University, Vancouver, B.C., 1 Oct. 1996.
2. Ibid.
3. Canada, "Highlights of Departmental Action Plans in Response to 'Science and Technology for the New Century'" (Ottawa: Minister of Supply and Services, 1996), 3.
4. Industry Canada, "Speaking Notes for the Honourable John Manley, Minister of Industry, Vancouver Board of Trade, Connecting Canadians," Vancouver, 17 Dec. 1998, 9.
5. Quoted in Roberto Gualtieri, "Science Policy and Basic Research in Canada," in *How Ottawa Spends: 1994-95: Making Change*, Susan Philips, ed. (Ottawa: Carleton University Press, 1994), 302.
6. John Polanyi, "Private Sector Can't Carry Research," *Globe and Mail*, 14 Jan. 1997, B2.
7. See Gualtieri, "Science Policy and Basic Research," 304.
8. Leslie Millin, "For 50 Years, Our Country Has Squandered Its Scientific Legacy," *Vancouver Sun*, 18 July 1995, A9.
9. Canadian Press, "Research Poisoned by Government Cuts," *Vancouver Province*, 30 July 1997, A12.
10. Gualtieri, "Science Policy and Basic Research," 304.
11. Ibid., 311.
12. Carey Goldberg, "Urging a Freer Flow of Scientific Ideas," *New York Times*, 6 Apr. 1999. Accessed on the *New York Times* Web site at www.nytimes.com/library/national . . . nce/040699sci-scientific-exchanges.html
13. Doug Saunders, "Murder and Money at the End of the University," *The Peak*, 19 Sept. 1994, 13.
14. Natural Sciences and Engineering Research Council, "2A.2 Research Partnerships Program." 7 Aug. 1997. Accessed on the NSERC Web site at www.nserc.ca/programs/resguide/tpp.html
15. Natural Sciences and Engineering Research Council, *Highlights* 1993, (Ottawa: NSERC, 1993), 10.
16. David Noble, "The Religion of Technology," Lecture, Simon Fraser University, Vancouver, 20 Mar. 1997.
17. Loka Institute, "The Community Research Network." Accessed on the Loka Web site at www.amherst.edu/~loka/ncrn/ncrn.html
18. Richard Sclove, "Science, Inc. versus Science for Everyone," *Loka Alert* 4, no. 4 (Aug. 1997). Accessed on the Loka Web site at www.amherst.edu/~loka/alerts/loka4.4.txt
19. ARA Consulting Group, "Evaluation of the Networks of Centres of Excellence Program, Final Report," prepared for the NCE Program Evaluation Committee, Jan. 1997, 12.

20. Ibid.

21. Ibid., 13.

22. Ibid., 14.

23. Ibid., 57.

24. Ibid., 23.

25. "At the Interface: Building University-Industry Relationships," *SFU Research Links* 5, no. 1 (Jan. 1996): 4.

26. Noble, "The Religion of Technology."

27. Networks of Centres of Excellence, "TeleLearning Network of Centres of Excellence," News Release, 15 Oct. 1998. Accessed on the NCE Web site at nce.nserc.ca/blurbs/teleleng.html

28. Chuck Hamilton, "IBM's Pacific Development Centre," Presentation at SFU Information Tchnology Workshop, Oct. 1997.

29. Linda Harasim, "Application, Network of Centres of Excellence – Phase II," 9 Jan. 1995, C5.

30. Ibid., C5.

31. Ibid., C7.

32. Ibid., C92.

33. David Rodger, "Virtual-U, Virtual Learning," *SFU Research Links* 7, no. 3 (Sept. 1998): 4.

34. Frank Armstrong, "CANARIE Singing a New Song of Next Generation of Internet," *Technology in Government* 4, no. 9 (Sept. 1997): 8.

35. See Andrew Bjerring and Bill St. Arnaud, "CA*net II: A Bold New Direction for Advanced Networking in Canada, Final Version," CANARIE, 21 Jan. 1997.

36. Tony Martell, "Researchers Set to Launch Next Generation Net," *Globe and Mail*, 2 Sept. 1997, C14.

37. CANARIE, "CANARIE and Partners Build Tomorrow's Information Highway Today," 25 June 1997. Accessed on CANARIE's Web site at www.canarie.ca/c2/launch/

38. William Boei, "U.S., Canadian Universities Leave Internet to Build Separate Link," *Vancouver Sun*, 21 Feb. 1997, A1, A2.

39. Industry Canada, Secretariat for Science and Technology Review, *Resource Book for Science and Technology Consultations*, vol. 1 (Ottawa: Ministry of Supply and Services, 1994), 7.

40. Canadian Advanced Technology Association et al., "The Federal System of Scientific Research and Experimental Development Tax Incentives: Renewing the Partnership through Consensus, Consistency and Predictability," submission to the Honourable Herb Dhaliwal, Minister of National Revenue, May 1998.

41. Claire Polster, "From Public Resource to Industry's Instrument: Reshaping the Production of Knowledge in Canada's Universities," *Canadian Journal of Communication* 23, no. 1 (Winter 1998): 100.

42. Information Highway Advisory Council, *Connection Community Content: The Challenge of the Information Highway* (Ottawa: Supply and Services Canada, 1995), 75.

43. Ibid., 82.

44. Ibid., 151.

45. Industry Canada, *Science and Technology for the New Century* (Ottawa: Ministry of Supply and Services, 1996).

46. Ibid., 4.

47. Ibid., 10-11.

48. Natural Sciences and Engineering Research Council, *Highlights 1994*, (Ottawa: NSERC, 1994), 5.

49. John McMurtry, "Letter to the Editor," *CAUT Bulletin*, Jan. 1998, 2. McMurtry cites William Graham, "From the President's Desk," *Ontario Confederation of Faculty Associations Bulletin* 6, no. 15 (1989): 2-3.

50. Keith Daursell, "University-Industry R & D Ventures Rising," *Financial Post*, 7 June 1995, 10.

51. Natural Sciences and Engineering Research Council, "NSERC Modifies Programs," reported in *SFU Research Links* 5, no. 1 (May 1996): 2. Accessed on the NSERC Web site at www.nserc.ca/news/modi.html

52. "University-Industry Project: Science and Engineering Funding Opportunities from NSERC Across the R&D Spectrum," *SFU Research Links* 5, no. 2 (May 1996): 2.

53. Randy Ray, "Collaboration Enables Researchers to Take Long View," *Globe and Mail*, 5 Dec. 1995, C7.

54. Canadian Institute for Advanced Research, "The Commercialization of University Research in Canada: A Review and Approach to a Strategy for Industry Canada," Toronto, 26 Mar. 1996.

55. Leonard Zehr, "Patent Spending," *Globe and Mail*, 22 Oct. 1998, C1.

56. Myriam Beaugé, "UBC Chooses Equity Over Cash in Spinoffs," *Business in Vancouver*, 11–17 Nov. 1997, 5.

57. Industry Canada, "Welcome to Trans-Forum." Taken from the Trans-Forum Web site at trans-forum.schoolnet.ca/english/admin/ welcome.html

58. Zehr, "Patent Spending," C1.

59. Ibid.

60. Julia Flynn, "Millionaire Dons," *Business Week*, 9 Mar. 1998, 98-101.

61. Virginia Galt, "NorTel Gives $8 Million for Institute," *Globe and Mail*, 5 Feb. 1997, A7.

62. Meg Murphy, "Policy That Allowed NorTel Deal Challenged," *Varsity News*, 3 Mar. 1997. Accessed on the University of Toronto Web site at www.campuslife.utoronto.ca/groups/Varsity/archives/117/mar03/news/nortel.html

63. Galt, "NorTel Gives $8 Million."

64. Richard Sclove, "Community-Based Research: Making a Difference," *Loka Alert* 3, no. 1 (Feb. 1996). Accessed on the Loka Web site at www.amherst.edu/~loka/alerts/loka3.1.txt

65. Richard Sclove, "Putting Science to Work in Communities," *Chronicle of Higher Education* 41, no. 29 (Mar. 1995): B1-B3.

66. Ibid.

67. Richard Sclove, "Community-Based Research."

68 Humanities and Social Sciences Federation of Canada, "Community Research and Information Crossroads (Phase 1)," July 1997. Accessed at the HSSFC Web site, www.hssfc.ca/PROG/CRICPropContentsEng.html

Chapter 7: Colonizing New Markets: IBM Goes to School

1. Greg Crone, "Study Ponders Teacherless Society," *Ottawa Citizen*, 9 Oct. 1997, A3; Wendy McCann, "Students Might Carry Computers to 'Paperless' Classes," *Calgary Herald*, 9 Oct. 1997, A20.
2. William Thorsell, "Threshold for Breaking the Law," *Globe and Mail*, 25 Oct. 1997, D6.
3. Michael Valpy, "Just What Is in Ontario's Bill 160?" *Globe and Mail*, 20 Nov. 1997, A23.
4. "High-tech Tools Open New Vistas in London," *Globe and Mail*, 8 Oct. 1997, C1.
5. Heather Menzies, *Whose Brave New World? The Information Highway and the New Economy* (Toronto: Between the Lines, 1996), 53.
6. Jennifer Lewington, "Plan for Spending Less Laid Out in Leaked Memo," *Globe and Mail*, 22 Oct. 1997, A10.
7. Lynne Ainsworth, "Class Conflict," *Financial Post*, 11 May 1996, 44.
8. David Shoalts, "This Is Not a Request for Money," *Globe and Mail*, 18 Apr. 1996, D4.
9. Veronica Lacey, "The Only Way to Travel: Lifelong Learning on the Information Highway," Nov. 1994. Accessed on www.epsb.edmonton.ab.ca/fast.learn/1995/sessions/fi.html
10. Richard Mackie, "Education Spending Cut Cited by Group," *Globe and Mail*, 26 Oct. 1998, A6.
11. Jennifer Lewington, "Closer Academic, Business Links Cautiously Favoured," *Globe and Mail*, 29 Sept. 1997, A7.
12. Lynne Ainsworth, "Class Conflict."
13. Industry Canada, *The Canadian Information Highway* (Ottawa: Minister of Supply and Services Canada, 1994), 9.
14. Ibid.
15. Ibid.
16. Robert Thompson, "Conservatives Commit $135 Million," *Computer Dealer News*, 1 June 1998, 12.
17. Samer Muscati, "Corel's Deals with Provinces Raise Some Eyebrows," *Globe and Mail*, 22 June 1998, C2.
18. "Focus on Educational Software," *Computer Dealer News*, 14 June 1995, 44, 46.
19. Gillian Shaw, "Why Your Child Needs to Be Computer Savvy," *Vancouver Sun*, 13 Aug. 1998, E1.
20. Economic Council of Canada, "A Lot to Learn" (Ottawa: Minister of Supply and Services Canada, 1992), 51, 54.
21. Information Highway Advisory Council, *Connection Community Content: The Challenge of the Information Highway* (Ottawa: Ministry of Supply and Services Canada, 1995), 57.

22. Ibid.

23. Ibid., 60.

24. Ibid., 138.

25. Ibid., 185.

26. "Guess Who's the Newest Component of Public Sector Funding? You, the Private Sector," *BC Business*, Feb. 1995, 43–48.

27. "How the Corporate World Is Entering the Classroom," *Today's Parent*, Oct. 1994, 67-73.

28. Lynne Ainsworth, "Class Conflict."

29. Muscati, "Corel's Deals," C2.

30. Ibid.

31. Brahm Eiley, "First in Their Class," *Report on Business Magazine*, Oct. 1996, 73.

32. Sheridan Centre for Animation and Emerging Technologies (SCAET), "4.0. Financial Plan," 18 Nov. 1997, accessed on the Sheridan Web site at www.sheridan.on.ca/news/scaet/finance.html

33. Paula Anderton, "Ontario Funding to Back Animation Field," *Computing Canada*, 9 June 1997, 16.

34. "Centennial College and Partners Hardwired for Future," Advertising Feature, *Globe and Mail*, 9 Dec. 1994, C2.

35. Jennifer Lewington, "The Classroom Can Be Glitch for Computers," *Globe and Mail*, 23 Mar. 1998, C6.

36. "Centennial College and Partners Hardwired for Future," Advertising Feature, *Globe and Mail*, 9 Dec. 1994, C2.

37. Kevin Robins and Frank Webster, *The Technical Fix: Education, Computers and Industry* (Basingstoke: Macmillan Education, 1989), 109.

38. Jennifer Lewington, "Arts Background No Handicap in Job Search, Study Finds," *Globe and Mail*, 26 Oct. 1998, A6.

39. Linda Harasim, "Application for TeleLearning Networks of Centres of Excellence," 13 Jan. 1994, C3.

40. David Shoalts, "New Brunswick Project Leading the Way," *Globe and Mail*, 26 June 1997, C4.

41. Tony Bates, *Technology, Open Learning and Distance Education* (London: Routledge, 1995), 231.

42. Robins and Webster, *The Technical Fix*, 112-18.

43. Ibid., 116.

44. Heather-jane Robertson, *No More Teachers, No More Books: The Commercialization of Canada's Schools* (Toronto: McClelland & Stewart, 1998), 174.

45. teenSizzle, "Young Businessman on the Net," 3 Apr. 1998. Accessed at www.teensizzle.com/bristow.html

46. "The Brainium: Your Online Science Education Destination." Accessed at www.brainium.com/_info.html

47. "Multiactive Group of Companies – Corporate Overview." Accessed at www.multiactive.com/multiactivegroup.html

48. David Vogt, "Science World," Presentation to the PowerUp Conference, Robson Square Media Centre, Vancouver, June 1996.

49. "The Latest on The Brainium." Accessed at corp.brainium.com/f_press.html

50. David Vogt, "Science World."

51. Patrick Johnston, "A Present for the Government? You Shouldn't Have," *Globe and Mail*, 23 Oct. 1998, A27.

52. Maude Barlow and Heather-jane Robertson, *Class Warfare: The Assault on Canada's Schools* (Toronto: Key Porter Books, 1994), 157-58.

53. Youth News Network, "YNN." Accessed on YNN Web site at www.ynn.ca/

54. Ijeoma Ross, "Educational Advantage or Corporate Manipulation?" *Globe and Mail*, 4 Mar. 1999, C10.

55. "An Offer to Canadian High Schools," *SchoolNet Today*, 8 Feb. 1999. Accessed on SchoolNet Web site at www.schoolnet.ca/today/

56. Teressa Iezzi, "Digital Renaissance, NB Tel Partner on VOD Test," *Video Innovations*, 1 Dec. 1997, vi-4.

57. "Less Talk, More InfoAction," *Dr. Dobb's Journal*, May 1994, 6. Accessed on teleeducation.nb.ca/articles/ddj-e.html

58. David Shoalts, "New Brunswick Project Leading the Way," *Globe and Mail*, 26 June 1997, C4.

59. Ibid.

60. TeleCampus NB, "NB Institutions Offering Online Courses." Accessed on telecampus.edu/learners/courses/index.shtml

61. Scholars.com, "Scholars.com." Accessed on scholars.com/about-us.asp

62. "Microsoft Allies with Government of New Brunswick to Take Education Online," *Technology in Government* 2, no. 8 (1995): 1, 9.

63. Canadian Press, "N.B. Offers On-line Education to Students," *Vancouver Sun*, 7 June 1995, A10.

64. "Microsoft Allies with Government."

65. Nathan Newman, "Microsoft Goes to College: The Education Software Market and Microsoft's Expanding Monopoly," *Micro$oft Monitor* 35 (Oct. 1998). Accessed on NetAction Web site at www.netaction.org/monitor/moni35html

66. Nathan Newman, "From Microsoft Word to Microsoft World: How Microsoft Is Building a Global Monopoly." Accessed on NetAction Web site at www.netaction.org/msoft/world/MSWord2World.txt

67. Scholars.com, "What's New." Accessed on scholars.com/Whatsnew_Content.html

68. Nathan Newman, "Action Alert: Stop CETI," *Micro$oft Monitor* 20 (Dec. 1997). Accessed on NetAction Web site at www.netaction.org/monitor/moni20.html

69. Simona Chiose, "Digital Bullies: Whose Kids Will Win the Game in the Information Super-playground?", *This Magazine* 31 (April/May 1994): 22.

70. Ibid.

71. Neil Postman, *The End of Education: Redefining the Value of School* (New York: Vintage, 1996), 43-44.

72. Robert Everett-Green, "Arts Boosts Scores," *Globe and Mail*, 6 Nov. 1997, A12.

73. Postman, *The End of Education*, 93–113.

Chapter 8: What Does Industry Want?

1. Alex Carey, *Taking the Risk Out of Democracy: Corporate Propaganda versus Freedom and Liberty* (Urbana, IL: University of Illinois Press, 1997), 20.

2. Ibid., 21.

3. Ibid., 2.

4. Ibid., 20.

5. Ibid., 81-82.

6. Larry Tye, *The Father of Spin* (New York: Crown, 1998).

7. See Edward Herman and Noam Chomsky, *Manufacturing Consent* (New York: Pantheon Books, 1988).

8. Carey, *Taking the Risk Out of Democracy*, 88-91.

9. Karen Rothmyer, "Unindicted Co-conspirator?" *The Nation*, 23 Feb. 1998, 20.

10. Lawrence Soley, "Heritage Clones in the Heartland," *Extra*, Sept./Oct. 1998, 20.

11. Alex Carey, *Taking the Risk Out of Democracy*, 90.

12. Murray Dobbin, *The Myth of the Good Corporate Citizen: Democracy Under the Rule of Big Business* (Toronto: Stoddart, 1998); Linda McQuaig, *Shooting the Hippo: Death by Deficit and Other Canadian Myths* (Toronto: Viking, 1995).

13. Heather Menzies, "Hyping the Highway," *Canadian Forum*, June 1994, 18-26.

14. McQuaig, *Shooting the Hippo*," 11.

15. Herman and Chomsky, *Manufacturing Consent*, 302.

16. Shawn McCarthy, "Canadians' Message to Ottawa: Keep Cutting the Debt," *Globe and Mail*, 8 Feb. 1999, A1.

17. McQuaig, *Shooting the Hippo*, 44.

18. Ibid., 55-63.

19. Ibid., 242-45.

20. Ibid., 249-50.

21. Ibid., 63.

22. Murray Dobbin, "We Don't Need a General Tax Cut – Just a Fair System," *CAUT Bulletin*, Jan. 1999, 2.

23. Barrie McKenna, "Canadian Productivity Posts Weak Growth in 1996," *Globe and Mail*, 6 June 1997, B5.

24. Andres Poon, "Information Technology Boosts Growth, Study Says," *Globe and Mail*, 10 July 1997, B4.

25. Christopher Farrell, "Why the Numbers Miss the Point," *Business Week*, 31 July 1995, 78.

26. James Brian Quinn and Martin Baily, "Information Technology: The Key to Service Performance," *Brookings Review* (Summer 1994): 37-41; "Information Technology and the Service Sector," *The Futurist*, July/Aug. 1994, 60-61.

27. Jessica Keyes, "So Where's the IT Payoff?" *Byte*, May 1995, 260.

28. Bruce Little, "The Industries That Will Define the Decade," *Globe and Mail*, 21 Apr. 1997, A6.

29. David Noble, "The Truth About the Information Highway," *Monthly Review*, June 1995, 50.

30. Deirdre McMurdy, "In Thick and Thin," *Maclean's*, 7 Aug. 1995, 35.

31. Carey, *Taking the Risk Out of Democracy*, 89.

32. Anders Schneiderman, "Three Myths About Government, Markets and the Net: A Special Report on the Clinton Administration's Plans for Global Electronic Commerce," *E-node* 2, no. 4 (July 1997). Posted to e-node@igc.org on 27 July 1997.

33. Information Highway Advisory Council, *Connection Community Content: The Challenge of the Information Highway* (Ottawa: Ministry of Supply and Services Canada, 1995), x.

34. Robert Kuttner, "The Limits of Markets," *American Prospect*, no. 31 (Mar.-Apr. 1997): 28-41. Accessed on wpn.org/prospect/31/31kutt.html

35. Ibid.

Chapter 9: Reclaiming Public Information

1. David Korten, *When Corporations Rule the World* (West Hartford, CT: Kumarian Press, 1995), 294.

2. Garth Graham and Leslie Regan Shade, "Rhetoric and Reality in Canadian Community Networking," paper presented to the INet 96 Conference, Montreal, 27 June 1996.

3. Ibid.

4. Saul Chernos, "Electronic Town Squares Getting Crowded: Community Networks in Canada," *Information Highways*, Apr. 1995, 34.

5. "Blue Sky Community Networks Embark on Full-Scale Expansion," 14 Nov. 1996. Accessed on www.freenet.mb.ca/info/press/infra-press.release.html

6. Mark Surman, "Free TM: Paying a Toll on the Infobahn," *This Magazine*, Dec. 1994/Jan. 1995, 6.

7. Neil Guy, "Community Networks: Building Real Communities in a Virtual Space?" (Master's thesis, Simon Fraser University, 1996). Accessed on www.vcn.bc.ca/people/nkg/ma-thesis/. This thesis provides a broad overview of community networking in Canada and British Columbia.

8. Surman, "Free TM."

9. Canadian Press Newswire, "Questions Raised About Death of City Free-Net (in Montreal)," 26 Dec. 1996.

10. Ibid.

11. Guy, "Community Networks," 42.

12. Murray Whyte, "Internet Service Provider Awarded Charitable Status," *Vancouver Sun*, 10 July 1996, A1.

13. Surman, "Free TM."

14. Telecommunities Canada, "Bylaw #1." Accessed on www.tc.ca/bylaw1.html

15. Guy, "Community Networks," 32.

16. "Communities Across the Country Set to Go Online," Canadian Press News Wire, 15 Aug. 1994.

17. Douglas Schuler, *New Community Networks* (New York: ACM Press, 1996), 25.

18. Guy, "Community Networks," 2.

19. Howard Frederick, "Computer Networks and the Emergence of Global Civil Society," in Linda Harasim, ed., *Global Networks: Computers and Communications* (Cambridge: MIT Press, 1993), 283-95.

20. Rosalva Bermudez-Ballin, trans., "New Ways of Social Struggle Attributed to the EZLN by Specialists of the United States," *La Jornada*, 6 Feb. 1999.

21. Madelaine Drohan, "How the Net Killed the MAI," *Globe and Mail*, 29 Apr. 1998, A1; Peter Morton, "MAI Gets Tangled in Web," *Financial Post*, 22 Oct. 1998, 3.

22. Kady O'Malley, "Grassroots in Cyberspace: Community Organizing on the Internet," *Canadian Forum*, Jan./Feb. 1998, 29.

23. Michele Landsberg, "Cyber-Mavens Harness Power of 'Net for Their Cause," *Toronto Star*, 18 May 1997, A2; see also O'Malley, "Grassroots in Cyberspace."

24. W. Alton Jones Foundation, "Circuit Riders: Pioneers in Non-Profit Networking," Oct. 1996. Accessed on www.wajones.org/circuit.html

25. Ellen Balka, "Resources for Research and Action: Computer Networking: Spinsters on the Web" (Ottawa: CRIAW/ICREF, 1997), 35-43.

26. Jagdish Parikh and P.K. Murphy, "The World Is Our Picket Line." Posted to rre@weber.ucsd.edu on 20 Mar. 1997.

27. Robert McChesney, "The Global Struggle for Democratic Communication," *Monthly Review* 48, no. 3 (July-Aug. 1996): 18.

28. Robert McChesney, "Market Media Muscle," *Canadian Forum*, Mar. 1998, 22.

29. Andrew Shapiro, "New Voices in Cyberspace," *The Nation*, 8 June 1998, 36-37.

30. Economic Security Project, "Recommended Links." Accessed on www.igc.apc.org/esp/relative.shtml

31. Stevie Cameron, "Getting Paranoid Over the Right to Privacy," *Globe and Mail*, 16 Mar. 1992, A4.

32. Nick Moore, "Rights and Responsibilities in an Information Society," *Journal of Information, Law and Technology*, 1998, 1. Accessed on elj.warwick.ac.uk/jilt/infosoc/98_1moor/

33. William Birdsall, "A Canadian Right to Communicate?" *Government Information in Canada*, no. 15 (1998). Accessed on www.usask.ca/library/gic/15/birdsall.html

index